The
History of England

Meeting of Edward III with the Black Prince after the Battle of Crecy.

p. 305.

The History of England

for Catholic Children

FROM THE EARLIEST TIMES
TO 1850

Copyright © Hillside Education, 2019
Originally published in 1850, Burns & Lambert. London

All rights reserved. No part of this publication may be reproduced in whole or in part, stored in a retrieval system or transmitted in any form or by any means, electronic, mechanical, photocopying, recording, or otherwise, without prior written permission of the publisher.

Cover and interior book design by Mary Jo Loboda

Cover Image: Catherine of France (Catherine of Valois) presented to Henry V of England, at the treaty of Troyes, 1799

incamerastock / Alamy Stock Photo

All interior images public domain via Wikimedia, except where noted.

ISBN: 978-0-9991706-9-4

Hillside Education
475 Bidwell Hill Road
Lake Ariel, PA 18436
www.hillsideeducation.com

to

THE CATHOLIC CHILDREN OF ENGLAND:

who, in their childhood

pursuing a silent course of dependent obedience,

follow the footsteps of the

HOLY CHILD JESUS,

that like him also they may, in their after life,

give themselves,

with an entire devotion and singular love,

to the work of God,

in winning back our country to the 'Old Paths'

of

The Catholic Faith.

Introduction

 VERY few words should perhaps be said here to those whose office it is to mold the understandings and desires of children—to train them, in fact, to the mind and character they are required to possess. This, as need not now be said, is the very highest, and also the most responsible and laborious part of education.

In order to fulfill this office in any competent manner, those who undertake it must themselves necessarily be trained so as not only to awaken and develop the faculties and understanding of children, but to seize the favorable moment to make lasting impressions upon their young hearts, and at every fitting opportunity to strengthen and establish these impressions until they become *habits*.

It is true that the characters of children differ as widely as the natural habits of animals, or the leaves and flowers of vegetation; but they can, after all, be resolved into classes; and amid this infinite variety we find familiar characteristics returning again and again to our view. We need never, then, be discouraged by the apparently endless nature of our task, and the less so because it is certain that, according to the nature and constancy of our training, so will the child be. It may require more or less stringent measures, or a longer or shorter time, or a more or less continual repetition of our efforts; but in the end, by repeated strokes of the hammer, the metal must become welded to the form we desire.

It need scarcely be said, that the foundation and continual food of such a training must be unwearied prayers for the souls committed to our charge.

When, then, we enter into the details of such an education as is here spoken of, and fix upon some one portion of instruction, as History, for instance, we have to determine in what manner we shall open this subject to children. If we make it a mere matter of memory, a storing-up of barren facts, our task, though wearisome enough, will be comparatively easy. The books being provided, and the necessary time for studying them allotted, the work is nearly done to our hands. A considerable quantity of matter will soon be stowed into the children's heads, where it will remain until other facts drive it out again; and in some cases, the very words learned and repeated at school will be retained by the memory till a late old age. But will the child's understanding be opened by this process? Will the facts which in one sense are possessed, take root and bring forth the fruit of mature thought and experience? Let those acquainted with the larger class of school-girls judge whether the fruits of such an education are not usually like the flowers plucked and stuck into a child's garden, whose rootless stalks and ephemeral beauty withers at sundown.

On the other hand, let us consider the effects of an education which, without putting aside the cultivation of the memory, acts powerfully also on the mind and heart. In this view, if we take History again as our subject, we should first of all begin with some great and leading principles—some end to be sought in the study; either by contemplating History generally as the ordinances of God's Providence upon different nations, or as the fulfillment of certain striking prophecies, as in Ancient History, or the rise and increase of the Catholic Church, and its various influences, as in modern times. Or again, we may view it as a great spiritual Drama, in which the world, with its kings and nobles, is made to group itself round, and to do the bidding of some otherwise hidden Saint; and, as it has often happened, to produce some violent convulsion—a revolution, wars, or the like—in order to bring out into clearer view the power of holiness, and the triumph of Faith over the exterior world.

In the history of our own country, how often do we not find striking instances of this fact? In the stories of St. Dunstan, St. Anselm, St. Thomas, St. Neot, and innumerable others, a thick veil is drawn aside for a moment, as if to show us glimpses of another and a higher world of motive and action, compared with which all that is visibly done, and forms the usual matter of the "great events" of history, is like the impotent and ludicrous movements of a child's puppet-show. To view History, then, with the eye of faith, and to instill the same great and noble apprehension of it into the minds of children, is surely a gain to us and to them.

Other lesser objects, but still excellent and useful, should not be lost sight of; such as the government, laws, institutions, and general character of a nation, whether it be our own or another. Innumerable subjects of thought and reflection, not only useful to exercise and strengthen the understanding, but also to correct the judgment and give a soundness of discrimination, will thus be opened; all of which, besides being turned to account in every lesser duty of life, may tend also to the greater glory of God, and the lasting good of His Church.

Such a mode of instruction is perhaps needed in a more special manner in a protestant country, where brilliant and fascinating works are continually pouring from the press, without any oneness of idea or solid ground of right faith, but in which every art and ingenuity of talent and genius is exerted to prop up a failing cause, or to dress a shining theory with the semblance of truth.

Against such a pressure of influence upon young, ardent, and untried minds, negative remedies are not sufficient. It is not enough to show that such and such principles or theories are false; it is necessary also to point out which may be acted upon as the true ones. In like manner, it is not enough to contradict or to clear up false statements in history, and to put into children's hands protestant historians accompanied with a series of denials. In this especially it is a nobler, higher, and safer plan to remodel it altogether, to take it from a different view, to throw aside entirely the petty, miserable manner of reasoning of the last century, and to begin at once from a new ground; new to us, but old as the "lasting hills" of the Faith, the ground of the Truth and of the Church.

With this view, the mere national prejudices which so cling to our island nature must be overcome, we must lose our country, as it were, in the Church, and clearly interpret, *in their Catholic and religious sense*, the bitter disputes between the spiritual and temporal powers in England, especially under William the Second, Henry the First, Henry the Second, John, Henry the Eighth, and Elizabeth. Similar struggles in other countries should be instanced, as those of St. Ambrose and Theodosius, Philip Augustus with Innocent the Third, Henry the Sixth of Germany with Gregory the Seventh, Pius the Sixth with Napoleon, and so on—to show that however much times, places, and all other circumstances may change, *principles remain unaltered*. By this multiplication of events bearing upon one principle, the child, instead of having his mind cumbered with a confusion of *facts*, will gain a clear and sound habit of generalizing, or reducing a variety of apparently dissimilar circumstances to one broad general rule. This is the quality chiefly prominent in all first-rate minds, and of any, indeed, who attain great excellence in their profession or occupation in life, whatever it may be.

It may he objected by some, that the habit of referring or reducing facts to principles, and to high and great principles in particular, gives the mind a theoretical and unpractical turn. But this objection will itself be considered a groundless and theoretical one, when we reflect upon the facts which history and experience afford in contradiction to it. From the stories of the Saints of the Old Law down to modern times, who have proved themselves the most useful, practical, and successful men? Evidently those who acted upon the highest principles, and who aimed at the highest ends. If practicalness, manifest success, and usefulness are the cherished idols of our times, and indeed of the world in all times, they will be best gained by aiming at the best and highest ends.

And it is only acting upon right reason to come to this conclusion; for it is clear that a chemist or a naturalist who collects only a mass of disjointed facts without rule or order will never do more than collect materials upon which others may labor; while one who reasons from fact to principles, and from those principles deduces another rich store of facts, may become a Cuvier or a Sir Humphry Davy, opening out and fertilizing new regions of science, and shedding a beneficial light upon what was before a useless chaos of disorder.

It need not be urged, that a training and habits of mind fitted to nerve and strengthen the character to a greater, and to the greatest excellence, are an end for which no care nor pains should be spared. In every rank and condition of life, from the statesman to the mechanic, labor thus bestowed would act in the most beneficial manner; is needed in the most urgent degree; and in all ranks, states, and classes, the influence through whom and by whom the Church most promptly and surely acts is the influence of women.

If, then, we may deserve in this matter to have ten talents committed to our care, shall we not be called to account for our lack of zeal and diligence if we are content to receive only two, or perhaps, with an unloving negligence, to bury our one in the ground?

It remains only to say, that the following History was attempted with some such intention as has been here pointed out; and no apology is offered for the slight and imperfect nature of the narrative, for this among many reasons, i.e. because so strong a conviction is felt, that however great may be the labor bestowed upon books of education for children, they are after all a dead letter without the cooperation, we may almost say the *interpretation*, of those who instruct from them.

If this History should be the means of helping one individual to take a nobler view of our condition as a country than that of mere national pride; if it excites a single child to perform his daily actions with a higher aim, as being one of a nation still separated from the Catholic Church, and whom he has a certain responsibility (as far as may be) to restore— the end sought for in it will be more than gained.

Contents

Introduction	ix
The Early Britons	1
Roman Rule in Britain	7
The Last Days Of Britain	13
The Fair-Haired Strangers	19
Our Anglo-Saxon Forefathers	23
The Heptarchy and the Mission from Rome	27
The Bretwaldas	31
The Sea-Kings	41
England and English Laws	47
The King and the Saint	53
The Anglo-Saxon Kings	63
The Danish Kings	77
The Last Anglo-Saxon Kings, And New Comers	85
Gang Roll's Children	95
The Red King	105
The Scholar-King	109
The King and the Empress	117
The First of the Plantagenets	121
The Church and the World	127
Henry's Wars, Troubles, and End	137
The Lion-Heart	143
The Church of the People	155
Peace In England	165
The Good Queen	169
The Wicked Queen and Bad Company	177
The Glory of England	181
The Sad End	195
Richard of Bordeaux	201
The Usurper	209
The Greatest Glory of England	215
The Maid of Orleans	221
The White and Red Rose	227
End of the Red and White Rose	237
The Hunchback, and the End of the Plantagenets	245
The First Tudor	251

The Splendid Chancellor..259
The Holy Chancellor 265
The Wicked King's End 277
The Misery of England 283
Mary The Good 289
The Court of Elizabeth...297
Mary Stuart...307
The Cruelties of Elizabeth, and the End of the Tudors............315
Foolish King James..323
The Cavalier King and the Civil Wars............................331
The Parliament Out of Place......................................343
The King Again, and His Bad Ministers.........................355
Holy King James...367
The Dutch King and England's Shame 377
Kind Queen Anne and the Fierce Duchess.....................389
The Hanoverian King..397
Prince Charlie..403
Better Times—The American War............................413
The French Revolution 421
Nelson and his Battles Peninsular War and Waterloo............429
The Breaking of our Chains 437
The Constitution Changed, But Yet the Same. 441
The End, and our Present Condition...........................451
Appendix..455

Chapter I.

The Early Britons.

From 500 B.C. to 55 B.C.

VERY one of us ought to know something about the history of our own country, which is, you know, the country in which we were born. There is a great order in charity; and Almighty God has given us this country to love and to serve, before all other countries, just as He has given us our parents and relations, whom we are to love above all our other neighbors. We are bound, therefore, to study and to make ourselves acquainted with the history of our country, that we may know how to fulfill our duties towards it and in it.

Besides this first or principal reason, which makes it a *duty* to know it, there is another, which shows us how *beneficial* the study of our history must be. All history is only the record of the providences of God upon a country. It is the account of His dealings with it, His favors, His rewards, and His chastisements, according to its deserts; and as it is necessary for each one of us to know the will of God in regard to ourselves, so it is deeply interesting and profitable to trace it in regard to the country in which He has placed us, and where our duties call us to act in such or such a manner. This knowledge helps us to fulfill those duties better and more completely in different circumstances, and by it we become, therefore, better able to act when we are called upon to do so, and to *fill our station,* that is, to do the will of God, in a more perfect manner. Each one of us ought to aim continually at this end.

We must, then, try to learn, first, of what religion our forefathers were; by whom, and when, they were rescued from pagan errors, and taught the knowledge of the true Faith; how they practiced their faith, and what effects it had upon them; and what saints and friends of God were raised up by it. Next, we must learn what government they had, how it was formed, for what end, and what influence it had upon the people; what laws they obeyed; and how justice was done among them. We must examine what kind of poetry, and painting, and music, and architecture, they had, which are called the *Fine Arts;* in what manner they lived, how they built their towns and cities, and how they improved their condition by inventions and manufactures. In short, how they looked, what they did and spoke and thought; for then we shall see in what things they were in a better or worse condition than we are now, and in what we should imitate them and follow their example, or the contrary.

Two thousand years ago, England was called Britain. It is an island 640 miles long (with Scotland), and from 150 to 280 (or 280) broad. It is bounded, as you know, by the North Sea, the English Channel, the German Ocean, and St. George's Channel. It has many large navigable rivers, the chief of which are the Thames, the Severn, and the Humber, and many fine harbors, which, together with the rivers and its being an island, show at once its fitness for becoming a great trading and maritime country.

Inland, Britain has always been famous for its fertility. It has very few mountains, and except in the east, very little marsh or bog land; and, in general, is composed of gentle sloping hills and fine corn or pasture land, which is watered by innumerable brooks and streams, and richly wooded with forests of oak, elm, and beech trees. The oak and the elm are the most valuable of the British trees, and the oak especially grows to a gigantic size.

Underneath the earth lie rich mines of iron, lead, tin, copper, and coal. The British tin was so famous, that our islands were known among the ancients by the name of the Tin Islands.

The first inhabitants of Britain were a race of Scythian or Celtic Goths, who must have travelled westwards from Asia, the great cradle of the human race, and settled in Britain. They brought with them their Eastern paganism, which contained both the worship of fire and the sacrifice of human victims; and their priests, who were called Druids, seem to have had a mixture of the learning of the ancient Chaldean Magi, and the more modern Paganism of the Roman Empire.

The Britons, our forefathers, built enormous temples to their chief idol, whom they called Dis, or Pluto; and the remains of these temples still astonish everyone who sees them. The chief of them is called Stonehenge, which is near Salisbury. There is another, which must have been very magnificent, at Avebury, on the Wiltshire downs: and there are many besides. No one can quite understand how they dug up such huge masses of stone, how they carried them

Stonehenge in Wiltshire England

from the quarries, or how they set them up in a circular or round form. But these temples are quite enough to prove that the Druids must have had a good deal of knowledge and education.

They taught three things, which it is very curious they should have known; and they called them the three principles of wisdom: 1st, Obedience to the laws of God. 2nd, Care for the good of others. 3rd, Fortitude under the trials of life.

They thought that their gods principally lived in the thick forests of oak with which Britain was then covered; and they loved and reverenced the oak so much, that they would never allow any of the trees to be cut down. They met together every year to cut off the mistletoe that grows on the branches; and when they had found it, the oldest, or Arch-druid, got up into the oak, and cut it off with a gold sickle. After the ceremony, they made a great feast and rejoicing.

The Early Britons.

When there was any event—such as a battle, or a new chief, or any disease among the people or cattle—the Druids sacrificed human victims. They took the captives whom they had captured in battle, or some of the British children, and either killed them with a dagger, and burnt their bodies upon large stones called Cromlechs, or put them into a wicker-work frame, representing a huge man, and burnt the frame and the people together. They thought that the death-shrieks of these poor victims were very pleasing to their gods.

Before we pass on to learn how Almighty God rescued our forefathers from their idolatry, we must hear how they lived at this time.

In the north of Britain the people were very savage indeed. They did not wear any clothes, but painted themselves blue with a plant called *woad;* and they lived upon acorns and beech-mast, and in holes and caves in the woods and rocks. But in the southern parts of the country they were more civilized, and not so wild and rude. They knew how to build houses of logs of wood, and rushes platted together and covered with mud, to keep out the wind and rain; and they made stone foundations to their wooden houses. The roof was roundish, or what is called *conical,* that is, like a sugar-loaf, with a hole in the middle for the smoke to go out; for the fire was always made on flat stones in the middle of the floor.

These southern Britons wore a tight waistcoat and trousers made of cloth, and braided with colored braid; and over them a large square cloak or mantle that hung down on all sides. They wore rings on their fingers, and chains round their necks, made of iron or brass. They made all these things themselves; for they had no ships, and they never went out of Britain. They were very skillful farmers, and grew a great deal of fine corn, which they kept in dry holes in the rocks, instead of in barns; and they spent their spare time in carving bowls and cups and spoons, and making little fishing-boats, called coracles, out of beechwood, and wicker-work, and leather.

The Druids really governed the country; for although the Britons had chiefs, they consulted the Druids upon all important matters. They made war and peace, settled the disputes between one chief and another; and when any of the chiefs disobeyed or insulted them, the Druids would not allow him to come to the sacrifices, and he was looked upon (as we may say) as a person excommunicated.

Some of the Druids made songs, and sang them upon their harps. When they did so, they were called bards, and the bards always went out to battle with the chiefs; and in time of peace they sang at the feasts and sacrifices. These songs were never written; they were handed down by tradition from one bard to another; and the people loved them better than any book that could be written. These songs were about the bravest of the British chiefs and his deeds in battle; and when any chief had many songs sung about him, he was honored and esteemed by all the others.

Chapter II.

Roman Rule in Britain

From 55 b.c. to 306 a.d.

ROME is now the capital of Italy, and we love it because it is the Holy City, and the capital of Christendom. But at the time we are writing of, which is about two thousand years ago, before our Lord was born, Rome was not the Holy City, the Mother and Mistress of Churches; she was the capital of the Pagan Roman Empire.

Julius Caesar had conquered Gaul, which is now called France; and as he was sailing along the northern coasts of Gaul, he saw in the distance the white cliffs of Britain. He had heard that it was a very fertile country, and full of valuable mines of tin. He knew, too, that the people were strong and brave, and he wished to make them Roman soldiers, and to make Britain a Roman province. Julius Caesar sailed across the English Channel, and landed in Britain; but he found the people ready to meet him, and they beat his famous legions, and killed their consul.

The next year Caesar came again to Britain; and this time he sailed down the Thames to London, which was called then Trinovantum, where he found the British king, Cassibelan, with a large army. Caesar took Trinovantum, and afterwards St. Albans, which was then called Cassibelan, I suppose from the British king.

There were a great many battles after this between the Romans and Britons. The Britons fought in chariots with scythes fastened to the wheels, which cut and killed every one who came within their reach; and the soldiers would often leave the reins with the charioteer, run along the pole between the horses, jump into the midst of the Roman soldiers, and then get back again into the chariot with such quickness and courage as to astonish the Romans, although they were so brave themselves.

One of the bravest of the British kings was Cassibelan, who first fought against Julius Caesar. Another was Caractacus.

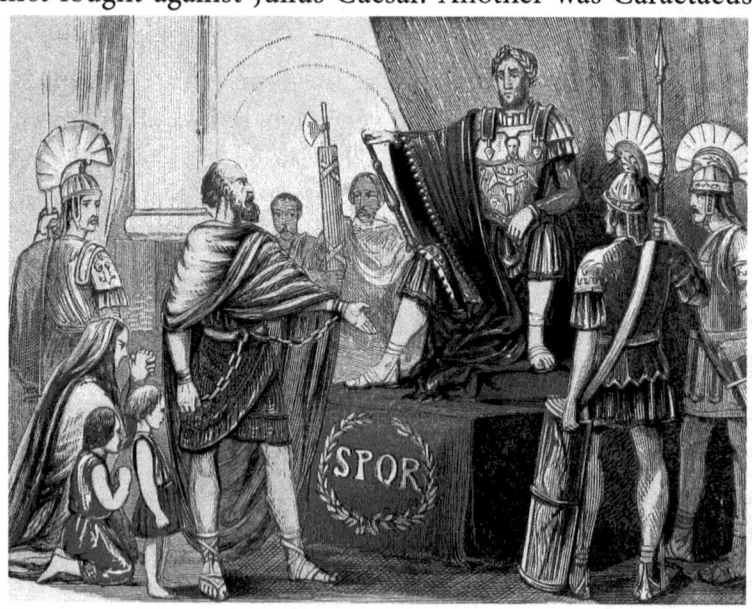

Caractacus meets Emperor Claudius

He was taken prisoner and carried to Rome; and when he was walking in the triumphal procession through the streets, and saw the marble palaces, and temples, and statues, and fountains of that magnificent city, he said: "I wonder very much that the men who live in such palaces as these should envy me my little cottage in Britain."

The Romans were very glad to have conquered Britain. They found the people strong and active and industrious, and that they made very good soldiers and servants. They sent a good many of them to Rome to fight for the empire, and they sent a good many Romans to Britain. They sent Roman governors, too, to rule the country; but after a while the British-Romans, or Roman-Britons, became governors of Britain.

The Britons learned a great many useful things from their new masters. They taught them how to build with fine brick and hewn stone, and they built larger cities, with better houses in them, at London, York, Bath, and Verulam, which was before called Cassibelan, and is now St. Albans. They built baths and theatres, and first planted gardens with onions, and cabbages, and other useful vegetables. They taught them how to make finer cloth, and to embroider in gold and silver, and to wear silk.

But the slavery of Britain was to answer a much higher end than to make them comfortable, and better fed and clothed; it brought them the true freedom of the faith of Christ. About fifty years after our Lord, St. Philip went to preach to the Franks in Gaul; and while he was in Gaul, it is said that he chose twelve companions from his disciples, and having laid his hands on them, he sent them to preach in Britain. One of these companions was his dear friend St. Joseph of Arimathea. They landed in Britain, and began to preach; and one of the Pagan chiefs or petty British kings gave them an island to live in, full of brambles, and thickets, and pools of water.

In this little islet they had a vision. The angel Gabriel appeared to them, and bade them build a church in honor of our Lady, which they quickly did. It was made of twisted willows covered with clay, and this poor little chapel was the first Christian church in Britain. While he was preaching near this church to the heathen people, it is said that St. Joseph stuck his staff into the ground, and prayed that Almighty God would show a miracle to prove that he taught the true faith. Immediately the staff took root, and shot out into green leaves, and became a beautiful thorn-tree with white blossoms upon it.

Upon the spot where that chapel of twisted willows was framed, a magnificent abbey was afterwards built, called Glastonbury Abbey; and a huge thorn-bush near the ruins is still called the Glastonbury Thorn, and is still believed to bring forth green leaves and white flowers on the same day.

Soon after St. Joseph's first preaching, King Lucius wrote to the Pope, St. Eleutherius, and begged of him to send some Christian priests to Britain to instruct him and his people. St. Eleutherius sent two holy men, named Phagan and Dannan, or, as they are commonly called, St. Fugatius and St. Damian, to Britain, who baptized the good king and his court, and very many of the Druids and people. The Druids, who were generally very learned men, became valuable instruments in converting their countrymen. So you see what a blessing it was that the Romans came to Britain.

After a while, when Diocletian became emperor, a great persecution arose, and the first glorious martyr in Britain was St. Alban. Dioclesian had ordered that all the Christian priests in the Roman empire should be put to death, and those in Britain were sought for among the rest. One evening, a poor priest was hunted in this way, near Verulam, by the emperor's officers; and he came to Alban's house, who was a Pagan nobleman, and asked for shelter. Alban generously gave him shelter at the risk of his own life, and hid him for several days. The priest, in return for this generous kindness, instructed him, and prayed for him day and night; and Alban received the grace of becoming a Christian, and was baptized.

Albans and Amphiblaus (Matthew Paris, Trinity College Dublin)

Time passed on, and the Pagan governor heard that Alban had a priest hidden in his house. He was enraged at this, and ordered the Christian to be brought before him. Alban sent away the holy priest secretly and in disguise; and then putting on the missionary's robe, he quietly waited for the soldiers. As soon as they saw him, they mistook him for the priest, and carried him away to the judge. The judge knew Alban, and was so enraged at his boldness, that he threatened him with instant death if he did not sacrifice to the Pagan idols. Alban bravely answered that he was a Christian, and gloried in being one; and he was carried away to martyrdom. He was to be beheaded on a hill outside the town, and he had to pass a river before he could get up the hill. There was only one narrow bridge across the river, and a great multitude of people had to cross it. Alban saw them passing over one by one, and he knew that it would be evening before he could get across the water to receive his crown. He was so very anxious to be martyred, that he prayed fervently to God to dry up the river, and it was dried directly; and he passed over its course, and went up the hill. The executioner, who was looking on, saw the miracle; and he threw away his sword, and falling at Alban's feet, said he would be a Christian too.

They passed on together to the top of the green and flowery hill, and there Alban prayed again, and a stream of fresh water sprang out of the turf. After all these miracles, St. Alban and the executioner, who had become a Christian, were beheaded together, and went to receive a glorious crown. The town of St. Alban's was afterwards built on this hill.

The Dioclesian persecution lasted ten years; but after that there was peace for the Church. Conatantius, the Roman Caesar, married Helena, the daughter of the British King Gael, who lived at Colchester, and their son was Constantine the Great. This was the glorious St. Helen, who found the true Cross at Jerusalem.

CHAPTER III.

The Last Days Of Britain

From A.D. 306 to 446.

THE Romans had now possessed Britain between four and five hundred years, and the Britons had married Romans, and the Romans had married Britons, till they had become like one people. The Britons had become, too, like the Romans, soft and fond of pleasure, and led a very slothful and luxurious life. The young men were taken away by the Romans to fight their foreign battles, and those who remained in Britain were not allowed to have arms, so that they had quite forgotten how to fight. When the Britons were reduced to this miserable condition, the Romans found that they could not stay with them any longer. Rome itself was in great danger from the vast hordes of barbarians who poured down from the banks of the Danube and the north of Europe; and the Romans were obliged to go home to defend their own country. Before they went, they built a wall from one side of Britain to the other, that

Hadrian's Wall

is, from the German Ocean to Solway Frith, to prevent the Picts and Scots from coming in, and then they sailed away, and left the poor helpless Britons to take care of themselves. As soon as they had set sail, the Picts and Scots appeared in great crowds, and laid the whole north of the country waste. The Britons were carried away to be made slaves, with their corn and cattle, and their houses and barns were burned.

In their misery the Britons sighed for the kind, gentle government of their old masters. They sent ambassadors to Rome, and begged help from their enemies. The Romans were very much troubled themselves; but they sent a fleet to Britain, and chased away the Scots and Picts, who fled in a great fright before the terrible Roman soldiers. When the Romans had established peace, they resolved to abandon Britain forever. They told the Britons that now they must defend themselves; and they built a stronger wall, with towns, along the northern boundary of Britain. They showed the Britons how to make good armor, and how to use their weapons; and then they sailed away from Britain, never to come back again.

The Scots and Picts soon found out this, and they came with larger armies to persecute Britain. The Britons wrote another letter to the Roman Consul; but he did not come any more. The letter was called "The Groans of the Britons," and in it were these words: "The barbarians drive us into the sea, and the sea drives us back again upon the swords of the barbarians: between both we are not allowed to live; for by one we are massacred, and by the other drowned."

The Romans were then at war with Attila, king of the Huns, and they could not send even one soldier to Britain; so the Britons did what they could for themselves; but the country was in so miserable a state that it gave wicked men an opportunity of indulging all their bad passions.

The king's name at that time was Constans. He was a monk who had been crowned by a nobleman named Vortigern for his own ends. Vortigern gave him a guard of Picts, as he pretended to take care of him, but in reality to betray him. One day Vortigern went into the hall where these Picts were drinking, and told them with tears in his eyes that he was going away, for he thought that brave men ought not to be treated as he was; and he bade them goodbye. When he was gone, the Picts got up enraged, and said, "Why should we not kill this monk, and let Vortigern be king?" And they went directly into the king's apartments, and cut off his head, which they took to Vortigern. Vortigern burst into tears, and ordered his soldiers to put all the Picts to death, pretending to be full of grief, but in reality he was delighted to be king.

This cruel and treacherous act was but the beginning of his crimes; for, as the old chronicler tells us, he was "a hater of truth, a despiser of God, an enemy to the noble, and a friend to the wicked."

The Scots and Picts soon spread again all through the country, and carried terror on all sides. They killed, and burned, and took away captives, without mercy; and, as if to show how displeasing Vortigern was to God, Britain was afflicted with famine and pestilence, besides its enemies. There was another worse misfortune even than these. This was the heresy of Pelagius, which sprang up and took deep root in Britain. The British bishops were so unhappy at the state of the Church, that they sent to Gaul to ask the bishops of Gaul to come to Britain, and teach them how to overthrow and convince the Pelagian heretics. The prelates of Gaul sent two very holy bishops, named St. Germanus, bishop of Auserre, and St. Lupus, bishop of Troyia, to Britain. They landed in our island, after being nearly lost in a violent storm, which was calmed by St. Germanus, who threw into the water a few drops of blessed oil. As soon as they landed, they began to preach; and the Pelagians were frightened at the numbers who returned to the true faith. For a long time they were afraid to meet St. German and St. Lupus, but at last they ventured.

It is said that this meeting took place at St. Albans, where the Pelagians came in rich and splendid robes, and surrounded by great crowds of their followers. An immense multitude gathered together to hear the contest, eager to know how the stranger missionaries would stand against these bold and positive men. St. German and St. Lupus came in the simple black habit of the Roman ecclesiastics, without gold, or jewels, or followers. The Pelagians spoke first; and then the Christian bishops answered with words of such moving truth and power, that the heretics could not say another word. While they were thus silent and full of rage, a British noble appeared, leading his little girl by the hand, and making his way through the crowd to the missionaries from Gaul. The child was blind; and he asked them to heal her, and restore her sight. St. Germanus begged him to take her first to the Pelagians, that they might show, by working a miracle, whether their faith was true or not. The heretics, quite confounded, said they had no power to heal, and the blind child was led back to the bishops. St. Germanus prayed fervently over her; and then, taking a little case of relics from his robe, he laid it upon her eyes, and immediately she recovered her sight. All the people then with one voice proclaimed that the faith which St. Germanus taught was the true one, and the Pelagian heretics were driven away.

While St. Germanus was in Britain, the Scots and Picts invaded the country again. It was Lent, and as St. Germanus preached every day, great crowds of people came to ask to be baptized. They were to be baptized at Easter; and a rustic chapel was built in the forest, of leafy boughs and roughly-hewn trees, for the ceremony.

Just then the Pictish army advanced against the place, and St. German said he would help his children to conquer their heathen enemies, but without shedding blood. He chose a narrow plain surrounded by hills, where he placed his men among the brushwood and rocky caves; and at night, when he gave the signal, he with his priests shouted with their whole strength, "Alleluia, Alleluia!" and the people too, all of them, shouted "Alleluia!" and the rocks echoed back the sound all round the frightened Picts, who thought some supernatural enemy was come upon them, and without striking a single blow, they threw away their arms and fled. Many were lost in the river, and many fell by the swords of their own countrymen, who did not know one another in the darkness. This was ever after called "The Battle of Alleluia."

The Aberlemno Serpent Stone, Pictish stone with Pictish symbols

Chapter IV.

The Fair-Haired Strangers

From 449 to 477

WICKED king Vortigern had now brought Britain to so miserable a condition, that he resolved to ask some strangers, who were cruising in three chiules, or long ships, in the English Channel, to come and fight the Picts for them. These strangers were called the Saxons; they were pirates or sea-robbers, a Teutonic race, who came from the shores of the Baltic Sea, and were called Saxons from the *saxes* or short swords which they wore. They were a tribe of the famous Scandinavian race, whose mythology, so full of grand and heroic symbolism, stamps them at once as a brave and dignified people. They were fearless and desperate men, and were renowned for always conquering when they attacked, and for escaping when they were attacked.

These pirates were commanded by two chiefs, named Hengst or Hengist, and Horsa, both which names mean a horse, which the Saxons especially venerated; and they always carried the milk-white charger embroidered on their standard. Hengst and Horsa willingly agreed to fight for Vortigern; but they asked to be allowed to have a piece of land in Kent for their reward. Vortigern gave them part of Kent, and they fought for him, and conquered the Picts completely; for their short swords and strong bright battle-axes broke the weak javelins of the Britons to pieces, and they could not stand against the fury of the fair-haired strangers.

Vortigern was so delighted at this, that he sent for a great number of Saxons, and gave them the Isle of Thanet for their own; but he soon found that he had raised up for himself worse enemies, according to the old British sons, "Woe to the day when we loved the Saxons! Woe to Vortigern and his cowardly advisers!"

For when the Saxons found that the wicked king and his people were so weak, they thought they would take Britain for themselves. So they sent for their countrymen, and for more ships; and then they were too strong for Vortigern. This time the ships brought with them Hengst and Horsa's sister, Alice Ronwen, or, as she is commonly called, Rowena, who was very beautiful; and as soon as Vortigern saw her, he divorced his own Christian wife, and married the pagan Saxon. After this, the Saxons by degrees took possession of the whole of Kent and the south of England, and carved their standard, the milk-white war-horse, upon the green turf on many of the downs on that coast. Under the turf, you know, lies the white chalk; and when the turf was cut off in the shape of a horse, it looked at a distance like a large white horse lying on the hills.

It would only puzzle you to tell you about all the battles that were fought between the Britons and the Saxons, and the names of the chiefs on both sides who fought them. It was some years before the whole of Britain was conquered; and it was divided into a great many small kingdoms, with a king for each. Vortigern and many of his subjects were obliged to fly into the mountainous parts of West Britain, which we now call Wales; and many others fled across the Channel to Gaul, and seized upon a part of it called Armorica, to which they gave the name of Bretagne or Brittany, in remembrance of their own dear island. The modern Welsh and the Britons are the descendants of our British ancestors; and they still speak, in many points, nearly the same language.

Many wonderful stories were told about Vortgern. It is said that he went to consult Merlin, the famous British bard, and that he foretold all the miseries the Saxons would bring upon England, as a punishment for Vortigern's crimes. However this may be, he certainly ended his long and wicked life in the greatest poverty and wretchedness, and was hated and despised by every one for his cowardice and his crimes.

After Vortigern, there were two British kings who prevented the Saxons from taking possession of Britain for a time by their wisdom and courage. The first was named Aurelius Ambrosius, a Roman-Briton; and the second was the great King Arthur, about whom so many wonderful stories have been told. It is said that he had twelve knights at his court, who were so brave, that he never could tell which was the bravest; so he had a round table made for them, because he could not tell which deserved to sit at the top of the table at the feasts. King Arthur was so brave that he never was beaten in any battle; and even when he was dead, the Britons firmly believed that he had only disappeared for a time, and that he would come back and help them to fight the Saxons. King Arthur was buried at Glastonbury Abbey;

and after his death, the Saxons took possession of all Britain. They had some tribes of Angles among them, and from them the whole island was named Anglelard, or England, which is a name we all love much better than Britain. There was another tribe called Jutes, who settled in Kent and in the Isle of Wight; and to this day the Kentish people look upon themselves as a different race from the rest of England.

King Arthur, Howard Pyle

Chapter V.

Our Anglo-Saxon Forefathers

So we heard before, the Saxons were heathens, and they worshipped false gods, the chief of whom were named Odin, Thor, Frigga, and Balder. Their mythology was full of a certain dignity and grandeur, which showed them to be a people naturally religious. They thought that Odin lived in a palace called Asgard, where they too would go, and be happy with him, if they were brave and generous in battle. At the gate of this palace stood the huge ash-tree Yggdrasil, on whose leaves all events, past, present, and to come, were written. They represented Balder, the son of Odin, the most beautiful and glorious of all their deities, and the leader of the armies of Odin, as being killed in the very prime of life, which signifies the going down of the sun, but which may also contain a faint traditional idea of the death of our Lord, as they had also of the battle between the angels and Lucifer.

The Scandinavian mythology represented the earth as being formed out of the body of a huge giant. The mountains

The Norse god Odin enthroned, flanked by his two wolfs, Geri and Freki, and his two ravens, Huginn and Muninn, and holding his spear Gungnir.

were made out of his bones, the earth of his flesh, the trees of his hair, and the heavens of his skull. The books in which these strange wild notions are found are called the Edda and the Sagas; and by and by you will like very much to read the books written by the Scandinavian historian Snorro.

Whatever the Saxons wrote or sang about was full of warlike and magnificent thoughts, which showed that, however wild and cruel their character might be, it had always something noble and dignified in it. There are other things about them, too, which it is very interesting to us to remember, as they, more than any of the other nations who conquered our country, became rooted in its soil, and brought in with them, and fixed in the most enduring manner, their government, customs, and ways of thinking; so that we look to the Saxons now as our first forefathers, and rather as the rightful possessors than the conquerors of England.

The first of these characteristics of our Anglo-Saxon forefathers was *the love of justice*. In their own forests, and even as pagan tribes, the Teutonic races were celebrated for their obedience to certain laws, and for respecting the rights and property of their friends and neighbors. This was a great natural virtue, and one which always accompanies a natural sense of religion. Another characteristic was a certain truthfulness, an integrity and sincerity of mind, which led them to shun deceit and to speak the truth; while the Celtic tribes, as a family, were untruthful and full of cunning.

A third distinguishing mark of the Anglo-Saxons was a great respect and honor for women. Instead of treating them as a better kind of cattle, which was the custom of all the tribes of the great family of Asiatic Celts, they looked upon them with a respect amounting to reverence. The *housfrau*, or mistress of the house, had always a particular chair kept for her; everyone got up and uncovered his head when she came in or went out; and she was always consulted on all matters of importance, and in many instances her words were supposed to have the meaning of an oracle. So, as the men were more courteous and polite than other pagan tribes, the women were more modest, and gentle, and reserved.

When you have the opportunity of studying German, you can read many very interesting books upon our Saxon or Teutonic forefathers, and their manners and customs. Then you will remember how you first learned to take an interest in them in your English history.

"The Ash Yggdrasil" (1886) by Friedrich Wilhlem Heine

Chapter VI.

The Heptarchy and the Mission from Rome.

From 477 to 604.

SAXON kings in England were not at first called kings, but Bretwaldas. They did not reign over all the country, but divided it into kingdoms. This is always called the Saxon Heptarchy, from the Greek word *hepta*, which means seven. The first bretwalda was named Ælla, the second Ceawlin, the third Ethelbert. I have nothing to tell you about the first two; but Ethelbert's reign was a very important and interesting one, and you will like very much to hear about it.

The Pope at that time was the great St. Gregory. Before he was made Pope, he was walking one day in the forum at Rome, and saw some boys standing in the market to be sold for slaves. They were very fair, with large blue eyes, and long curling yellow hair; and he asked who they were. He was told that they were Angles. "Justly are they so named," said he; "for their face is angelic, and they ought to be co-heirs with the angels in heaven. And how is their province named?" The boys answered, "Deira," which was the name of Northumberland. "De ira Dei" (from the wrath of God), he replied, "they must indeed be torn, and called to His mercy. How is the king of their country called?" The boys replied, "AElla." Then said Gregory, "Alleluia in praise of God shall be surely hymned in that portion of the earth." When he was made Pope, St. Gregory remembered the poor Saxon boys; and he sent a holy monk named Augustin, with several others, to England. They landed in the Isle of Thanet in Kent, and asked leave to preach before King Ethelbert, promising him as a reward a lasting kingdom, whose joys should never decay.

Ethelbert had heard a great deal about the Christian faith; for he had married a French princess named Bertha, the daughter of Charibert king of France, who was very pious and good. He said that the missionaries might come and preach to his people, and that he would feed them as long as they stayed in England.

Then St. Augustine and his companions walked in procession into Canterbury, carrying a silver cross and a large picture of our Blessed Lord before them, and chanting as they went. I am sure you would like to hear what it was they sang. It was "Kyrie eleison, Kyrie eleison! We beseech Thee, O Lord, in all Thy mercy, that Thy anger and wrath be turned away from this city and Thy sacred mansion; for we have sinned. Alleluia."

It was not in vain that the voice of these litanies ascended to heaven. King Ethelbert was baptized with all his court, and many thousands of his subjects; and by degrees other kings

St. Augustine preaches to King Ethelbert

too were converted to the faith; so that all the southern parts of England were restored to the Church. The king gave to St. Augustine and his monks his own palace at Canterbury for a monastery, and went to live at Reculver himself. St. Augustine was made Archbishop of Canterbury by St. Gregory: he had the old British churches cleaned and repaired, and the idol temples sprinkled with holy water, and the idols in them broken in pieces; so that they could be used as Christian churches. And now you see that the great St. Gregory's words came true, and Alleluia was sung all through merry Catholic England.

St. Mellitus and several other companions were sent by St. Gregory from Rome to help St. Augustine; and they brought vestments, and chalices, and everything that was necessary for the use of the priests, and to serve as models for all the churches. St. Augustine made one of his companions Bishop of Rochester; and a great many missionary priests were sent out through England to preach and instruct the people.

The little church of St. Martin, in which St. Augustine

first said Mass at Canterbury, was rededicated by him to our Lord; and this, Christ's church, he made his own and his monks' residence. There was an idol temple outside the town, which he dedicated to St. Pancras. The king also built a beautiful church to St. Peter and Paul; and a monastery for a community of monks, to whom he gave it forever. If you ever go to Canterbury, you will see the old church of St. Martin, and remains of St. Augustine's monastery, and *the very altar* St. Augustine used to say Mass upon in St. Pancras' church.

King Ethelbert built also a church in London in honor of St. Paul, and St. Mellitus was made Bishop of London in his reign. Before he died, by the advice of St. Augustine, this wise king drew up the Anglo-Saxon laws into a regular code, and established order and justice throughout his kingdom.

Canterbury Cathedral

Chapter VII.

The Bretwaldas
From 616 to 728

HE fourth bretwalda was named Redwald; the fifth Edwin. Edwin lived in Northumberland, and he married Edilburga, the daughter of King Ethelbert; but he himself was a Pagan for a long time. Edilburga, however, took with her to Northumberland a Roman priest named Paulinus, who persuaded the king to renounce his idols. Paulinus was afterwards made Archbishop of York; and Edwin gave him a house and lands in the city: so that there were now two Archbishops in England. King Edwin set his kingdom in order, like Ethelbert; and built stone cisterns and fountains along the highways; and fastened, with a chain, a brass cup to each fountain, that the thirsty travellers might drink and be refreshed on their way.

The next bretwalda's name was Oswald. He was a saintly and a brave king; and in his reign St. Aidan, a Scotch monk, built a monastery in Lindisfarne, which was thence called Holy Island, and converted all the north of England. Oswald married the daughter of the King of Wessex, who was named Cynegils; and he persuaded Cynegils and his brother Cuichelm to become Christians. Cynegils gave the city of Dorchester in Oxfordshire to St. Birinus, and he built a cathedral there, which afterwards became very magnificent. On the Berkshire downs there is still a large barrow or mound of earth, which is now said to be King Cuichelm's tomb.

King Oswald very often went about with St. Aidan to preach to the people; and when he could not explain himself well (being a Scot) to them, the king was his interpreter, and repeated what St. Aidan had said. And this most beautiful sight of the king helping and forwarding the Church, as her eldest and most devoted son, was not seen merely once or twice, but many times in this holy king's reign.

One day, as he was at dinner, Oswald was told that a great crowd of people had come to ask alms. The king's dinner was spread out upon a very large silver tray, and he pointed to it, and told the servant to take all that there was and give it to the poor, and to break up the tray into small pieces and to divide it among them. St. Aidan, who was sitting next to the king, seized the hand which had pointed to the tray, and said, "May this hand never perish for thy charity!" It was a prophecy; for after the holy king's death, the hand which the saint had touched, and as it were consecrated to be a relic, was cut off and kept uncorrupt for many years.

King Oswald's habit of prayer was so constant that it passed into a proverb; and this proverb tells us that his last words, like his life, were words of prayer, and that his heart as well as his words was full of charity. This Northumbrian proverb is, " 'May the Lord have mercy on their souls!' as Oswald said when he fell on the battlefield."

The seventh bretwalda was Oswio or Oswy. He had a relation named Oswin, who was a very holy man. He was, too, very kind, and generous, and handsome, and everyone loved him better than Oswy, who was jealous of him, and hated him. At last he gave Oswin part of Northumberland, and sent him away; but he only watched for an opportunity to put him to death. St. Aidan loved Oswin very much, and Oswin loved St. Aidan, and did all he could to help him in his diocese, as Oswald had done. He gave him once a very beautiful horse, that he might make all his journeys safely at all times in the year.

Very soon after the king had sent him this horse, St. Aidan was riding it along the highway, and a beggar asked alms of him. The Bishop immediately got off his horse, and gave it, just as it was, with a fine saddle and bridle, to the beggar. St. Aidan dined with the king that day, and Oswin was vexed at his giving away his beautiful horse, and told him that he had chosen it for him especially. St. Aidan very quickly made the king this beautiful answer: "Can it be then, my king, that the son of a mare is dearer to you than the son of God?"

The king had been so vexed at his favorite horse being given away, that he would not sit down with the bishop, but stood by the fire, and eat his dinner there. But after a few minutes' thought he unbuckled his sword, and put it away, and, throwing himself humbly at the bishop's feet, he begged of him to pardon him, and said that henceforth he would be silent, and that St. Aidan might give as much of his money as he pleased to the *sons of God*. They then dined together as usual; but St. Aidan was soon seen to weep; and being asked by his priest aside why he did so, he said he knew that the king's death was near, for as he had never seen so humble a monarch, so he knew that the nation was not worthy of him. His words, like his words to Oswald, proved to be another prophecy. Oswy very soon after treacherously took him prisoner and murdered him, and St. Aidan died twelve days afterwards.

In the reign of Oswy there were some disputes about the discipline of the Church upon two points, which caused a great deal of anger and trouble. The calendar was so bad at that time that it was difficult for people in different parts of the world to know when it was really Easter and when it was not. This was so inconvenient, as well as irregular, that the Pope had it newly arranged according to the Alexandrian cycle, and ordered that Easter should be reckoned everywhere from the same calendar. Everyone was glad to agree to this except the British clergy, who liked their own customs and their own old Sulpician Calendar, and perhaps their own way too; and they would not agree to keep the Roman Easter with all Christendom, but kept their own Easter by themselves.

Another point of dispute was the manner of giving priests the tonsure. All priests have some hair shaved off from the back of their heads, in remembrance of the crown of thorns which our blessed Lord wore. This is called the *tonsure;* and priests love to have it, because it crowns them with His crown, and reminds them of the cruel mocking of their King, which they too must share.

The Roman clergy cut their tonsure at the back of the head, as I have described; but the British clergy cut theirs like a crescent in front. The Roman clergy said that this was the tonsure of Simon Magus, and they begged of the British clergy to leave it off, that they might all alike follow St. Peter and the customs of Rome. It was a sad and foolish thing, and showed a self-willed and obstinate spirit, to refuse to do as Christendom did, and to follow Rome, the seat of the Vicar of Christ, and the Mother and Mistress of all the churches: this seems to have been the predominant fault of the British clergy.

King Oswy was obliged to interfere, and he seems to have acted well and wisely in this affair. He called a council, and sent for St. Wilfrid, the Bishop of York, and St. Colman, and all the bishops of his kingdom. St. Colman said that he had the authority of St. Columba, the apostle of the north, for the crescent tonsure of the British clergy; St. Wilfrid said, on the other side, that St. Peter sanctioned and established the Roman usage. Oswy decided that St. Peter, who was Head of the Church, was more to be followed than St. Columba; and it was wisely settled that all should follow the discipline of Rome.

St. Wilfrid's is a beautiful and wonderful history. After converting most of the north of England, he was banished by the King of Northumberland, Alfred, and went into Wessex. Afterwards he was driven out of Wessex into Sussex, where he preached to the pagan fishermen. He went twice to Rome, and was at last restored to his own diocese of York. The history of the kings of Northumberland, from this time, is only a tale of murders and cruelty. But although there is nothing worth telling about the Northumbrian kings, you must learn the names of two Northumbrian scholars, who were known and loved all over Europe. They were Bede and Alcuin. Bede was born at Sunderland, and was brought up at Jarrow, where he spent a long life in learning and teaching others. He wrote a great many learned books, which were spread and read with great delight all through Christendom.

Alcuin was not a monk; he was a schoolmaster. The Archbishop, Egbert, of York made him master of the large grammar-school in that town; and he was so famed for his learning, that crowds of French and German students came to learn at his school. The Emperor Charlemagne sent to him to come and live in France; and he went and lived at Paris for many years; but when he grew old, he was tired of so many fine and worldly people, and he went to Tours, where he taught till he died.

A page from a copy of Bede's *Lives of St. Cuthbert,* showing King Ethelstan presenting the work to the saint. This manuscript was given to St. Cuthbert's shrine in 934.

Whenever you hear any one talk about the ignorance of the "dark ages," as those times are called by some people, you can remind them of the two Englishmen, Bede and Alcuin.

I will tell you now about two kings of Wessex, and then we shall finish the time of the Saxon Heptarchy. The first of these was named Cadwal or Cadwalla. He had reigned for two years with great renown as a pagan, conquering all the neighboring states, and behaving very cruelly to them; but at the end of that time he felt a strong desire to be a Christian and to be baptized. And he resolved not only to be baptized, but to be baptized at Rome; for the grace of God was so strong in him, that he said he had only two desires. One was, to get to St. Peter's shrine, and to be washed from his sins at the tomb of the Prince of the Apostles; and the other was, to die in his baptismal robes, that he might carry them unstained to heaven. He left his earthly kingdom without the least regret; made his long and difficult journey through France and Lombardy, and got to Rome, where he was baptized in St. Peter's by Pope Sergius, and took the name of Peter, out of love for the Head of the Church. And as the first of his prayers was heard, so too was the last; for the newly-baptized Peter was seized with a mortal sickness, and dying soon after, was buried, as he desired, in St. Peter's, and in his baptismal robes.

The king who succeeded Cadwalla was named Ina. He was one of the wisest men and best kings that have ever reigned. Besides governing his kingdom with great prudence, he built a great many churches and monasteries, and always helped the clergy as much as he could. He had a queen named Ethelburga, who was afterwards canonized, and who persuaded the king to do a great many of his good deeds. Amongst others, King Ina founded a new monastery at

Glastonbury; and he often went there to make a retreat, and to spend some time in prayer.

Ruins of Glastonbury Abbey

Ina was very fond of learning and of learned men. He asked every master of a house who could afford it to send him a penny; and when he had collected a great many pence, he sent them to Rome, to build a school for the English who went to Rome to be educated. This was the first foundation of the English college which is at Rome now, where many of our English priests go to study. The money which Ina collected was called *Peter's Pence*, or *Romescot;* and it was the very greatest benefit to the Anglo-Saxon clergy and people, and one which, no doubt, contributed more than any other circumstance to that docile, childlike faith which so distinguished them, to have a college in Rome, which cherished in the students not only a spirit of enlightened learning, but also, what is more valuable, a constant intercourse with Rome, and the fond devoted love which grows out of that intercourse.

But now you must hear a beautiful story of King Ina and

Queen Ethelburga, which will make you love them even still more. St. Ethelburga wished very much to become poor for Christ's sake; and she asked the king to leave their royal crown and their kingdom, and give up all the dignity of their state, and become poor in some distant land, where they might serve God in peace. King Ina was a very wise and prudent king, and he knew well how many duties he had to perform to his people; so he said 'No' very often; so often, that St. Ethelburga was tired of hearing it, and she resolved to ask in another way.

One night she made a great feast at the king's castle, and invited everyone to come; and there was music and dancing, and a great feast, and everything that the world calls pleasant and delightful. No one looked so bright and happy that night as St. Ethelburga, and everyone loved to be near her, and to look at her kind and gentle and beautiful face. The next morning she ordered all the king's beautiful horses to be brought out; and she and the king and all the guests went out into the green forests, to hunt and amuse themselves in the fresh spring air. When they had ridden about all day, and talked and laughed till they were tired, they returned to the castle. To their amazement, it was desolate. No guards stood at the gates; no warder blew his horn to say they were coming; no grooms waited to take their horses. All the doors stood wide open, and the rich hangings were pulled down from the walls, or hung in tatters upon them. As the guests walked in silent wonder through the empty halls, they came to the king's own apartments: a litter of pigs lay there upon some straw. Every one looked at his neighbor, but no one could explain the mystery.

Then St. Ethelburga spoke. She spoke of the riches and splendor of yesterday, the gay scene of mirth and shortlived pleasure. She asked the king where his feasts, his dances, and his music now were; and what they availed him. And what, she said, in a few short years would be their lot? They must go, and leave all these delights, all this vanity.

Would they not desire that they had devoted themselves to God, and served Him only?

She did not speak in vain. The great and wise King Ina, victorious in so many battles, and who for seven-and-thirty years had been looked up to by all the neighboring kings as their model, listened to his dear and holy queen. He called a council of his nobles, stripped off his royal robes, laid down the golden sceptre which he carried, put on a pilgrim's weeds, and, amid the tears of all who beheld him, set off with St. Ethelburga for Rome. There he built a church in honor of our Lady, near to the English College, and, with his faithful queen, lived poor and unknown in the Holy City all the rest of their lives.

Chapter VIII.

The Sea-Kings

From 800 to 835

MOST of the histories of England that have ever been written have said that the Saxon Heptarchy ended in the year 800, when Egbert became king, and that he was the first king of all England. It has been doubted, however, lately, whether Egbert really had more land or authority than the bretwaldas; and the later histories seem to agree that though he called himself king of all England, he certainly was not. But as you have not the time to read all these, nor are able to judge for yourself, we had better conclude that Egbert had at least more power than the kings who reigned before him, and that the Saxon Heptarchy began to break up and disappear about his reign. And as he was a very wise and powerful king, it is most likely that he helped to break it up; and as he got more of the country into his hands, he was looked up to as in some sort the sovereign of the other lesser princes whose kingdoms surrounded his.

Egbert was a brave and handsome prince, which pleased the people, and he fought a great many battles; he even took possession of parts of Wales and Cornwall, so that his name became very famous. But in the very midst of his victories, when everyone thought he would take peaceable possession of all England, and that the land would rest, a new and cruel enemy appeared, more revengeful and mischievous than the heathen Saxons had been.

These were the Danes, who came from the islands of the Baltic Sea, and the continent round it, as the Saxons had done; and who were, in fact, part of the same great Scandinavian family, but with different characteristics, and habits, and customs. They hated their relations the Anglo-Saxons, because they had become Christians, and they were determined to seize upon their fertile and beautiful island. They gloried in calling themselves the faithful sons of Odin; and made it a rule to put to death all the priests they could find, and to burn all the Christian churches. Whenever they had done such a deed as this, they used to sing a wild wicked song, beginning with these words:

"We have sung the Mass of Lances, and it lasted from sunrise till night"

The Danes were governed by a chief, who had the authority of king only in time of battle. When the battle or the war was over, the chief sat with the other soldiers round the fire, and they saluted one another as brothers, and drank beer together, and sang wild loud songs. Their chiefs were called "Sea-Kings," or *Vikingsr*[1] and they boasted that their kings "never slept under a raftered roof, nor sat by the sheltered hearth-stone."

The ships of these terrible Norse men[2] (as they were often

---

[1] Vikingr—coasters, or lyers-in-wait in creeks and straits.

[2] Norse men, northern men. Scandinavia was often called Nordland, as parts of Norway and Sweden are to this day.

called) were as wild-looking as themselves. The fore-part, or beak, was carved into the form of enormous horses' or snakes' heads, painted in bright colors, and gilded; while the stern, or hind-part, was coiled and curved into a tail like that of a serpent or dragon. The sides were often covered with plates of brass, like scales; so that the whole ship looked like some terrible sea-monster. Their standard was a black raven, which was woven or embroidered upon the silk at noon-day, by the three daughters of the greatest of all the Sea-Kings, Ragnar Lodbrog; and whenever this raven appeared, horror and dismay spread on all sides, for it was well known that the terrible Vikingr spared neither man nor woman, house nor land.

Ragnar Lodbrog

This was the enemy that came pouring in upon England from the North Sea, in King Egbert's time, headed by Ragnar Lodbrog himself. They landed in Northumberland, where they burned and destroyed all the corn and houses, and barns and churches. But Ragnar was taken prisoner by Egbert's armies; and it is said that he was put into a dungeon filled with serpents, who stung him to death, which was a most barbarous and unchristian punishment. While the fierce Sea-King was dying, tradition says that he sang a wild extempore song, as the Scandinavians were used to do, which was called

"Ragnar's Death-Song," and which has been preserved and handed down till now. Two or three verses of it are written down here, which will give you a good idea of the mixture of courage, ferocity, and the love of mystery, which are always to be found in the Scandinavian race:

> "We smote with our swords on the day when I saw hundreds of enemies stretched on the sands beneath an English headland; dew-drops of blend fell off our swords; our arrows sung in the wind when they sought the helmets, and it gave me delight. *   *   *   *
>
> "We smote with our swords in fifty-and-one battles. I doubt if among men there ever was a king more famous than I am. From my boyhood I have shed blood, and have longed for such a death as this. The hours of my life are fast ebbing. I am smiling under the hand of death."

The death-song of Ragnar was carried by the Danes to the shores of the Baltic; and his fierce people were so angry when they heard it, and remembered how many times he had led them to victory, that they were resolved to revenge their beloved chief's death. They came again to England, and marched from Northumberland to Croyland in Lincolnshire, burning and destroying whatever lay in their way.

There was then a beautiful and massive abbey at Croyland, which they determined to burn; because, as they hated the very name of the Christian religion, and they hated priests and monks above all. The monks of Croyland were just going to sing Matins when they heard that the Danes were coming. The aged abbot ordered that all the young and strong monks should go out of the monastery, and hide themselves in the fens; while he with the old monks would stay behind and share the same fate, rather than desert the altars of God.

The central door of the Croyland Abbey's west front of the ruined nave. The quatrefoil above the central door depicts scenes from the life of Saint Guthlac.

So the young monks set out, and took the chalices and consecrated vessels with them into the fens; and the old grey-haired abbot, and some very old brethren and some little boys, remained in the church, and began to sing Matins. Mass was said, and they went to Holy Communion. Their communion was scarcely over, when the Danes rushed in, and after torturing the old abbot and the monks, put them most cruelly to death. No one was left alive except a pretty little boy named Ingulf, who had been serving Mass. He was crying bitterly to see his dear father-abbot lying bleeding on the ground, and one of the Danish soldiers, who seems to have been less like a wild beast than the rest, took pity on him, and saved his life. The Danes then tore up and broke all the monuments in the church, and went away. As they were going along, Ingulf escaped from them into the fens, and when he grew up to be a man, he wrote this account of the burning of Croyland Abbey.

Not long afterwards, the Danes left England for a while; but they again landed, once on the southern, and once on the south-eastern coast, in Cornwall. King Egbert then got all his soldiers together, and beat them in a great battle at Hengston Hill, where an immense number of Danes, and British rebels who had joined them, were killed. The rest sailed back to their own country, and Egbert soon after died.

Egbert King of the West Saxons, first Monarch of all England / desig. et sculpt. G. Vertue. *Abstract/medium:*1 print: engraving.

Chapter IX.

England and English Laws

From 836 to 860

GBERT'S son, Ethelwulf, became king after him. He had been well brought up by St. Swithin, and was a very good and pious king. Besides St. Swithin, St. Alstan was his prime minister and counsellor; and as he was accustomed always to ask, and to follow, the advice of holy and prudent men, his reign was a happy and useful one for his subjects. The Danes at first gave him a good deal of trouble; for as soon as Egbert was dead, they came back to England, and covered the sea all round our island with their ships. They landed, nearly at the same time, in Lincolnshire, at Southampton, and in the Isle of Thanet. They burned Canterbury and London, and did a great deal of mischief; but Ethelwulf was very brave, and he would not let his soldiers be disheartened. He waited for the Danes at Okelev in Surrey, where he fought a very famous battle. More Danes were killed there than had ever before been killed in

England; and they were so afraid of Ethelwulf afterwards, that as long as he lived they never came again.

When they were gone, Ethelwulf had time to think about his people, and to set his kingdom in order. And now you must attend very carefully, while you hear a little about the laws and customs of the Anglo-Saxons, that is, of our early English forefathers.

I told you before, that even when the Saxons lived in the forests of Germany, they loved justice very much. That is, when one man murdered another man, they liked that the murderer should be punished, either by being put to death, or by being fined some money, which he was to pay to the relations of the person he had murdered. This money was called the *were,* and according as the rank of the person was high or low, so the *were* was greater or less. The Anglo-Saxon laws on this subject were very wise and just, and it is from them that we have learned to love that justice should be strictly done to all kinds of persons.

At present, you will not understand perhaps why such and such laws were important, and why such and such others should be altered. Perhaps even you do not quite understand as yet, why there should be laws at all. You must be satisfied in this case with *believing* that they are necessary, without understanding. Almighty God spoke to the Israelites on Mount Sinai, and gave them His laws, which we call the Ten Commandments. He spoke them so that all could hear and understand them, and whoever broke them would be punished. Those laws can never be changed. They are divine laws, and we are bound to keep them just as much as the Jews were bound.

Men, too, must make laws. They have the power of choosing how they will be governed, whether by a king, or by a king and a parliament, or by a council. They may alter a government when once they have chosen it. But whatever kind of government they choose, and whatever wise or foolish alterations they make in it, they must still have laws; and if there is to be any order or peace, those laws must be obeyed. But there is always this difference between the laws of God and the laws of man; that the first, which are divine, are framed by infinite Wisdom, and intended for all ages and people. They cannot be changed. The second, which are human, are framed by men who can only see what is best for the time they live in, for a few short years, and in general have to be soon changed for others, or altered to suit other times, greater knowledge, and a fresh race of men.

The Anglo-Saxon laws, therefore, have been most of them either changed or quite done away. But their spirit was so wise and just that it has sunk into the soil, as it were, instead of being rooted out, and grew up into a whole system of English law, which was distinguished for its mildness, equal justice, and moderation. The people thought that many heads were better than one, and as reading and writing were not common, they settled their disputes by calling in a great many witnesses. By this means the truth generally came out, and was made clear to all. They thought, too, that old heads were better than young and giddy ones; and they chose old or elderly men to speak in their meetings or councils, which were called *motes*. The whole country was divided into hundreds, or divisions; and for each hundred there was a *mote*, where justice was done, and offenders were punished. Each division, or number of divisions, chose an elderly man to speak for them, and to represent their wants to the king at the great *mote*, which met three times a year, and which was called the *Witan-a-gemote*, or the meeting of wise men;

Witan-a-gemote

and the elderly men who were chosen were called eldermen or *eoldermen*. Our word alderman comes from this, and also earl, because the eldermen were always *ethel*, or noblemen. There were certain towns in the hundreds called *burghs*, or boroughs, which chose someone to speak for them also. They chose a gentleman of lower rank than the eorls, called a *ceorl*, who was afterwards called a burgess, from his having to speak for a town or borough. Whenever the witan met, all the eldermen and burgesses came together, and told the king what his people wanted, and how they were behaving; so that from the very first times of the Anglo-Saxons, the kings of England knew the condition and wants of their people in such a way that they were able to govern them better; and, as far as lay in their power, to make them happy. This is a great benefit to the government as well as the people. It helps to make it strong and lasting.

When the aldermen and burgesses went home again, they told the people what new laws were made, and remedied what was wrong, as the king had ordered; and this was the first beginning of the English Parliament, which you will take great interest in by and by. This will show you that there was very early in our country a great confidence between the king and the people.

King Ethelwulf called a witan very often; and at one of their meetings a law was passed which gave the tenth of the produce of every man's land to the Church. The bishops ordered a solemn service in all the churches on Wednesdays and Fridays, to ask help of Almighty God against the Danes, in return for the dutiful love the king always showed them.

During his reign, St. Swithin went to Rome upon a pilgrimage, and the king sent his little son with the bishop. He was not more than five years old, and was a very dear little boy, named Alfred. The Pope was very glad to see him, and gave him, with his own hands, the Sacrament of Confirmation, and anointed him with holy oil. The king was not satisfied with sending St. Swithin to Rome; he resolved to go himself, and to take Alfred with him. He got together a good many courtiers and soldiers, and set out on his pilgrimage. On his way he passed through France, and went to visit Charles the Bald, who was then king. He stayed with him some time, and then journeyed on to Rome, where he spent a good deal of time in praying at the tombs of the Apostles, and in visiting the Seven Churches, and other holy places in Rome.

On his way back, Ethelwulf married his second wife, Judith, the daughter of Charles the Bald; and this marriage offended the English. His second son, Ethelbald, seized the crown for himself, and was helped in his rebellion by a good many of the nobles, who perhaps thought Ethelwulf too pious and fond of the clergy. The good old king seems to have been a true peace-maker, for he gave up Wessex to Ethelbald, and kept only a small part of his kingdom for himself. He spent all the rest of his life in acts of piety and devotion; and died two years after, leaving a sum of money to the Pope, and the churches of SS. Peter and Paul at Rome, to show his love for Rome and the Vicar of Christ. He was buried in Winchester Cathedral.

Winchester Cathedral

Chapter X.

The King and the Saint

From 871 to 900

ING ETHELWULF had several sons. The three elder ones reigned after him, each in his turn; for they all died without children. They were named Ethelbald, Ethelbert, and Ethelred I. But there is nothing worth telling about them, for they were neither good, nor brave, nor wise. Whilst Ethelred was king, the Danes invaded England again; and his young brother Alfred fought all his battles, and beat the Danes so thoroughly at a great battle at Aston in Berkshire, that they went away for a while. Just after the battle of Aston, Ethelred died, and Alfred became king of England.

And now we must go back to the time when he was quite a boy, that we may see how he was brought up, and how he learned to become what he was, the greatest and the best king that ever ruled our country.

His mother's name was Osburga; she was Ethelwulfs first

wife, and was a very pious and learned queen. She knew what very few people then knew—she knew how to read and write. She loved reading, and liked to have learned men at her court. One day, her boys were sitting with her, and she was reading a beautiful book, which was painted all over and gilt, and had pictures of Our Lady and the Saints in it. She told the boys, who were delighted with the pictures, that she would give it to the one among them who could first read it. The elder ones did not care to take the trouble, they liked rough sports and play better; but Alfred ran away directly to one of the scholars who lived at the court, and asked him to teach him to read. He soon learned to read the beautiful book (which was written in Latin), and it was given to him as his reward.

When he grew older, he loved to listen to the tales that were told by the Anglo-Saxon bards of his father's court, and he eagerly learned them by heart. But best of all he loved to hear the tales which the *palmers,* or pilgrims, brought from the Holy Land or from Rome. They would all sit round the blazing hearth, and tell of the Holy Child and His blessed Mother, who on such a night was found in the grotto at Bethlehem by the Magi; or would speak of the House of Nazareth, which they had seen, where He was so obedient to His parents. Then, again, they would tell of many brave soldiers of Christ, who, leaving the world, had followed His footsteps, and put off their crowns, to live as pilgrims and wanderers upon earth.

Such were the tales which fed young Alfred's heart, and made him burn to do the like.

Hearing stories and songs gave him a good deal of knowledge, but it was not enough for him. He wanted books, and there were none to be had, excepting what were written in Latin. He began by translating pieces of Latin into Anglo-Saxon, till he was quite master of the language; and then he asked the most learned men he knew of in Europe to come and help him to teach his people.

The chief of those who came were the monk Asser, from Wales, the monk John, from the great Benedictine monastery of Corbie in Saxony, and Grimbald, the learned superior of the monastic college at St. Omer in France. There were, besides, three or four learned Anglo-Saxons, who came to live at the court; and by their help Alfred built schools and colleges, and provided them with books and masters. The king himself translated the Ecclesiastical History of the Venerable Bede, an Ancient History, the Consolations of Philosophy by Boethius, the Pastoral of St. Gregory the Great, and the Lord's Prayer. He sent a copy of St. Gregory's Pastoral to each of his bishops, and asked them to have it chained in some convenient place in the church, where all their priests might see and read it.

Alfred had now done a great deal for his people; but I am sorry to say that he soon began to grow proud and overbearing, and then he fell into grievous sins. For several years he led a very bad life, was very cruel and harsh towards his subjects, and careless about their good. He was so severe, indeed, in punishing the least offence, that his people feared and hated him. But you will see how he made up afterwards for his conduct, and how Almighty God brought him back again, like holy David.

Alfred had an elder brother whom we have heard nothing about. He was the eldest son of Ethelwulf, and his name was Athelstan. He had been a very brave prince, and had fought well against the heathen Danes; but after one of those bloody battles his heart was touched, and he resolved to leave the world, and go and live as a hermit. He kept his resolution; and Prince Athelstan became a hermit and a saint, St. Neot. St. Neot in his hermitage performed many miracles, and converted many souls; and among those who sought his cell at Neotstowe in Cornwall, was his brother Alfred. St. Neot, like Nathan, rebuked the king sternly and sharply for his evil life, and his harsh treatment of his people; and Alfred listened to him, and repented, though his heart was not thoroughly changed yet. Alfred came again and again, without really changing his life; and at last St. Neot told him that he should suffer terribly from his enemies, and that they would drive him from his throne; but, *by his prayers,* he should be restored to it again. This was the last meeting between the king and St. Neot, as brothers, for very soon after the saint died.

The prophecy of St. Neot soon came true. When the Danes came again, and Alfred sent out the usual Saxon messenger—a soldier carrying an arrow and a naked sword, and saying, "Let every man that is not worthless, whether in the burghs or out of the burghs, leave his house, and come forward,"—the king found, to his great sorrow, that his sins and harsh treatment of his subjects had made them hate him; and they would not come and fight against the Danes. He was very unhappy at this, and was obliged to fly into the woods and marshes, to escape being killed. He fled to a part of Somersetshire, between the Parret and the Thone, full of wood and tangled brushwood. One day, while he was there, he went into a swineherd's cottage, and asked for a piece of bread. The swineherd's wife was a thrifty soul, and she thought he was a strong able man who ought to do something for his supper, so she asked him to mind the cakes which were roasting on the hearth, while he was mending his bow and arrows. The king sat down by the hearth, but he was thinking about his poor country and the Danes, and he forgot all about the cakes, and let them burn to a cinder. When the good woman came back, she scolded the king soundly, and perhaps gave him a box on the ear. She was still scolding, when some of Alfred's nobles came in, and brought their king news that the Danes had been defeated in a great battle, and that now was the time to attack them.

Alfred's time, however, was not come yet. He remained in the lonely island of Athelney, where many strange and wonderful things happened to him. One day, when all his followers were out fishing, and he, for pastime, was reading in a book, a poor pilgrim came to him, and asked an alms in God's name. The king lifted up his hands to heaven, and said: 'I thank God of His grace that He visiteth this poor man this day by another poor man, and vouchsafeth to ask of me that which He hath given me.' Then the king anon calleth his servant, that had but one loaf and a very little wine, and bade him take the half thereof to the poor man, who received it thankfully, and suddenly vanished from his sight, so that no step or sign of him was seen on the moor he passed over; and also what was given him by the king was left as it had been given unto him. Shortly after, the company returned to their master, and brought with them great plenty of fish they had caught. The night following, when the king was at his rest, there appeared to him one in a bishop's weed, and charged him that he should love God and keep justice, and be merciful to poor men, and reverence priests; and said, moreover, 'Alfred, Christ knoweth thy mind and thy conscience, and now will make an end of all thy care; for tomorrow strong helpers will come to thee, by whose aid thou shalt subdue thy enemies.' 'Who art thou?" said the king. 'I am St. Cuthbert,' said he, 'the poor pilgrim that yesterday was with thee, to whom thou gavest both bread and wine. I am busy for thee and thine, wherefore have thou mind thereof when it is well with thee.' And after this vision Alfred was more comforted.

He grew bolder in the promise of the saint, and went in disguise to the camp of the Danish king Gothrum, and played upon the harp in his tent. When he had made his observations, he gathered his men together in Selwood Forest, at King Egbert's Stone, to do battle with the Danes; and there one night, as he was lying in his tent, a glorious sight appeared. This was his brother St. Neot, dazzling like an angel, and shedding a sweet odor round him. He brought a suit of armor in his hand, and bade Alfred take courage, and go forth in God's name to overcome the Danes, for he should win a great victory.

The Anglo-Saxons came gladly at King Alfred's summons. They had suffered most terribly from the Danes; and they now knew that their king was changed by his adversity, and that they could trust him again. He spoke to them on the field, and reminded them that, on this day, they must either overcome, or submit forever to the hated Danish raven, and become slaves to the sorcerous and bloodthirsty heathens. He said they had all deeply sinned, but they were now forgiven; therefore they could fight with fresh courage. His voice sent a new strength into their hearts. They cried out, "The Lord shall give strength to His people. Blessed be God!" The battle was a very fierce one, and was doubtful for a long time. Just when it was most doubtful, a strange hand seized the standard of the Snow-white Horse, and urged on the Anglo-Saxon soldiers with a voice which no one could resist. The stranger was robed in dazzling white, and his brow shone with such majestic splendor, that the affrighted heathens fled in terror and confusion before him. It was a day of holy vengeance and retribution for the blood of the just, which the Danes had poured out like water in England. St. Neot, for it was he, led the victorious Saxons forward to the thickest ranks of the enemy; and wherever he went the ground was strewed with dead. So many thousands of the Danes lay dead on that field, that the place is still called Slaughter Ford. And when the work was done, St. Neot returned to his place in heaven, and never was seen again on earth.

In that great battle the Danish king Gothrum was taken prisoner, and very many of his nobles also. And not long after the battle, he and his nobles, with King Alfred and all his court,

Baptism of Gothrum

were gathered together at Westminster,[3] clothed in white, and with white fillets on their foreheads, to beg the grace of baptism. And there the fierce Gothrum became changed into the Christian soldier Athelstan, St. Neot's ancient name, for he took it at the font, as King Alfred stood sponsor for him. He and his Danes settled in the east of England, and became good and peaceful English subjects.

---

[3] There is every reason to think that the ancient Wedmore was Westminster.

And now at last Alfred had leisure to attend to his subjects; and it was with a changed heart and a changed life that he came back to reign over them. The first thing he did was to re-establish order among them. A number of petty magistrates had got power into their hands in many of the towns and villages, and treated the people very unjustly, taking money from bad rich men who bribed them, and behaving tyrannically to the poor. The king sent all these bad magistrates away, and put some of them to death; so that the rest were frightened, and they never dared take money again for doing justice as long as they lived.

Then, with the help of his witan, Alfred made such good laws, and caused them to be so well kept, that, as an old Saxon chronicle says, "golden bracelets were hung up by the roadside, and no one dared to touch them."

Next, the king had the people taught how to build better houses, and to make more comfortable furniture; and he founded schools for both the rich and the poor all through England. One of these schools was built at Oxford, which afterwards became a famous University. In these good works the king was helped by the learned men whom we spoke of before. The Welsh monk Asser tells us that he never left the king, either in joy or in sorrow; and it is he who has told us so many beautiful things about Alfred. Alfred next built a great many ships; and he invented several new ways of building them, by which they were greatly improved. In fact, the first founder of our English navy was King Alfred. He sent messengers to the Baltic Sea, to the North Cape, to Hungary, and to Germany, to hear about these countries; and when they came back, he wrote down what they said, to instruct and amuse his people. He sent the good Bishop of Sherborne also to Malabar in India, where some poor Christians were

King St. Alfred the Great

in great want, with money for their necessities; and they, in return, sent back some spices and pearls by the bishop.

Alfred could never have done so much if he had not been very exact about his time. He divided the day into three parts of eight hours each; so that he had eight hours for his prayers and study, eight hours for business, and eight for meals, sleep, and recreation. To make himself more exact, Alfred invented a clock, which it will amuse you to hear about. He had a certain weight of wax made into six candles, each twelve inches long; and the inches were marked upon them. Each candle burned four hours. So you see the whole six candles would last exactly four-and-twenty hours.

Alfred divided his revenue as exactly as he did his time. He put one share apart for the expenses of his court, his servants, and public buildings; another was kept for donations to convents, monasteries, and schools, in a word, for alms. But indeed I cannot tell you all that this great and good king did; for it is time to end this long chapter.

Alfred at last fell very sick, for he was quite worn out with pain and many labors. When he found that he was going to die, he divided all his money between his relations, his bishops, some priests, whom he loved very much, and a great many poor. Then he called his son Edward to him, and gave him some good advice about his people; and spoke to him about some serfs or slaves whom he had freed. When you can read larger histories, you will like to know all that Alfred said. It seemed as if he very much wished there were no serfs, for nearly his last words were to his son about these serfs. "For God's love, my son, and the advantage of my soul, I will that they be masters of their own freedom and their own will; and, in the name of the living God, I entreat that no man disturb them; *and that they should be as free as their own thoughts to serve what lord they please.*"

CHAPTER XI.

The Anglo-Saxon Kings

From 901 to 1016

UNDER the name of Edward the Elder, Edward now became king; and he had a very rough and warlike reign. The Danes came to England again, as soon as Alfred was dead; and the king spent all his life in fighting with them. He was helped in every way by his sister Ethelfleda, who governed Mercia, and is always called "The Lady of Mercia." Edward was not so great or wise a man as his father; but he was brave and successful; and at last he forced the Danes to retreat to the very north of England; and made even the king of Scotland do him homage as his fief-master.

Instead of following the history of all these bloody battles, I will tell you a story of Edward's little daughter. She was called Eadburga, and she was the youngest of the king's children. One day, when she was about three years old, the king took her into his room, where he had spread out a quantity of cakes and sweetmeats and trinkets upon one end of the table;

and had caused the Chalice and Paten, with the Book of the Gospels, to be put at the other end. He then told Eadburga to choose which she liked best. The little girl did not even look at the cakes and toys, but ran immediately to the other end of the table, when she stretched out her hands for the Chalice. The king, who was delighted to see how early God had chosen his dear child to be His own, sent her immediately to the convent at Winchester, where her grandmother, King Alfred's widow, was abbess; and Eadburga died a very holy nun.

When Edward the Elder died, his son Athelstan was made king; and he is sometimes called the first king of all England, because he was the first who possessed Northumberland, which used to be a kingdom by itself. Athelstan was a very brave and warlike king, whose name became famous all through Europe. He was rather short, very fair, and wore a gold net round his long yellow hair. When he was only a baby in the cradle, his grandfather Alfred had knighted him, and had given him a beautiful purple robe and a bright sword.

Athelstan made the Welsh and Cornish Britons pay him tribute; and the princes of Scotland came to do him homage as their "hlaford" or lord. The king met them every year at a place called Eadmote; and there the Scottish princes knelt before him, and put their joined hands into both of his, to show that they acknowledged him for their sovereign.

No doubt these princes were very unwilling to pay homage to Athelstan; and he had plenty of enemies. Aulaff, the son of the king of Northumberland, whose kingdom Athelstan now possessed, came to England with a great fleet, and some of the sea-kings, to try and get his kingdom back again. But Athelstan got a great army together, and when he was ready for battle, he went into the church at Beverley, and offered his dagger upon the altar, which he then vowed to redeem (according to the custom of that time) at a royal price, if he won the battle. Aulaff, who was very brave too, dressed up like a bard, and went into Athelstan's camp, playing the harp. One of Athelstan's soldiers knew him, but he would not betray him; though, as soon as Aulaff had gone, he told the king, and advised him to choose another place for the battle. It was well that he did so; for Aulaff had studied the ground so well, that every one of the king's soldiers that were in that place the day of the battle were killed.

Soon after the great battle of Brunanburgh was fought, and Athelstan won a splendid victory. It was such a battle, that both Danes and English made songs about it, and sang them on their harps. Here is a little bit of one of their songs.

> "Olaf (Aulaff) has fled, followed by few, and has wept upon the waves. The stranger, when seated by his fireside, surrounded by his family, will not relate this battle; for in it his kinsmen have fallen, and from it his friends have never returned. *   *   *   •

> "Never did more men perish by the sword since the day when the Saxons and the Angles came from the east across the ocean, when these noble practicers of war came into Britain, who conquered the Welsh (the British), and took their country."

After the battle Athelstan went back to Beverley, and paid his vow by ransoming his dagger for a large piece of land, which he gave to the Church.

The defeat of the Danes at Brunanburgh was so famous, that it caused Athelstan to be respected by all the princes and kings of Europe. Harold Harfager, the king of Norway, sent his son Haco to be educated in England; and when he had finished his education, he took some good priests back to Norway with him, to teach his people the true faith. Alan of Brittany was another of the king's wards, or pupils; and Athelstan had him so well educated, that he became a very good and wise king. Athelstan's sister had married Charles the Simple, the king of France, and they had one son, who was sent to England; and because he lived in our country so long, the French called him Louis d' *Outremer,* or Louis from beyond the sea. Louis d'Outremer became afterwards king of France. The king had seven other sisters, four of whom married princes, and the other three became nuns. One married Hugh Capet, king of France; and when he sent to ask Ethelda for his wife, he sent some beautiful presents for Athelstan,—relics, perfumes, jewels, and fine horses, with the sword of Constantine the Great, and a spear that had belonged to the Emperor Charlemagne. All these rich and precious gifts were shown to the king and his nobles at the witan at Abingdon; and Ethelda was sent back with the ambassador to be Hugh Capet's wife.

The emperor of Germany, Henry the Fowler, asked Athelstan to let him marry one of his other sisters, and Athelstan sent two of them to Germany, that he might choose which he pleased, which seems very strange to us now. They both stayed, and married in Germany. The last and most beautiful of Athelstan's seven sisters married Lewis, prince of Aquitaine.

At last Athelstan died, and the English people were very sorry to lose their brave and wise king. He had built many a beautiful church, and given land to many a monastery and house of canons, and the clergy loved him very much. He had paid great attention to the state of his kingdom, and had called a witan very often, that he might hear how justice was administered, and that offenders were punished. If any of the nobles broke one of the laws, he was fined a large sum of money. But if any poor man broke a law, he had to pay less; which was quite just, because he was poor, and because he was not so well taught as the nobles. So that, for his justice and his kindness, both rich and poor loved King Athelstan, and grieved when he died. He was buried, according to his wish, in Malmesbury Abbey; and a long train of bishops and nobles followed his body to his tomb in that place, where he was buried with great pomp, and with tears, which were better than pomp.

A.D. 940: The next king's name was Edmund. He was Athelstan's brother, and he began his reign well, so that the people were consoled for their dear King Athelstan's death. But Edmund had reigned only a very short time, when he was murdered. As the king was feasting on St. Augustine's day, a robber named Leof came into the dining-hall, and stood by the fire. Edmund was so angry at his insolence, that he rushed towards him to turn him out; but the robber stabbed him with a dagger which he had hidden, in his breast, and the king died directly.

A.D. 946: His brother Edred was made king in his stead, because Edmund's two little sons were too young to be good kings.

Edred's reign was not very remarkable for anything, except for the final subjection of Northumberland, which the Danes had seized again. Eric the Dane was conquered and slain by Edred in a great battle, and the king put Northumberland under the government of an eorl, who now began to be called an earl. Edred was very sickly himself, and could not attend to business, but he had two of the wisest ministers that have ever governed England. These were his chancellor Turketul and St. Dunstan. Turketul was a priest, and the grandson of King Alfred, for he was Athelstan's brother. When he was young he was a brave soldier as well as a priest, and he helped Athelstan to win the battle of Brunanburgh. He was now grown old and grey-haired; and as he was one day going through the Lincolnshire fens, he came to the ruins of the great abbey of Croyland, which had never been rebuilt since the Danes had burned it. The monks showed the chancellor the relics of St. Guthlac, and lamented over their dear abbey, and Turketul felt a strong desire to restore it, and to go there himself to die. He did rebuild the abbey, and when it was finished, he asked Edred to let him go and end his days in it. He was obliged to ask a great many times, for the king valued his wise and prudent chancellor too much to part with him easily; but at last he consented, and Turketul went to end his life in the green and quiet solitude of Croyland, where he became abbot of the monastery.

St. Dunstan was of noble birth too, and he was abbot of the great abbey of Glastonbury, of which we hear so much in our history. We shall learn more of him in the next reign.

A.D. 955: When Edred died, the eldest of Edmund's two sons succeeded him. His name was Edwy, and he was so handsome that he was called Edwy the Fair. It is a pity that he was not as good as he was handsome. He was very young when he became king, and was foolish and good-naturedly weak, so that he fell into very bad company, and was never happy unless he had a number of wicked and foolish young people round him. These wicked friends persuaded Edwy to spend his time in eating and drinking, and all kinds of wicked pleasures. He ruled his kingdom very badly, and treated his poor grandmother Edgiva so cruelly that she died of want, while he was rioting and feasting. St. Dunstan tried all he could to prevent the king from behaving so ill, but he would not listen to him. St. Dunstan was at this time the chief support of the kingdom. He was not only a very holy man, but a wise and active minister too. He taught the people to make organs and bells for the churches, and to sing and play church-music, and to make vestments, and to paint beautiful pictures in books. All this made the people love St. Dunstan very much.

And indeed everyone loved him except the foolish young king and his bad companions. The king hated him because St. Dunstan often told him he was leading a wicked life, and was displeasing God; and courtiers hated him because he told the king to send them away, and to choose better friends, and they were afraid of being punished.

So they persuaded Edwy to banish St. Dunstan out of the kingdom. He went to Flanders, and lived there a year; and all the Flemish clergy and people grew as fond of him as the English were, and begged of him to stay and live with them. But as soon as he could St. Dunstan went back to England, because that was his own country, and he liked to teach the people over whom God had placed him.

While he was in Flanders the English grew so angry with their foolish king, that they sent him away, and said he should not be king any longer. So Edwy was banished in his turn; and I hope when he was away from all his bad companions, and in trouble, that he began to think and to repent of his wickedness.

A.D. 959: His younger brother Edgar was made king instead of him; and he is sometimes called Edgar the Pious, sometimes Edgar the Peaceful, and sometimes Edgar the Magnificent. As soon as he became king, he sent for St. Dunstan, and made him his chief friend and councillor; so that he never undertook anything in his kingdom without asking if he approved of it. He made him, first, Bishop of London, and then Archbishop of Canterbury, and the Pope made him his legate, or minister in England. St. Dunstan then began to work very hard, and he was helped by the other bishops and the good king. The clergy had become very disorderly from the Danes so often invading and upsetting the country; and Edwy had stolen a great deal of land from the Church, and had made some very bad men abbots and canons. St. Dunstan sent away these bad priests; and he spoke to them in such a manner, that some of them were very sorry indeed, and became good men. He also sent away a good many secular canons from the cathedrals, and put monks in their place.

The secular canons of Winchester were so angry at these changes that they made a petition to the other bishops to let them stay. The bishops met together to consult what should be done; and while they were debating they heard a voice from the crucifix speak to St. Dunstan these words: "Dunstan, thou hast judged well; to change thy decree is not good."

Then the bishops determined to send away the secular canons.

Besides this, the good king helped St. Dunstan to rebuild the beautiful abbeys which the Danes had pulled down or burned; and they were built much more splendidly than before, and in larger numbers. It is said that no less than fifty beautiful abbeys were built from the ground in Edgar's reign; and as fast as they were built, crowds of young men of all ranks, even soldiers and noblemen, came to offer themselves as servants of God in religion.

You may believe, that as King Edgar did so much for the Church, everything prospered with him. He was able to build a fleet of more than three hundred ships, to send against the Danes; and his fleets and armies were so successful, that Scotland conquered Northumberland again from the Danes who had seized it, and finally united it to the crown, while the king of Scotland came to do him homage, as he had done in the time of Athelstan. He was obliged to do this, because he had laughed at Edgar, who was very thin and short, and said, "He wondered how the English could have so little spirit as to obey a dwarf." Edgar led the Scottish king into a wood, and, drawing his sword, made him soon acknowledge that he was very fit to command.

Besides being successful in war, Edgar set the whole country in order. He ordered a new coinage of money, punished every crime that was committed, prevented the piracies that were carried on in the Isle of Thanet, and made *progresses,* or journeys, every year through the kingdom, to find out the real state of his people, and whether justice was administered or not. Wherever he went, he was beloved and feared; and never, since Alfred the Great, had there been so powerful a king.

But, as we so often see, this great esteem made Edgar's heart swell with pride, and he fell into a very grievous sin. He carried away a nun from her convent, and married her. His faithful minister St. Dunstan, like the prophet Nathan, went to him, as St. Neot went to Alfred, and rebuked him severely for his scandalous sin; and Edgar, whose generous heart was so unlike his brother Eilwy's, touched with contrition, knelt down humbly before the archbishop, and, confessing his guilt, begged a penance for it. St. Dunstan saw that he could bear it, and he gave him a severe penance. He was not to be crowned for seven years; to fast twice a-week during all that time; to give great alms to the poor, and to found a convent of nuns, in reparation for his sacrilege. King Edgar performed his penance faithfully, and even prolonged it, for he was not crowned till thirteen years afterwards. At the end of that time, all his princes and nobles were gathered together, and St. Dunstan put the crown on Edgar's head at Bath. After his coronation, the king went round the coast, and landed at Chester, where the Scottish, Welsh, and other northern princes came to do him homage, and rowed him in barges to the church of St. John the Baptist, where the ceremony was performed.

This wise and good king lived only two years after; and when he died, an old chronicler wrote of him these beautiful words: "He reared up God's honor, he loved God's law, he preserved the people's peace. And God was his helper; so that kings and earls bowed to him, and obeyed his will. Without battle, he ruled all as he willed."

A.D. 975: As soon as Edgar was dead, his little son Edward became king. He was only thirteen years old, and was very good and brave. Like his father, he made St. Dunstan his counsellor and friend, and never did anything without his advice. Everyone thought that he would have a long and glorious reign, but their hopes were soon cut short. Edward's mother-in-law, Elfrida, hated him, because she wished her own son, Ethelred, to be king. One day, as he was hunting in Dorsetshire, he stopped at Corfe Castle, where Elfrida lived, and asked for a cup of wine. While he was drinking, Elfrida ordered one of her servants to stab him in the back with his dagger. The poor king spurred his horse, and tried to ride away, but the wound was too deep. He fell from his saddle, and was dragged along the road till he died. His servants buried him at Wareham; but St. Dunstan, who grieved very much at his death, took up his body some years afterwards, and buried it in Shaftesbury Abbey. This king is always called Edward the Martyr.

A.D. 978: The wicked Elfrida did not gain any thing by her cruel murder. Her poor little son became king, it is true; but she had treated him so cruelly for crying when Edward the Martyr was murdered, that he became half an idiot, and was one of the worst and most miserable kings that ever reigned in England. Elfrida herself was so unhappy, that she went to a convent, where she spent all the rest of her life in public penance.

Ethelred was scarcely seated on his throne, when the Danes came again, and ravaged the country more dreadfully than ever, while at the same time there was a famine and a terrible pestilence, so that, as the chroniclers of that time say, never before had England been in so wretched a state. Ethelred too was never ready to meet the Danes when they came; and for this slowness and folly he was nicknamed "Ethelred the Unready." Like most weak and undecided men, Ethelred was cruel and treacherous, and as he was too slothful and cowardly to beat the Danes in battle, he made a wicked, plan to get rid of them. This plan was soon followed, and on St. Brice's day (November 13th), he ordered the Danes to be put to death every where at once. Not one was spared, even of those who had been settled in England so long as to have become like Englishmen. This cruel massacre only made the Danes more enraged against Ethelred, and they soon came with a larger and stronger fleet, the ships of which were wilder and more frightful than ever. Some were carved into the figures of bulls and lions, and some of horses; and the king's ship had a long twisted tail, like a dragon. The ships were all covered with bright plates of copper, and had birds carved and painted on their masts. It was a fearful sight for England; for the people well knew that the army brought by that awful-looking fleet was fiercer and more awful still in their savage and diabolical desire of revenge. In four years from its landing, almost all the corn and cattle were carried away and burned; the fields, which had been so well tilled and fertile, were a barren waste, and the beautiful abbeys and monasteries which had sprung up on all sides were heaps of smoking ruins. Among the horrors of that dreadful time was the martyrdom of the old Archbishop of Canterbury, St. Elpheg.

Surely the blood of young Edward the Martyr had cried to heaven for vengeance, and it was fearfully avenged.

Sweyn, the Danish king, had a son named Canute, and he was so brave that he won many of the English nobles over to his side; for they were tired of their wicked and foolish king, who gave himself up to pleasure, while his kingdom lay desolate. So there were two parties in England; one for the Saxon, and one for the Danish king. The Danes were just going to besiege London, when Ethelred the Unready died, leaving five sons.

A little before these wretched events, the great and wise St. Dunstan had died. He foresaw and prophesied their coming as punishments for the sins and scandals of his countrymen; and he gave the foolish king all the advice he could, and tried to show him how to reign wisely, as he had shown Edred, and Edgar the Pious, and young Edward the Martyr. But when he found that his advice was only scoffed at, and quite weary of living so long among the quarrels and intrigues of the court, he went away to his own dear abbey at Glastonbury, where he could spend the rest of his time in praying and preparing for the end he so ardently desired.

On the Feast of the Ascension he preached three times upon that mystery; and during his last sermon the people saw streams of glorious light shining round his venerable head. At the end of his sermon he begged their prayers, and said, like St. Paul, that very soon they should see his face no more. Then they all began to weep and sob, and pressed round him to kiss the hem of his vestments, and to beg his blessing. In

A picture of Christ by St. Dunstan with his self-portrait at the bottom.

a day or two afterwards, St. Dunstan saw a troop of bright angels coming to fetch him, and, shutting his eyes, he died very joyfully, and was buried in Canterbury cathedral.

A.D. 1010. The eldest of poor foolish Ethelred's sons became king when his father died; and as he was very strong and brave, he was called Edmund Ironside. Poor Edmund did all he could to win his kingdom back from the Danes, and to put it into some kind of order; but though he fought and won five great battles, he could not withstand the power of Sweyn's son Canute, and he was himself killed in the last great battle of Assington, where the magic standard of the Raven, by its movements, inspired the great Danish chief Thurkill with hopes of success. There can be little doubt that, however the influence of this standard was increased by the superstition of the heathen invaders; still it was woven by magical arts, and endued with magical power by diabolical agency, and that it was for the punishment of the sins of our country, and the decay of piety and faith among the once saintly Anglo-Saxon race, that the kingdom was about to pass away into strange hands.[4] For as it is with individuals, so it is with races; and if favors or privileges are despised by either, they will be visited by the loss of them, if not by heavier misfortunes; and if they grow tepid in the service of God, their kingdom will be given to another. It is for this reason that we ought to think more about the favors and advantages of our country, and of its sins against them, than of its riches or prosperous conquests, as we usually do.

---

[4] The Raven embroidered on the standard, without which the Danes never engaged in battle, was first woven at noon by the daughters of Ragnar Lodbrog; but must have been constantly renewed, as it had been more than once taken in battle. It was always said to possess the same properties (given to it by invoking the enchantress Aslauga) of flapping its wings and uttering shrill cries of joy when victory was about to fall on the Danish side, and of hanging its wings in sullen sadness when the English were about to conquer. There seems reason to believe that much of the extreme horror of those Danish victories was frequently owing to the supernatural help often visibly afforded them by evil spirits during the combat.

CHAPTER XII.

The Danish Kings
FROM 1016 TO 1042

TWO little baby-sons, and several brothers, were left by Edmund Ironside; but Canute the Dane had not fought five great battles for the sake of allowing them to reign. He sent the little princes to Norway; and their uncles having fled to Normandy, Canute was left in quiet possession of the crown. Perhaps Canute intended that the Norwegian king should put the English princes to death, or at least shut them up in prison; but if so, Clave was more merciful than he supposed, for he sent the boys to Hungary, and put them under the good King Stephen's protection. Their names were Edmund and Edward. Edmund soon died; but Edward grew up and married, and we shall hear of him again by and by. Their two uncles who fled to Normandy were Edward and Alfred. The next thing Canute did was to ask Ethelred's widow, Emma, to marry him, which she did; and although many of her countrymen blamed her very much, it was a wise measure, for it helped to make the Saxons and Danes friends with one another, and prevented a great many quarrels. It was settled by the witan that Canute and Emma's children and grandchildren should be the kings of England, instead of Edmund Ironside's brothers.

It turned out that Canute was a very good king indeed. He made peace between his English and Danish subjects, and sent away his army of Danes, which was so unpleasant to the English. He kept only the crews of three ships for a guard, which was called his *thingmanna,* and sometimes the *huscarles,* or men (carls) who guarded his house. Canute employed his huscarles as policemen, and sent them about to take up every person convicted of murder; for, in consequence of the long and terrible Danish ravages, England was no longer King Alfred's England, and murders and cruelties of all kinds had become so common, that no one was much shocked at them. Canute was very anxious to reform the administration of justice; and when one day he killed a soldier himself in a fit of passion, he came down from his throne, and fined himself a *hot,* or fine, nine times larger than any one else would have paid.

Canute had been baptized when he was young, and now it appeared that that seed of divine grace which had by that sacrament been infused into his soul was still alive, and now shot up into fresh strength and beauty. He became so changed, that no one would have known him to be the same. He was very sorry for having treated the English so cruelly, and he became kind and gentle in his manner to all his subjects. He caused all the English and Danish nobles to meet together, and forgive one another at a witan at Oxford. At this witan he also confirmed the laws and customs of King Alfred, and promised to keep them; and he made some very good new laws. He ordered that the judges should spare life as much as possible, and that they should punish the rich and great men who did wrong more than the poor, because they were better taught, and had less excuse for committing crimes. He forbade English serfs to be sold out of England, for fear they should fall into the hands of pagan masters; and he forbade all kinds of pagan worship among his subjects, or remains of the superstitious practices of the Danes. He also forbade his officers to seize money or provisions for his use, and ordered that no one should be compelled to marry against his will; for it had often happened, when the daughters of rich men had succeeded to their father's estates, that wicked and greedy nobles came and married them by force.

King Canute the Dane, https://www.rct.uk/collection/600052/king-canute-the-dane

Canute often went to visit his other kingdoms of Denmark and Norway; and when he went he took missionaries with him to instruct his poor heathen subjects in the true faith. He sent numbers of young men to Alfred's schools at Oxford, and to the English college at Rome, to be well educated, and to be brought up as good priests; and he did much good by spreading the knowledge of religion, and by bringing a great many holy bishops and priests into his kingdom. He restored the great abbey of St. Edmund at Bury St. Edmund's, and built a magnificent church at Assington, in memory of his victory over Edmund Ironside. He encouraged all the learned men he knew of to come and settle in England, where some of them taught our countrymen how to build better churches, and how to stain beautiful colored glass windows, and to paint pictures, and to write music and hymns for the Church services. The king understood and loved music himself, as the Teutonic nations have always done; and there is a quaint old song, or rather rhyme, still preserved, which speaks of his rowing in the great fen-pools of Ely, and listening to the monks in the Minster singing.

Canute re-established the payment of Peter's pence, or the Roman silver, which King Ina had begun; and as he had committed so many crimes, and was so truly penitent, he made this tribute larger than it had ever been before. Besides paying this royal alms or offering to Rome, Canute made a pilgrimage himself to the Holy City; for he longed to visit the tombs of the Apostles, and to obtain the Pope's blessing. He went through France; and as he went along, he visited all the celebrated churches on the way, and left such magnificent offerings to each, that an old chronicler says everyone cried out, "Blessings upon the king of the English!" as he went along. While he was in Rome, he wrote a letter to all his bishops and people. This beautiful and noble letter begins with these words:

"Canute, king of all Denmark, England, and Norway, and part of Sweden, to Egelnoth the Metropolitan, to Archbishop Alfric, to all the bishops and chiefs, and to all the nation of the English, both nobles and commoners, greeting." He goes on to say that he returns humble thanks to Almighty God, that He has allowed him to visit the tombs of the blessed Apostles Peter and Paul, and every holy place within and without the city of Rome, and to honor and venerate them in person. "And this I have done, because I learned from my teachers that the Apostle St. Peter received from the Lord the great power of binding and loosing with the keys of the kingdom of heaven. On this account I thought it highly useful to solicit his patronage with God."

He then tells them how many kings and lords there were assembled to keep Easter with the Pope at Rome; and that he had laid all his grievances before the Pope, and they were redressed. He asked that his archbishops should not be obliged to pay so much money when they went to receive the pallium; and that his pilgrims and men should be allowed free access through other countries to the Holy City, which was also gladly granted. He concluded with this beautiful sentence, which is a model and example for the conduct of Christian kings in all ages: "Now, therefore, be it known to you all, that I have dedicated my life to the service of God, to govern my kingdoms with equity, and to observe justice in all things. If, by the violence or negligence of youth, I have violated justice heretofore, it is my intention, by the help of God, to make full compensation. Therefore I beg and command those to whom I have confided the government, as they wish to preserve my friendship, or save their own souls, to do no injustice either to rich or poor. Let all persons, whether noble or ignoble, obtain their rights according to law, from which no deviation shall be allowed, either from fear of me, or through favor to the powerful, or for the purpose of supplying my treasury. *I have no need of money raised by injustice.*" He finished by exhorting the bishops and clergy and officers to enforce the payment of the tithes which were due to the Church; and then bade them farewell while he went to Denmark.

Canute's courtiers thought that as he did so many good actions, he would like to be praised for them; so one day they told him he was so powerful that the waves of the sea would obey him, if he would command them to go back. The king pretended to believe them; and when he was at Southampton, he ordered a chair to be carried out and set down upon the beach at the edge of the sea, when the tide was coming up. He then sat down in it, and in a loud voice ordered the waves to retire, that he might not be wetted. The waves, of course, came up higher and higher, till the king and his foolish lords were completely drenched with spray. Canute then turned to the downcast courtiers, and said to them: "Learn from what you have now seen, that there is One only who can say to these waves: 'Hitherto shall ye come, and no farther, and that One is God." He was so sorry for the foolish and wicked words these lords had spoken, that he took his crown off his head, and hung it on the great crucifix in Winchester Cathedral; nor did he ever wear it again as long as he lived.

The good and great Danish king reigned three years after his pilgrimage to Rome. He died at Shaftesbury abbey, and was buried in Winchester cathedral, which was then the usual burial-place of the kings of England.

A.D. 1036. Harold Harefoot succeeded his father Canute. He was named Harefoot from his great swiftness in running, which was such, that he could run down and catch hares and foxes on foot; but besides this single quality of body, there is nothing good to be told of Harold, for he was a cruel man and a bad king. The most remarkable circumstance of his reign is his sending, or allowing some of his nobles to send, for Ethelred the Unready's sons, from Normandy. The youngest of them, Alfred, came to England, and was received with great honors by Earl Godwin, and soon after treacherously and barbarously murdered, with all his soldiers. The archbishop Egelnoth refused to crown Harold after this dreadful massacre; and it is said that Harold insolently put the crown on his head with his own hands, and became afterwards a bitter enemy to the Church. When it was time to hear Mass, he used to call for his hounds, or order the hall to be spread for a feast, to show his contempt for religion. You may judge by this what kind of king he was. In fact, the Danes remained, even when Christians, half-heathens.

A.D. 1040. When Harold Harefoot died, he left no children, and his brother Hardicanute (or Hardacanute) became king. He was not much better than Harold; and he began by savagely ordering his brother's body to be taken up, its head cut off, and thrown into the Thames. Some fishermen, who were in the river, fished up the head and the body, and buried them in St. Clement's church in London; which, from being used as a burial-place for the Danish kings, came to be called St. Clement of the Danes. It stands now in the Strand.

Notwithstanding this barbarous act, Hardicanute was a better man than Harold. He was very kind to his half-brother Edward, and made him very happy in England. In his reign, the great and powerful Earl Godwin was accused of being the cause of Alfred's murder; but he cleared himself of guilt by what was then called a Compurgation, that is, by his own oath, and the oath of twelve of his peers. In token of being reconciled with the king, Earl Godwin gave him a magnificent ship, manned by eighty warriors in armor, covered with plates of gold and silver; and even the stern of the ship was covered with plates of gold. This shows us that our country was then rich, and had recovered most wonderfully from the miserable Danish wars. We know this also by hearing of the grand show that was made when the king's sister, the Princess Gunilda, was sent to Germany to marry the emperor, as Athelstan's sister had been. Gunilda is described as being the most beautiful princess of the time; and when she went down to the shore, a crowd of nobles and ladies attended her, dressed in grand silken robes, embroidered and fringed with gold and jewels.

It was thought, indeed, that now the Danes were peaceably settled, there would be rest in our country; but as Hardicanute was at a wedding-feast of one of his nobles, named Osgod Clapa, he died quite suddenly, as he was lifting his cup to his lips. The place was afterwards called Clapa's *Ham,* or house, and is now Clapham near London.

Chapter XIII.

The Last Anglo-Saxon Kings, And New Comers

From 1042 to 1066

As Hardicanute, like Harold Harefoot, had no children, every one turned their eyes with joy to the remaining half-brother of Edmund Ironside, and thought, with great delight, that the old Anglo-Saxon line was restored again, and that they should once more have a descendant of Alfred for their king. The crown belonged of right to Edmund Ironside's son, who was in Hungary; but Edward was older, and he had lived in England a long time, and everyone who knew him loved him very much; so all England was delighted to have him for their Saxon king again. Edward was a very wise and holy man, who had learned many things by his troubles, and the uncertain life he had led. He married Earl Godwin's daughter, who was named Edith, and who was so sweet and beautiful that she was called "the Rose among thorns." She was altogether so unlike the rude people of that unsettled time, and especially so unlike her fierce father, that an old writer says of her, "It is a marvel how so sweet a flower could have sprung from so sour a stem."

Edward found great difficulty in contenting every party. The country had, in fact, been split into five petty kingdoms, which were ruled by five great earls, some of whom were of Danish blood. Their names were Siward, Leofric, Godwin, and his two sons, Sweyn and Harold. The mild and gentle king, who hated war and bloodshed, was no match for these fierce nobles. It was well for him and for the country that all these great earls were at this time loyal, and did what they could to fix their new king firmly upon the throne. They united together, and drove all the Danes who opposed him out of the kingdom; and gave him time to set the country in order, and to make new laws, or rather to alter and mend the good old laws of Ethelwulf and Alfred. But almost as soon as peace was made, a new enemy appeared, who caused quarrels and divisions among the five earls. This was Magnus the king of Norway, who sent King Edward word, that unless he would give up the English crown peaceably, he would come with a large army to England, and take it from him. King Edward answered, that he inherited the English crown from his ancestors; that the English people had crowned him king; and that he would not give up his crown, because it was his duty to defend it. But soon after the warlike message of the Danish king, his own kingdom was seized by a cousin, and he sent another humbler message, begging for some English ships to defend it. Earl Godwin, who was related to Magnus, wished to send the ships, but King Edward refused.

This caused the first quarrel between the king and Earl Godwin and his troublesome sons, which was carried on for a long time. At last, Sweyn, who was the fiercest and worst of them all, and who had murdered his cousin Biorn, was outlawed. He became a sea-king, and ravaged the coasts, carrying off everything that he could lay his hands upon. But, in the end, his guilty soul was touched with remorse; and he went on a pilgrimage to the Holy Land, and died in Asia Minor.

King Edward loved Godwin and his sons, though they gave him so much trouble. He pardoned them all their faults, and received them at court again. He loved Harold most of all, and by degrees gave so much power into his hands, that he was called the *Under-king*. Harold was so brave and bold and truthful, that it is no wonder the king loved him so much, and the people loved him too; but there were still favorites at court whom the people did not love at all. These were the Normans whom Edward brought to England, because, as his mother was a Norman, and he had lived in Normandy so long, the Norman language and manners pleased him more than the English, which seemed to him rough and fierce. The Norman priests were much more learned, and altogether better educated than the English clergy; and Edward loved their society, and wished to bring enough of them to England to improve and soften his English subjects. The English were not wise enough to see the benefits of this mixture of other nations with their own; and they ridiculed all the Normans who came, and laughed at their dress, and language, and manners. Earl Godwin and his sons were foremost in disliking them; and there was a serious battle between the men of Dover, who were Godwin's feudal "men," and a Norman count named Eustace of Boulogne. At last, the powerful and turbulent Earl Godwin died. It is not certain whether the story is true or not, but it is said, that after the king had pardoned him, as he was dining with him on Easter-Monday, one of the servants' foot slipped, and he was only saved by his other foot from falling down with the cup. "Ah," cried the earl, "see how one brother comes to help the other!" "Yes," answered the king, looking at him; "and if my brother were now alive, he would help me." Godwin complained of this speech, and declared, that if he had been guilty in any way of Alfred's murder, he hoped the piece he was now going to eat would choke him. He put the piece of bread into his mouth, and fell down dead. This story is now generally believed to be false; but whether false or not, it is certain that Godwin fell down speechless as he was at dinner with the king, and died soon after. He was a wise and brave soldier, and was very much feared by all the robbers and evil-doers who swarmed at that time in England.

Another of the earls died about the same time. This was Siward the Dane, who, like a Dane, declared that he would not die in bed like a tame beast, but in his arms as a warrior should. So he put on his armor, and with his plumed helmet on his head, and his shield and spear in his hands, the stern, half-heathen old warrior gave up the ghost. It is wonderful to see how strong and almost invincible was the Scandinavian hatred of civilized life. "To live under a raftered roof, and to die a quiet death," were things which Danes, even long converted, held in abhorrence.

Harold was now the most powerful earl in the kingdom; and he fought a good many battles with the Welsh, and took their lands for the king. He was of great use to King Edward at this time, for he disliked fighting himself; and though he went with the army whenever he thought it right, he hated bloodshed and strife.

He was much more occupied in arranging his kingdom, so as to obtain the real good of his subjects, than in conquering fresh countries, or in humbling foreign princes. He revived and strengthened the laws of the Anglo-Saxons, and made such new ones as had become necessary, in the same spirit. He settled the administration of justice, and never allowed a poor person, or a widow, or orphan to be oppressed. Whoever was wronged, or ill-treated, or in trouble, always found King Edward ready to hear him, and prompt to do him justice, and give him relief.

We cannot wonder, then, that if some of his half-heathen nobles pretended to despise him, and to say that he was more fit to be a monk than to be king of England; still the poor loved him with all their hearts; and that they and the shopkeepers, and farmers, and gentry, all joined together in calling him " Good King Edward."

"Good King Edward" spent most of his spare time in building churches and monasteries, which he richly endowed. He sent several of the bishops on pilgrimage to the Holy Land; and when he had quieted the quarrels of his fierce nobles, and made them join their hands in peace and Christian forgiveness, he wished to go with some of them himself to visit the Holy Sepulchre. But when he had called a witan, and proposed this to the members of it, they all agreed that it would be more for the good of the kingdom, in its present state, that the king should remain at home; and they advised him to perform some other good work instead of this pilgrimage .So the king sent to the Pope, and asked him to allow him some other labor instead of this one which he was advised to give up.

The Pope replied, that the king acted rightly in remaining in his kingdom; and that he ordered him, instead of going to Jerusalem, to build a new church.

King Edward accordingly laid the foundation of a magnificent church in honor of SS. Peter and Paul, which was afterwards called *West Monastery*, and is now

Westminster Abbey.

And so, while all kinds of wars and quarrels were going on in the rest of the world, good King Edward used to go, day after day, to see his beautiful church; and as it rose higher and higher in its beauty and strength, he could sit quietly by, meditating on the vain and foolish strife of this world, and upon the rest which he ardently desired in heaven.

The under-king, Harold, in the meantime went to Normandy, where he was stranded on the coast, and seized by the Lord of Ponthieu, who gave him up to Duke William. William was very glad indeed to get hold of Harold; and he told him that King Edward and he had always lived like brothers together, and that he had promised to leave him his kingdom of England after his death. Harold was very sorry to hear this, and he wished to get away as quickly as he could; but the duke would not let him go till he had sworn to help him in getting England for his own, and in letting him into Dover Castle secretly. Harold intended to swear, making an exception in his own mind, which was a false and cowardly act, and was prevented by the duke, who took the cover off the table upon which Harold had laid his hand to swear, and showed him that he had sworn upon a casket quite full of the relics of saints, and that it was a true and solemn oath he had taken. Harold was then both grieved and frightened, and he wished he had at once boldly refused to be a traitor, but it was too late. It was very sad too that there was no successor of the Anglo-Saxon race for Edward. His nephew, young Edward, had come over from Hungary, where, as you remember, Sweyn the King of Norway had sent him; but soon after he came to England, he died without any visible cause; and the people, who grieved at his death, thought it came about by unfair means.

However that may be, and whether Harold had any share in such wickedness or not, we cannot tell; but it became clearly the will of God, that the long and glorious line of the Anglo-Saxon kings should now fail, and that the days were few and short before their crown should be given to another race. And meantime, that church which King Edward so loved, which he had watched with such earnestness, and a kind of foreknowledge that it was his last work, was finished, and was dedicated on Holy Innocents' Day. But after all his watching and fostering cares, he was not there to take part in the splendid ceremony, for he lay sick on his death-bed. And when, a very few days after, good King Edward gave up his holy soul into the hands of God, and his body was laid in the much-loved Abbey, it seemed as if the finishing of it were the token he had looked for to depart, and the sign that the last Anglo-Saxon king had gone to his place.

It cannot be denied, that the gentle King Edward was not the fittest king to govern England at that time; for the power of the great earls, and the strife between Saxon and Danish blood, required a very strong hand to restrain their violence, or to keep up any peace or union between them. Perhaps if Alfred or Edgar had been king, instead of Edward, the Norman Conquest might have been delayed some years longer; perhaps there might have been one or two more Anglo-Saxon kings in England.

But, as we have already seen, it was not so *designed*. The evil day might have been put off, but it would have not been put off for long. Instead, therefore, of blaming King Edward for not having a character which God had not given him, perhaps it would be wiser, juster, and more useful, as well as reverent, to look upon him throughout, rather as he is now, a blessed Saint and Confessor, and therefore likely to have been guided in, his whole earthly conduct by the inspirations of Divine grace. It would perhaps be more according to right reason, to look back with a devout joy upon our last Anglo-Saxon king as he was, holy, just, and mild, full of love to God and zeal for His honor in the real welfare of his people, than to lament (as some do) that a more stirring and active character had not filled his place. It may, with truth, be said, that when we have waded through the bloody, or mischievous, or melancholy reigns of some of his successors, we turn back to the life of "Good King Edward," the last Anglo-Saxon king, with much the same feeling as a weary traveller who halts in the desert, parched with sultry heat, and recalls the broad green meadows of his home, watered with cool and refreshing streams.

The king who succeeded to St. Edward was the powerful son of Godwin, Harold; and he was scarcely seated on the throne, when the fierce and angry Duke William of Normandy got an army together, to punish him for his broken oath upon the relics of the saints. Besides the angry duke, Harold's own brother, Tostig, came with the Norwegian king, Harold Hardrada, to try to get back the earldom of Northumberland, which Harold had taken from him. Harold sent word to Tostig, that if he would swear to live peaceably in England, he would give him back the earldom. Tostig consented; but he asked also what his brother, the king, would give to his friend, Harold Hardrada? "Seven feet of ground for a grave!" was the fierce and determined answer. "Then," exclaimed Tostig generously, "bid my brother prepare for battle; for never shall it be said, that the son of Godwin forsook the son of Sigurd" (Harold Hardrada's father).

The two armies met, and Harold Hardrada rode up and down the ranks on his great black charger, dressed in a bright blue tunic, and singing a wild Norse song. It is curious, that the whole account of this English battle is told by an Icelandic historian, whose wild but interesting chronicle will delight you to read some day.[5]

The brave Harold Hardrada, and his generous friend Tostig, were both killed in this battle at Stamford Bridge; and so many Danes and Norwegians lay dead on the field, that, for fifty years afterwards, the ground was white with their bones.

Directly after he had won this victory, Harold heard the news that Duke William of Normandy had actually landed at Pevensey in Sussex, and was taking possession of the country. Harold marched his army quickly southward, and met the duke at Hastings, where the two armies fought a great battle, which, on account of Harold's oath, and his having sworn homage to William, is called by the old historians the "Assize of God's judgment;" that is, they looked upon it as a kind of trial by ordeal, in which God would give victory to the just conqueror. The Norman war-cry was *Dieu est nostre ayde!* ("God is our help"); and the English answered with "Christ's Rood! the Holy Rood!" and met the Normans with flights of arrows, as thick as hail. The battle lasted all day, from sunrise to sunset; and when the sun was going down, the brave Harold was shot in the eye by a chance arrow, which went into his brain, and he died. His body was taken up, and buried so privately in Waltham Abbey, that for many years the English in some parts of the country believed that he had only fled to some foreign land to get help, and would come back again. As soon as he fell, the English began to fly; and such a number of nobles lay dead on the bloody field of Hastings, that the old Saxon families nearly all became extinct in one day. Harold's

---

[5]   Snorro's Heimskringla

two brothers, Gurth and Leofwin, fell with him. This famous battle was fought on the hill on which Battle now stands, and was called Senlac, or *Sangue-lac,* from the dark streams of English blood which flooded the green turf of the down. It was said that no rain would wash out the stains of this blood, and that strange sights and sounds were heard floating round those hills. Perhaps it was partly to do away with the sad and gloomy associations connected with this final "Assize of God's Judgments" upon the Anglo- Saxons, that William of Normandy built an abbey on the very spot where Harold's banner was cut down, and filled it with holy Norman monks, whose prayers and good works might wash away the stains of Sangue-lac. The abbey still remains, and is called Battle Abbey.

Battle Abbey

Chapter XIV.

Gang Roll's Children.
From 1066 to 1087.

ET us now go back some years, in order to trace the beginnings of the Norman power in France, and to see *where* this bold and chivalrous people came from, for they were not of the French race, as we too commonly suppose.

About the time of King Alfred, there was a king in Norway named Harold Harfaga, or Harold with the beautiful hair. He had a noble named Rognvold at his court, whom he loved very much; and Rognvold had several sons, who were brave and famous sea-kings. The bravest and most famous of those was named Rollo, who was so tall that he could never get any horse big enough to ride, and being therefore obliged to go on foot, was called Rollo the Ganger (walker), or *Gang Roll*. Gang Roll was banished from Norway by Harold for what was called *Strand-hug*, that is, for landing his men, and seizing whatever cattle and corn he wanted. He gathered a number of friends round him, and sailed away in several ships, plundered and seized every country he came near, and at last descended upon the north-west coast of France, where he landed his men, and took possession of the country. The Northmen, or *Normans,* sailed up the Seine, took possession of Rouen, and besieged Paris; but they made peace with the French without taking Paris; and Gang Roll married a French wife, and agreed to become a Christian, and to do homage for his new dominions, which he called Northman, or *Normandy.* When Gang Roll went to do homage to the king of France, who was then Charles the Simple, he was too proud to kiss the king's foot himself, but called one of his tall Northmen to do it for him. The fierce Norman would not kneel either, but pulled the king's foot up towards his lip, till the poor king lost his balance, and fell backwards flat on the ground, which made all the rude Normans shout with laughter. However, the French do not seem to have been really angry, or they were too much afraid of the Normans to show it; and Gang Roll was named Duke of Normandy, and settled peaceably there with his Northmen. He first endowed seven churches, and then divided the lands between his followers. He was called *Rou*[6] by the French; and his name became so famous for justice and severity, that wherever it was named, all robbers and oppressors trembled.

Besides France, the Normans settled in Italy and Sicily; and after burning and destroying all who opposed them, they became the possessors of large colonies and tracts of land in both those countries.

Duke William, Gang Roll's descendant, was as severe and warlike as his ancestor. As soon as he became King of England, and was crowned William the First at St. Edward's

---

[6] It was upon the exploits of Gang Roll that the famous romance was written called " The Roman de Rou."

Church of Westminster Abbey, he made great changes in our country. He set aside the laws and customs of good King Edward, which he promised at first to keep, and brought in Norman laws and customs instead. The old witan, which the English loved so much, was swept away, and the "King's Great Council" was established in its place. But as the chief

William the Conqueror, A portrait from the Welsh Portrait Collection at the National Library of Wales.

members of this council were Norman barons, they did not at all fulfill the same duties to the people as the eoldermen and burgesses had done.

In all the law-courts, French was the language used, and

the lawyers were obliged to plead in that language; and they, in consequence, being mostly Normans, the English came but poorly off in their lawsuits. At court and in the army, in the same manner, French was spoken; and Norman barons and knights were put in command; so that the poor English found themselves every where robbed, ill-treated, and trampled upon. It was not for some time afterwards that the languages were so mixed up as to become what we now call English; but if you take pains, and observe the words which we use, you will see how many of them come from the French. Thus 'flatter' comes from *flatter*, 'pierce' from *percer*, 'current' from *courant*, 'penetrate' from *penetrer*, and so on. But wherever you find words which are quite unlike the French and Latin, and like the German, you may know that these words are part of the old Anglo-Saxon language, which was spoken in our country before the Norman Conquest. Thus 'mother' comes from *mutter*, 'king' from *könig*,[7] 'speak' from *sprechen*, 'alone' from *allein*, and so on of numberless others. That kind of writing and speaking is the best and purest English which has the greatest number of these Anglo-Saxon words in it.

You may believe that all the English did not submit at once to William the Conqueror. London, Lincoln, Salisbury, Exeter, Cambridge, and York, resisted all his efforts, and Exeter in particular made such stout battle, that William offered all the citizens life, property, and full pardon, with all their privileges, if they would submit; and on these terms the people gave up their city to him. He was so angry at the northern risings, that, swearing his terrible oath, "By the splendor of God!" he marched an army northwards, and laid waste a tract of fifty miles every way with fire and sword, sparing neither man, woman, nor cattle. About 100,000

---

[7] König (konnen, verb), a strong man; one who is able, or who can.

people perished in this bloody ravage; and even the Normans called it a cruel and wicked deed.

But it was near Cambridge especially that the English resisted. In the middle of the fens near Ely there is an island, surrounded with fen-lakes and pools, where the English, under a brave noble named Hereward the Saxon, entrenched themselves, and which they called the Camp of Refuge. Hereward the Saxon did such wonderful deeds of bravery as can scarcely be believed, and with a few hundred fenners and peasants, kept the great conqueror at bay, till at last William offered him life, full pardon, and liberty to live where he pleased; so Lord Hereward thought it was best for England that he should submit, and he swore fealty to William. William had no sooner subdued his enemies than he began to take an account of all the lands, towns, and inhabitants of his kingdom, and to see how much money he could get from

Domesday Book has been rebound at least five times.

them. All the accounts and numbers were written down in a book called *Dooms-day-book (Domesday)*, or *Judgment-day-book*, because from it he was to *judge* how much they were to be taxed. There were new taxes made on markets and fairs and on land, and from all these taxes King William received more than a thousand pounds a day, which was an enormous sum in those times. The old customs of the lords and their men were changed for the feudal customs of the Normans, which were partly taken from the Roman ones; and altogether the English were very heavily burdened. Above ninety miles of country in Hampshire and Dorsetshire were laid waste to make a forest for William, and to get rid of men whom he knew to be badly inclined to the Normans. This was called the New Forest; and there are beautiful remains of it still in Hampshire, called the New Forest and Bere Forest. Everyone was forced all over England to put out fire and candle at eight o'clock, and to go to bed, whether they would or no; which was a vexatious tyranny, but which prevented many plots and risings. The bell which rung was called the *couvre-feu* or *curfew-bell*, and is often spoken of by poets as if it still existed.

Notwithstanding all the cruelties and hardships of William's reign, the Norman conquest was of the greatest and most solid benefit to our country. The people had become gross and sensual, the nobles ignorant and fierce, and the clergy, who were chiefly nobles, were careless and slothful. There was scarcely one learned man amongst them; and the general pursuits of all, both high and low, were hunting and field-sports, and excessive eating and drinking. The Norman nobles who came into England were, *as a body*, brave, chivalrous, and temperate gentlemen, whose high sense of honor and courteous manners greatly improved the English nobility, and acted in a different manner and more gradually even upon their rude and sensual vassals. The Norman clergy and monks whom the conqueror established here were men of learning, talents, and great piety, whose stricter and more enlightened discipline quickly raised up the English clergy to a more spiritual life.

The English Archbishop Stigand, an ambitious and deceitful man, was turned out of the Archbishopric of Canterbury, to which he had got himself named by unfair means, and the Italian Lanfranc was made Archbishop in his place. This one exchange alone more than made up for all the miseries of the Conquest. Lanfianc was born at Pavia in the north of Italy, and became a monk. His great talents soon caused him to be known; and when he went to France on business, Duke William asked him to stay in Normandy, and after he had conquered England, he made Lanfranc Archbishop of Canterbury; knowing that the influence of his holy life and wise and prudent conduct would soon win and raise the English clergy. He was not mistaken. At first Lanfranc was opposed, because he was a foreigner; but very soon the clergy began to see how holy and wise he was, and how much they gained by having so saintly an archbishop. Lanfranc made great and important reforms among them, and was always the constant and firm advocate for justice and mercy from William towards the English people. His advice and remonstrances saved the king from committing many acts of cruelty; for stern and terrible as he was, the conqueror loved and reverenced the Church, and never failed in his obedience to spiritual authority.

William had three sons, Robert, William, and Henry. They were very badly brought up; and Robert was so spoiled by his mother, Queen Matilda, that he gave his father more pain and trouble than all England put together. He was very strong and brave, but so short, that his father named him *Curthose*. This made him angry; and he hated his father, and was always rebelling against him. One day, as he and his brothers were at a little inn in France, he was walking under the balcony

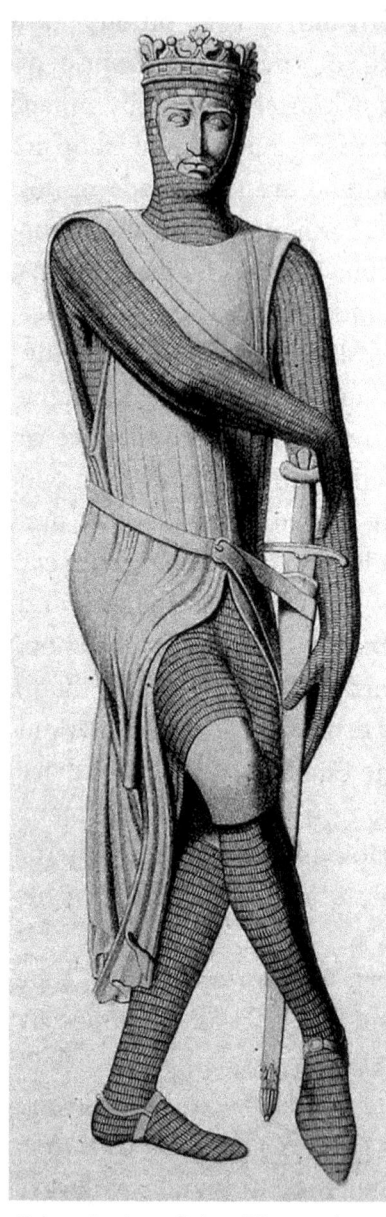

Robert Curthose, Duke of Normandy and Son of William the Conqueror

in which William and Henry were sitting, and they poured some water upon him, and wetted him through. Robert was so enraged at this insult, that he flew upstairs with his sword drawn, and would have killed them; but his father came out and separated them before he could do any mischief. However, he went away and raised an army, and fought against his brothers. Robert afterwards went to Italy, and married an Italian lady named Sybilla.

At last, the Conqueror went to fight the king of France, with whom he was very angry; and as he was besieging Mantes in Normandy, his horse trod on some burning cinders, and plunged violently. William was grown old and fat, and he was so much hurt, that he was carried to Rouen, where he lay on his death-bed, and was very unhappy to think of all the churches and monasteries he had burned. He gave large sums of money to restore as many of them as he could, and he distributed great alms to the poor. One morning he heard the bell ringing for Prime, and he asked what it was. They told him it rang Prime of our Lady; and then, lifting up his hands, he said, "I commend myself to that blessed Lady, Mary the Mother of God, that she may reconcile me to her most dear Son, our Lord Jesus Christ!" and then he died. As soon as the soul of the terrible Conqueror had left the body, the servants stripped it of its jewels, and even clothes; took away all the hangings, furniture, and plate out of the rooms, and went away, leaving the body by itself on the floor. At last, however, the monks of Caen buried it in their cathedral.

William was a head and shoulders taller than any of his subjects, and so strong, that he could bend a bow on horseback which no one else could bend on foot. He was very stern and terrible in his anger; but when he pleased, he was mild and winning. He was a good and kind husband, and always revered the Church.[8] His greatest passion was hunting, which caused him to commit many cruelties. The chroniclers of that time say that "he loved the tall deer as if he had been their father and it was to preserve them that he made the cruel law:

> "*Whoso slayeth hart or hind,*
> *Him man shall blind.*"

For whoever in this reign killed a deer had his eyes put out, or his hand chopped off.

When William lay on his death-bed, he said that his son William should be king, and that Henry should have five thousand pounds out of the treasury. Henry, who wished to

---

[8] As he showed by doing in all cases as the Pope advsed him, and being treated by him as a friend. When he was in compay with his bishops and clergy, William put off his fierce looks, and his manners became gentle and submissive.

be king himself, said, "But of what use is money to me, when I have no house to live in?"

"Be patient," replied his father, "and thou shalt inherit the fortunes of both thy brothers." William set off directly to England, when he heard this; and Henry went to the treasury, and asked for his money. Certainly, you will not like either of these selfish princes.

William the Red, "Rufus"

Chapter XV.

The Red King.

From 1087 to 1100.

AS soon as young William came to England, he made haste to get himself crowned, that he might be beforehand with his elder brother Robert, who was coming home to England. But Robert loitered so much on the way, and spent so much time in his courtship and marriage, that William was crowned, and his kingdom lost. William had fierce glaring eyes, and a red face and hair, which made his subjects name him *Rufus*, or red. He was good-natured at first; but he soon became cruel and avaricious, and led a most wicked and profligate life. As long as Lanfranc lived, he was a little restrained; for that great and powerful prelate influenced everyone, whether bad or good, and they feared as well as loved him. But Lanfranc died; and then the Red King did just as he pleased, and was ten times more cruel than his father had been. Indeed, as you know how badly he behaved to his brothers when he was young, you may think that he was not very good when he grew up.

When Robert came home, Red William tried to get

Normandy from him; for he was so greedy, that he was not satisfied with England. Then he joined with Robert in fighting against Henry, and they both besieged him in the castle of Mount St. Michel. Henry's soldiers had soon no water to drink, for which William was very glad; but Robert, who was more generous, sent some water into the castle, and some casks of wine for Henry to drink.

About this time, the Saracens, an infidel people who had overthrown the Lower or Greek Empire, and had established themselves in Asia Minor, took Jerusalem; and the Pope was very unhappy, and asked all the kings and princes of Europe to go to Palestine, and get the Holy Sepulchre back again. Most of the kings were very glad to do this good work, or to send some of their nobles and soldiers; and Robert was one of the very first, for he had a generous heart, which was not eaten up with avarice and selfishness, like his brother's. He pawned his Duchy of Normandy to Red William for a sum of money, and set out for the Holy Land. As soon as he was gone, his treacherous brother persuaded the Normans to choose him for their duke instead of Robert, that he might never have to give up the duchy again.

I told you that when Lanfranc died, the king lost all restraint, and became like a wild beast. That great and wise archbishop foresaw the misery he would cause, and he spent his last days in great sorrow on account of the country which he had, like a faithful shepherd, done everything to protect. When he was dead, however, God raised up another in his place. This was St. Anselm, the abbot of Bec in Normandy, where many of the new monks were brought from. St. Anselm did all he could to prevent the king from making him Archbishop of Canterbury; but it was of no use. He told them that the Church in England was like a plough drawn by two oxen—one the spiritual, and the other the temporal or kingly power. "And now," he said, "you wish to yoke me, a poor wretched sheep, with a furious wild bull to that plough. How can it be?" He suffered himself to be led, however, like a sheep to the dangerous post; and he soon found that he was right. The Red King had expected that Anselm, being a Norman, would give up all the lands and money of Canterbury to him, whenever he chose to ask for them; and when he found that the saint defended his rights, and the rights of his see, he was furious with rage. One day, before St. Anselm set out for Normandy, he went to see the king; and the king was so angry and enraged, that when he was told of it, he said: "Let him go. I hated him yesterday, and I hate him still more today; and I will hate him more and more bitterly every day that I live."

When St. Anselm found that, do as he would, he really could not defend his poor flock, he determined to go to Rome and take counsel of the Pope. Before he sailed, he went to take leave of the king, and to give him his blessing. He went in to his apartments when he was holding a court, and standing before him with his crosier, he said: "Sir, as this is the last time we shall ever meet, I am come, as your father and archbishop, to give you my blessing once more." The rude, fierce king was so struck with the dignity and charity of the man whom he injured so much, and in injuring whom he had injured God also, that he bowed down his head, and St. Anselm made the sign of the cross over him with his crosier, and went away; while the king was too much ashamed to say a single word.

It was soon seen that St. Anselm was right; and that it was really a prophecy, when he said he should never see the king again. The wicked man gave full loose to his passions, as soon as the archbishop was gone; but soon afterwards, he woke up shrieking in the night, and declared that he had seen a dreadful sight. What he saw is not known; but he went out to hunt one day in the New Forest, to drive away the remorse which struck him; and his courtiers were soon scattered through the wood to look for deer, and left the king alone. They looked everywhere for him for some days; and at last his body was found quite stiff in the forest, with an arrow sticking in it. Some charcoal-burners took it up and carried it to Winchester, where the monks buried it, without any ceremony, in a common piece of ground. Some people reported that Sir Walter Tyrrell had shot him by accident, but no one saw him do it; and Sir Walter, when he died, declared that he had never been with the king that day at all. Whether he was shot by some English serf, or whether his brother Henry had a hand in his death, we cannot know now; but this is certain, that a fitter retribution could not be found for a king who had fought against and hated the Church all his life, than to die without repenting of his sins, and without the help of her sacraments and priests, and to be buried without Christian burial, and, like a dog, in unconsecrated ground.

During Red William's reign Westminster Hall was built, which stands now opposite the Abbey. It has one of the finest roofs in the world; being quite without support throughout its length. He built a strong stone bridge also over the Thames, where London Bridge now stands. In his time the barons began to build beautiful castles and churches all over England; and the Norman style of architecture began to be used everywhere in our country, instead of the low and more clumsy Saxon.

CHAPTER XVI.

The Scholar-King
FROM 1100 TO 1135

WHEN the Red King's body was buried in a hole by night at Winchester, Robert, his eldest brother, was loitering in Italy at the court of Count Conversana. Robert was passionate and foolish, but he was brave and generous; he had fought more bravely than any of the other crusaders, except Godfrey of Bouillon; and he and that famous knight were generally together in the field. And when Jerusalem was taken by the crusaders, and the Holy Sepulchre was freed from its infidel masters, the crown of Jerusalem was offered to Robert, who was wise enough not to take it, and it was given to Godfrey of Bouillon. On his way home, Robert seemed to forget his duties and his subjects in Normandy in his love for the beautiful Sybilla, who at last married him, and they came home together. Then he found that he had lost all chance of being King of England; for Henry had gone before him to Winchester, and had forced the treasurer to give him up the royal treasures, and had got himself crowned in his place. Robert was very angry at first; but afterwards St. Anselm made peace between him and his brother, and he came and stayed at Henry's court at Winchester, where he enjoyed himself very much. Almost the first thing Henry did was to ask Matilda Atheling (as she was called) the daughter of Malcolm, king of Scotland, and St. Margaret, to be his wife. This showed how wise he was; for Matilda was of royal Saxon blood, the great granddaughter of Edmund Ironside; and she was, besides, so good and gentle and beautiful, that everyone loved her, and she was always called Mold, or Maude, the Good.

Matilda had been in the convent at Wilton; but as she declared solemnly that she had never even wished to be a nun, but disliked the idea, she was married to the king. But before they were finally married, St. Anselm had a pulpit out up at the gates of Westminster Abbey; and he told the people how Matilda had fled to Wilton to escape being obliged to marry a Norman husband, but had never even put on a veil,

Marriage of Matilda of Scotland and King Henry I

except when she was obliged. And he asked them if they were satisfied of this, and agreed that Matilda Atheling should marry King Henry.

And all the multitude of people cried out, and shouted, "We are satisfied. Let it be so." So, after this beautiful and singular scene, Henry and Matilda were married.

King Henry was very tall and handsome, with bright dark eyes, which sometimes looked very terrible. He was very learned, and fond of books and study, which caused him to be called *Beauclerc*, or *fine scholar*. Besides being learned, he was a very clever man; but he was also crafty and deceitful, cruel and profligate, though not nearly so bad as the wretched Red King, his brother. One of the first things he did was both good and wise. He sent away from his court all the bad and idle young lords and ladies who had helped Rufus to be so wicked. These foolish young lords curled their hair, and let it grow long, and some of them even had false curls, exactly like women. They wore twisted peaks to their shoes, like rams' horns, which were gilt and colored. It was wise of Henry Beauclerc to drive away these ridiculous milksops, and to take good and prudent men for his counsellors. Amongst other powerful and cruel nobles whom Henry banished was one named Robert Belesme, earl of Shrewsbury. He was so cruel as to delight in looking on when the miserable knights and people whom he imprisoned were being tortured; and he often caught men and women, and put them in prison, for the pleasure of seeing them suffer and hearing them cry out. Henry banished this wicked nobleman out of England, and he was never allowed to come back again.

Henry had agreed to pay his brother Robert a thousand marks a year, and he was to have Normandy besides. But Henry was so deceitful and treacherous as to pick a quarrel with his brother, and then to complain that he had broken the treaty, and must be punished. He fought against him, took his castles, and at last took Robert himself, and put him in prison in Cardiff Castle, where he died. This was the base return he made for his brother's generous kindness to him when he was shut up in the castle of Mount St. Michel.

When he had settled himself in his ill-gotten Duchy of Normandy, King Henry began to quarrel with St. Anselm, his great and wise archbishop, who, as you remember, had gone to Rome to complain to the Pope, and to ask his advice. After that he stayed at Lyons; but when Henry Beauclerc became king, St. Anselm came back again to England. Henry behaved very well to him for a time; but after a while he began to try to get all the power over the bishops into his own hands; and as we shall have to read a great deal about these battles between the Church and the kings of England, it will be well for you to try now and understand how they began.

A very long time ago indeed, when the number of Christians was smaller, and their manners purer, whenever a bishop died, all the canons, and priests, and people met together, and chose the best man they could find to be bishop in his place; and when they had chosen him, and given their reasons for thinking he ought to be bishop, the archbishop *invested*, or dressed him, with his ring and pastoral staff, which are the symbols of a bishop's spiritual power over his diocese or flock.

After a while, the kings in several countries began to think that, as the bishops were their *subjects*, they ought to have some share in making them bishops; and when they had said this to themselves, as we naturally love power, they went a little further, and thought that they would like to *invest* them too. They wished this, because they thought the bishops would show their gratitude by robbing their people, and paying sums of money for their investiture—in which they were not mistaken. The consequence was that these kings chose men to be bishops whom they knew would be false to the Church and servile to them.

It was this office which the Norman kings of England, who were very fond of power, tried to usurp, and which was a great crime, because our Lord gave it only to the Apostles and their successors, and never to any layman. Henry Beauclerc invested several bishops; and when he found that the Pope would not acknowledge them, he was very angry, and blamed St. Anselm for opposing him. In the end, after many violent disputes, in which St. Anselm remained firm to his opposition of Henry's unlawful exercise of investiture, he went to Rome, and the Pope threatened to excommunicate Henry. The king was very sorry for this, and he promised to give up his right. He met St. Anselm on his way home at Bec, and swore to invest no more bishops with the ring and staff. The weak old grey-haired Saint had beaten the proud and strong king, and had won a great victory.

The patient and unwearied St. Anselm did not live long after he came back to England. On Palm Sunday he was sitting with his monks, and one of them said to him: "Father, you are going to keep Easter with our Lord." On Tuesday in Holy Week they read the Passion to him; and when they came to the words, "Ye are they who have continued with Me in my temptations, and I dispose to you, as my Father hath disposed to Me, a kingdom," they saw that the aged Saint was dying. They laid him in the ashes, and he breathed out his soul in great peace.

Where the Church was not concerned Henry made good laws. He wrote down a great many of the laws of Alfred and

St. Edward, and said they should be kept. These laws were written on a large parchment or *charta*, which is the Latin for paper; and as laws were always written in this way, charta came to be used as an English word, and these laws are always called Henry the First's *Charter*. The people were very glad of this charter; and they were glad too of another thing which the king did. The pennies at that time had a cross upon them, and there were no halfpennies or farthings coined. Whenever anyone wanted a halfpenny, he broke the penny in two down the cross; and if he wanted a farthing, he broke it in four. This was a very clumsy contrivance; and King Henry ordered that round halfpence and farthings should be made, like what we now use.

Besides these useful things, the king did a great act of justice to the poor. Some of the nobles were accustomed to commit great cruelties when they went round the country to *purvey*, or get provisions for the king. At that time, instead of taxes, the king used to send out *purveyors*, or noblemen who collected horses, cattle, hay, corn, and meal for the king. Henry's purveyors used to seize all the corn and cattle they could find; and when they had taken the best for themselves, they used to burn and kill the rest, and wash the horses' feet with the ale and mead when they could not carry it all away, and very often burned the house of the farmer or tradesman to whom it belonged. If anyone complained of these wicked men, he was sure to be punished by them with greater cruelty; so that the poor and the farmers were robbed and ill-treated by everyone who was more powerful than themselves. But King Henry sent some good judges all over the country, and they listened to what the poor said, and tried the wicked nobles, and punished them. Some were put to death, and all of them were punished so severely that they did not dare

The Scholar-King

commit such wicked actions again.

The last years of Henry's life were very sad. As long as his queen—"the good Queen Mold"—lived, he was less cruel and tyrannical. It was Maude who persuaded or advised him to grant the charter, and to protect the poor, and to make peace, and submit to the Church. But when this good and pious queen was dead, Henry became more cruel; and though he married another good queen named Adelais or Alice, she was too young and childish to advise him as Maude did. He had an only son named William, whom he loved better than anything else in the world. Prince William had been fighting with his father in Normandy, and had behaved in a brave and generous manner to the French, whom they were fighting against. When they were just going to sail to England, a Norman captain came and asked leave to bring the prince in his ship, which was larger and faster than the others, and was called *la Blanche Nef,* or the White Ship. King Henry agreed, and Prince William and all his merry young companions went on board the White Ship, where they behaved in a foolish, wild manner, dancing and singing, and giving wine to the sailors till they were drunk. Then, to make up for lost time, they rowed as fast as ever they could—for in those days ships had oars as well as sails—and the Blanche Nef struck against a dangerous rock named the *Catte Raze,* which made a hole in her side, and she filled with water and sank. The sailors had jumped into the boats when they felt the ship strike, and Prince William and his friends were rowing ashore as fast as they could, when William heard his sister's voice calling to him out of the sinking ship. The generous young man told the sailors to row back again; and though they warned him that it would be dangerous to take any more persons into the boat, he would go and save his dear sister. But when they got within reach of the sinking ship, it happened as the sailors had told him; for so many of the poor people who had been left on the wreck jumped into the boat, that it overturned and sank, and they were all drowned together. The only people who remained alive were the captain and a French butcher from Rouen; and when the captain heard that the prince was drowned, he was so grieved that he let go of the mast he was holding, and was drowned too. The butcher was the only one who escaped, and who told the sad story.

King Henry was so unhappy at the prince's sorrowful end, that he fainted away for three hours, and never was seen to smile again as long as he lived. He had many troubles after this. As he had no other sons, he tried to make all his barons promise to make his grandson king. His daughter Matilda, or Maude, had married the emperor of Germany; and when he died, she married Count Geoffrey of Anjou, and had a little son named Henry, who was called Henry *Fitzempress*, or the empress's son. Count Geoffrey used to stick a sprig of yellow broom in his cap when he went out hunting, perhaps that he might be known more easily; and as the Latin name of this broom is *planta genista*, he was called *Plante-genêt*, or Plantagenet.

Some of the barons promised to obey young Henry Fitzempress as their king; and others said they would choose Stephen of Blois, King Henry's nephew, because he was a grown-up man, and fitter to rule than a child and his mother. In the meanwhile, before these disputes were settled, the king, who was very fond of doing exactly as he liked, ate too many potted lampreys, which he was advised not to touch, and he had a fever, and died in France. His body was brought to England, and buried at Reading Abbey, a very favorite place with him.

Chapter XVII.

The King and the Empress.

From 1135 to 1154.

IMMEDIATELY Henry Beauclerc was dead, his nephew Stephen of Blois, came to England, and all those lords and gentlemen who had said they would not be ruled by a child and a woman, went with him to Westminster Abbey, and he was crowned king. Stephen was very brave, and handsome, and polite, and taller than any of his friends; he had, too, very kind and pleasing manners, so that everyone who knew him loved him, and the people were glad to have so fine a king. He found a great deal of money in the treasury, all of good pure silver, and he soon gathered together a great many soldiers, and seemed to be quite settled on the throne. Stephen would have been a very good king, and would most likely have had a useful reign, if the crown had really been his; but as it was not, it caused the terrible wars which lasted all his life, and which made England a place of misery for nearly twenty long and sad years.

For the Empress Maude and her little son came to England, and their friends gave them money and soldiers to fight against Stephen, and Stephen got together an army to fight against Maude, and so there was a *civil war*, as it is called; that is, a war in which two parties in the same country were fighting against one another. This is the most dreadful of all the kinds of war, because brothers fight against their brothers, sons against their fathers, and neighbors against one another; and even when peace is made, and the people go to their homes again, they do not forget that they have fought together, but hate one another still, and teach their children to carry on this hatred, which is very dreadful.

The king of Scotland had promised Henry Beauclerc that he would fight for Maude; and he kept his word now, and was the first to march his army into England to fight against Stephen. The Princes of Wales, who did homage to the king of England, were very glad to take the opportunity of rebelling; and there was nothing but confusion and bloodshed from

Battle of the Standard

against the savage Scots, who were burning and destroying one end of England to the other. The old Archbishop of York, whose name was Thurstan, gathered the northern barons round him, and bade them fight for God and their country against the Scots who were burning and destroying everything they came near. Thurstan took the mast of a vessel and made a standard in the shape of a cross, with the blessed Sacrament hung under it in a silver pix, and the banners of St. Peter, St. Welfrid, and St. John of Beverley floating round it. The archbishop gave absolution to all the soldiers; and after a very fierce battle, the Scots were completely beaten. Soon after, Matilda took King Stephen prisoner, and shut him up in Bristol Castle, where she treated him very badly. But she was so haughty and cruel that, no one loved her; and even her own friends went away, and joined the king. Stephen escaped from Bristol, and fought against Matilda again, and very nearly starved her and all the soldiers of her garrison to death at Oxford. Matilda only escaped by dressing in white, with one or two knights, and walking six miles in the deep snow to Abingdon, where she got swift horses and rode to Wallingford Castle. This is one of the most daring and curious escapes ever read of in history.

King Stephen's brother Henry, who was the Pope's legate, and Theobald the Archbishop of Canterbury, did all they could to put an end to the war, and at last they succeeded. The proud empress and her friends agreed that Stephen should be king while he lived, and that young Henry should be his heir, and reign after him. Everyone was glad that peace was made, and especially Stephen's queen, who was named Matilda too, but who was kind and good, and beloved by everyone, as the empress was fierce and revengeful, and disliked.

I cannot tell you how shocking the state of the country was

at that time. All the miseries of William the Conqueror's and the Red King's reigns were nothing compared with it. Besides the civil war between Matilda and Stephen, and the corn and cattle their soldiers burned and carried away, nearly every baron who had a castle made a war of his own upon all his poor neighbors. These wicked nobles took them prisoners, shut them up in the dungeons of their castles, and tortured them till they gave them some money to let them out. Some of them were hung up in smoky fires, others had knotted cords twisted round their heads, others were pulled by a rack, and others crushed and mangled in a box filled with sharp rough flints, called a *crucet house*. So you see that those cruel tortures which pagan emperors gave the Christian martyrs were given to our poor countrymen then by Englishmen and Christians like themselves; and this was because the old laws and customs of the good and just Anglo-Saxon kings were forgotten; and the poor had no one like Lanfranc and St. Anselm to stand up for them and do them justice.

There were as many as 126 castles built and fortified by wicked barons in this reign; and some of them were churches or monasteries, which they seized upon and kept for themselves.

King Stephen did not live to do justice to the poor wretched subjects, whom he had made so miserable by taking a crown which did not of right belong to him. He died at Canterbury, after a reign of nineteen years.

Chapter XVIII.

The First of the Plantagenets

From 1154 to 1158

THAT which the Archbishop of Canterbury and the Bishop of Winchester had settled was done; and when Stephen was dead, Henry Fitzempress, the grandson of Henry Beauclerc, became king. He was young, brave, and handsome, and one of the cleverest, richest, and most powerful kings in Europe; so that Henry II began his reign with every prospect of doing a great deal of good. When he was only Count of Anjou, he married a very beautiful and witty lady named Eleanor of Aquitaine, who had a great deal of land in the south of France; so that, together with what Henry had, a very large part of France belonged at that time to England. If you will take your Atlas and look at France as it was when it was divided into provinces, you will see how much it was, when you read these names;—1. Maine. 2. Touraine. 3. Anjou. 4. Angoumois. 5. Poitou. 6. Perigord. 7. Saintonge. 8. Limousin. 9. Guienne. 10. Normandy. You will see by these names, that the kings of England had some right to be called, as they were when they were crowned, kings of England, Scotland, *France,* and Ireland.

Everyone was heartily tired of the cruel wars between Stephen and Matilda, and longed for peace, and time to sow corn and reap it, without the risk of its being carried away; and when the young king landed in England from Harfleur, all the bishops, and great numbers of the nobles and gentlemen, went joyfully down to the beach to welcome him; and there were rejoicings all through England at his coming. I will tell you what Henry's chaplain says of him, that you may picture to yourself what he was like. He says that he was neither tall nor short, but very well made; rather dark, and with clear sparkling eyes. His hair was cut short, with mustachios, and no beard; a "lionous visage," that is, a lion-like face; and when he was angry, his eyes flashed so terribly, that everyone ran away. His whole face then became distorted, his hands clenched, and he rolled on the floor, biting and tearing sticks, rushes, or whatever he got hold of. These terrible fits of rage made the great Henry II like a wild beast. Henry always stood during Mass, council, meals, and all kinds of business; and rode long journeys, galloping as fast as his horse could go. So that he never rested all day long; and often got up in the night, and set out on a long galloping journey, to see if his soldiers, or nobles, or judges were doing their duty. I think his courtiers and his horses must have had rather a hard life; for the nobles complained that they could scarcely ever keep up with the king. He wore plain clothes, a short Angevin cloak, and no gloves; so that his large hands were brown and untrimmed. And he generally held either a sword, or a spear, or hunting-staff in them. Every day he held a kind of council of learned and clever men, whom he asked to explain certain questions, or difficult subjects; and gave his own opinion about them, which was generally a very good one. He overlooked his judges in their office; and if they were unjust, they were severely punished. "No man was more wise in council, more *dreadful* in prosperity, nor more steadfast in adversity. When once he loved, scarcely ever will he hate; when once he hates, he scarcely ever receives into favor." These are the very words of Peter of Blois, the king's tutor and chaplain.

You may see very plainly from this, that Henry Plantagenet had great qualities, and that he might have been a very great and wise king; but he was unfortunately so crafty and deceitful, that Cardinal Vivian, after talking to him once for a long time, exclaimed: "Never did I see this man's equal in lying!"

The first thing he did was both a good and a wise act. This was to order all the castles which had been built in Stephen's reign to be pulled down or *dismantled* (that is, to have their fortifications destroyed); and those that were not pulled down, he took for himself. By doing so, the cruel barons, who had so long oppressed and illtreated their poor neighbors, were justly punished; and their ill-used power was taken from them. Next, the king sent away the good-for-nothing foreign soldiers whom Matilda and Stephen had brought into England; and this delighted his subjects even more than pulling down the barons' castles; for these soldiers had behaved in the cruelest manner to the people, and had always taken delight in burning and destroying everything they did not want for themselves. Having got rid of two chief troubles in this manner, the king found that the money which his grandfather Henry Beauclerc had made was spoiled and mixed with bad money; so he ordered fresh good money to be coined, and used instead of it; which was of great service to the tradesmen and merchants, and to all other classes of his subjects. Because, when money is bad, no one knows exactly the value of it; and when the farmers bring their corn and cattle and sheep to market, perhaps they get less for their goods than they ought to get; which is not fair, and which makes them sell them in some other country, or eat them themselves. This, again, causes a scarcity; and then everything becomes dearer than it ought to be, which is a misfortune to all the people in the country. By and by you will be able to understand this better, for it is difficult to understand well; but what I have told you is enough to show you why the coining of new money is always spoken of in history as a benefit. Besides this, Henry confirmed his grandfather's charter; that is, he too promised to keep the laws of "good King Edward;" and all these things made the people very glad indeed.

Just at the time when Henry Plantagenet became king of England, an Englishman was made Pope. His name was Nicholas Brakspeare; but he was called Adrian IV when he became Pope. He was a poor monk of St. Alban's, who went to France and studied, and was chosen abbot of a monastery in Provence. The monks, however, found that he was too strict for them, and they complained to the Pope. The Pope was sorry for their folly; and he told them to choose another abbot, for he had taken their's to be a cardinal. He sent Cardinal Brakspeare to Norway and Sweden, where he preached, and converted many of the poor country people, who were not much better than pagans. When he went back to Rome, he was chosen Pope instead of his old friend, who was dead.

The English were very glad indeed to have an English Pope; and they sent three English bishops to congratulate

Pope Adrian IV

him, together with a learned monk named John of Salisbury, who wrote a nice account of it and what Nicholas said to them. He told them, when he was thanking them for coming so far to see him, that his crown was a fiery one; meaning, that his office was full of trials and difficulties.

King Henry was one of the very first to make it difficult; for he began again the old quarrel about investitures, which his grandfather had settled with the great St. Anselm. He not only wanted to invest the English bishops himself, but to punish them too. Now, it had always been the custom, of course, for the bishop to punish his priests, and for the archbishop to punish the bishops; because the archbishop is the spiritual lord over all the bishops, as the bishop is over his clergy. But Henry II said that the clergy should be punished in his courts of justice, just as if they were laymen, and by his judges. The bishops told him that this was unjust, because the judges were not able to decide in spiritual matters; and the Archbishop of Canterbury said he never would agree to what the king wished. And now I am going to tell you the archbishop's story, in which I am sure you will be very much interested.

Henry II sculpture on Canterbury Cathedral

Chapter XIX.

The Church and the World

From 1158 to 1171

AMONG the English who went to the Crusades when the Normans took possession of England, was a citizen of London named Gilbert Becket, who was taken prisoner by the Saracens. He would most likely have stayed there, and died and been forgotten, if it had not been that a Syrian lady fell in love with him, and helped him to escape out of prison. Gilbert came back to London; and soon after, the Syrian girl came to London too, to find him. She knew only two English words, "Gilbert" and "London" but with the help of these and her persevering love, she really found out Gilbert Becket; and after having been baptized Matilda, he married her. They had one son, who was named Thomas, who was a very quick and clever boy, and tall and handsome like his mother. Thomas went to study at the schools at Oxford; and afterwards he was sent to the University at Paris, which was then the most famous in the world. When he had finished his education, few men in Europe could match him in great talents, learning, and energy of character. The Archbishop Theobald of Canterbury was a friend of his father, and took the young Becket into his household; but afterwards sent him abroad again, to study canon law at Bologna, because at that time one of the most famous lawyers in Europe, named Gratian, was teaching there. When Becket came back from Italy, the archbishop recommended him to the king for his chancellor; and Henry became so fond of him, that he could not bear to be away from him, and gave him large presents of land and money. The Chancellor Becket was so rich that, when he went once to France on the king's business, this was the way he travelled. First came two hundred and fifty singing boys; then his hounds, in couples; then eight wagons, with all his furniture, and the vestments for saying Mass; then his horses, led; then the squires of his gentlemen, leading their masters' horses; the gentlemen's sons who were brought up in his household, clergymen, knights, officers, and falconers, all riding two-and-two, according to their rank; lastly came the chancellor himself, with his own friends. When the French people saw all this grand procession, they said to one another, "What kind of man must the *king* of England be, if his *chancellor* rides in such state?"

Becket was a layman at that time, and quite a soldier and man of the world in his habits and looks; but when the good old Archbishop Theobald soon after died, the king said that his chancellor should be Archbishop in his stead. Becket did everything he could to persuade the king not to choose one who, he said, was so unfit for the high office; for he does not seem to have wished then to be a priest; but the king persisted, and said that no one but his chancellor should be Archbishop of Canterbury. When Becket saw that it was really settled, he fasted and prayed all night, and took a firm resolution to change his life entirely. And then it was seen, as has often been known in the history of the Saints, how much one strong resolution offered to God can do. The Archbishop sent away all his knights and squires, and pages and falconers, and horses and hounds. He put off his scarlet cloth and silken robes, put on a hair-shirt and a coarse cassock, and ate only plain and scanty food. He asked a few holy and simple priests to live with him; and they led together the life of monks, rising early, praying at set times, and living in common. He went to the king, and gave back the chancellor's seal into his hands; and said he could not now be chancellor any longer, for he had greater and heavier duties to fulfill.

Everybody was astonished at this wonderful change in the gay and worldly chancellor; but no one was so much astonished, and so angry, as the king. He was angry, not only because he had lost his merry and amusing companion, but because he feared that now his favorite friend was so changed, he would take part against him in the matter of investitures, and support the Bishops and the Church. And so it was with him as it usually is with worldly people, that when their friends leave off bending to their humour, and stand against their wicked designs, their love changes to bitter hatred.

The king was determined to carry out his plan of making the Bishops give up judging their clergy in the ecclesiastical courts; and he ordered them all to send the clergy to be tried in the common courts, by his judges. He made his lawyers write down a number of laws, which he called the Constitutions (or Customs) of Clarendon; and he asked the Bishops to sign this parchment, and promise to keep the laws written in it. I will not tell you all these Customs, as the king called them (to make the people believe that they were old laws); but in reality they were not old laws at all, but inventions of the Norman kings. The most unjust of them all was, that when a Bishop or Archbishop died, the king was to take all the money belonging to the see till there was a new Bishop; so that if the king was bad, he could keep the see without a Bishop for a long time, that he might get more money.

The Archbishop Becket would not sign the Customs for a long time; but at last he promised that he would, because the king was so angry that he swore to put all the Bishops to death if he did not. But some time after, he was so sorry for having made this promise that he wrote to the Pope and asked absolution for it. Pope Alexander said he was quite determined not to allow the Constitutions of Clarendon; and the king was in such a violent passion, that he resolved to banish the Archbishop, and not let him live in England any longer. I am sorry to say, that all the other Bishops were so cowardly as to be afraid to help their Archbishop to defend the Church; and they asked him to sign the Customs, lest the king should kill him.

St. Thomas was too brave a soldier to leave his post because it was a dangerous one. He said the Mass of St. Stephen the Protomartyr; and, vesting in his pontifical robes, and carrying the crozier in his hands, he went to the king's palace. As soon as he went in, the king and all his barons got up and went into another hall, to show how displeased they were; and the cowardly Bishops soon after went to them. The noble Archbishop sat down quietly at one end of the hall, waiting in silence to hear what the king would do; for he had now told him positively that he would never sign the Customs of Clarendon. He knew that the palace was full of barons and soldiers, who were all his enemies, because the king was his enemy. He knew that his blood might be shed the next moment, and that he was alone, without any human help; but still he sat there calmly waiting, just as our Lord waited at Herod's court to hear what the world would witness against Him.

Soon some of the Bishops came out, and were base enough to go up to the Archbishop, and say that they could not obey him any longer, because he had disobeyed the king, and that they appealed to the Pope to support them.

"I hear," replied St. Thomas; and he said no more.

Then all the Bishops, not daring to say any more to him, sat down on the opposite side of the hall, and there was a long silence—a silence which was fearful to the poor cowardly Bishops, but which was without any kind of terror to the great Archbishop, who was most likely thinking how our Lord was left alone by His Apostles, and that, as the servant is not above his master, so he must always be ready to suffer, to be despised, and to die; in a word, to drink the same bitter Chalice as He drank for us.

This wonderful scene was changed by Lord Leicester coming into the hall, and bidding St. Thomas "hear his sentence."

"My sentence!" replied the noble Archbishop, with dignity. "My son and earl, hear *me;* know that you are my children in God. Neither law nor reason allows you to judge your father. I decline your tribunal; I refer my quarrel to the decision of the Pope. To him I appeal, and, under the protection of the Catholic Church and the Apostolic See, I depart hence." So saying he got up, and passing through the midst of his enemies, who stood looking at him like raging lions disappointed of their prey, he left the hall. Some of the basest among them threw wisps of straw at him as he passed along, and one of them cried out that he was a traitor. At that vile word the Syrian blood that flowed in his veins seems to have once more mounted within him, and turning round, with a look that made them shrink, the Archbishop said, "If it were not that my order forbids me, that coward should repent of his insolence." As soon as he gained the gate, the people, who everywhere adored him as their best friend and father, received him with shouts of triumphant joy.

The next morning St. Thomas sailed away to France, where he went first to the king, and then to the Pope, who was living in France at that time, because there were great troubles, and a false Pope, at Rome. The Pope received him with tears of joy, and ordered him to live at the abbey of Pontigny.

The cruel King Henry would not let him rest even there. He banished every one who was related to St. Thomas, or who was his friend, or who had even known him; and he sent all these people, amounting to several hundreds, to Pontigny, to show St. Thomas how much his "obstinacy" had made them suffer. And not satisfied with this, he sent word to the Abbot of Pontigny, which was a Cistercian abbey, that if he allowed St. Thomas to stay there any longer, he would send all the Cistercian monks out of England.

So the holy Archbishop was obliged to leave his quiet rest, and to wander away again; but King Louis, who was very fond of him, gave him the city of Sens to live in. Here he spent all his time in prayer, and in reading the lives of the Martyrs; and here it was revealed to him that, as a reward for his glorious defence of the Church against her strongest enemies, he should obtain the Martyr's crown.

After a while King Henry went to Sens, and paid a visit to the Pope and to the king of France, and there St. Thomas knelt once more at the feet of the master who had so cruelly and ungratefully repaid his love and his services; and Henry's proud heart was touched, and he forgave his faithful servant, and said that they would always be friends.

But unhappily, when Henry went back to England, St. Thomas's enemies got round him again, and persuaded him that the Archbishop only wanted to be rich and powerful, and that his love for the Church was only a crafty pretense to hide his own pride and ambition. And then the king listened, and gave some of the other Bishops leave to take the revenues of Canterbury, and to use them for their own dioceses.

When St. Thomas heard this, he could rest no longer. When the king attacked himself, or him through his friends, he bore all that was done as patiently as a lamb; but when the Church and his beloved flock were touched, he became like a lion roused from his lair. He made up his mind to go back to Canterbury, and to defend it till he died. He went to bid King Louis good-by, and said that he was going to seek his death in England. Accordingly he set sail, and arrived at Canterbury a little before Christmas. On Christmas day he preached a beautiful sermon to his people about *peace to men of goodwill;* and when he ended he told them, in a few solemn and touching words, that he should soon leave them and go to his rest. All the people, who loved him with a passionate love, and who had rejoiced at his return to protect them, wept aloud upon hearing these words, so that the great cathedral resounded with their sobs and cries, and St. Thomas could not help shedding many tears himself; for he knew, as he told the Abbot of Pontigny, that "his poor people would be scattered like sheep without a shepherd."

The next day four gentlemen, Hugh of Hornsea, Reginald Fitzurse, and two others, came down to Canterbury, and threatened the Archbishop with death, if he did not give up his opposition, and submit to the king in every thing. These gentlemen had heard the king swearing and foaming with rage because St. Thomas had brought letters of excommunication from the Pope for some Bishops who had disobeyed him; and this enraged King Henry so much that he cried out, "Will nobody rid me of this troublesome priest!" So the four knights thought he would reward them richly if they committed so foul a deed. When they threatened the Archbishop, he only answered, " I am ready;" and as it was the vesper-time, he robed himself, and went into the cathedral when they began to chant vespers.

The four wicked knights put on their armor as if they were going out to battle, and then came into the cathdral crying out with a loud noise, "Where is the traitor? Where is the traitor?" No one answered; and then they cried again, "Where is the Archbishop?" St. Thomas then came forward, and said calmly, "I am here; the Archbishop, but no traitor." The people then all fled to the altars to save themselves, and St. Thomas remained alone but quite unmoved.

One of the murderers said to him, "Now you must die." He answered, "I am ready to die for God, for justice, and for the liberty of the Church; but I forbid you, in the name of Almighty God, to hurt in the least any of my religious, clergy, or people. I have defended the Church, as far as I was able, during my life, when I saw it oppressed; and I shall be happy if by my death, at least, I can restore its peace and liberty."

So saying, this noble shepherd of his flock knelt down, and commended his brave soul to God, to our Lady, and to the patron saints of Canterbury, and prayed for his murderers. Then, as he was praying for them, they struck him with their swords, and scattered his holy blood and brains upon the pavement. While, with a calm and joyful countenance,

The death St. Thomas Becket

praying to the last, the most glorious of all the English Martyrs went to receive his crown.

It is impossible to say how all the kings and princes of Europe cried out with grief and indignation when they heard what King Henry had done; and he was so struck with remorse himself that he would not eat or speak, and shut himself up for four days; for he was frightened to think what a dreadful crime he had committed. The Pope excommunicated every one who had any share in the martyrdom; and the king offered to do public penance to atone for having caused it. He was summoned to Avranches in France to prove his innocence, and there, in the great cathedral, before the Pope's legates, the king of France, and his bishops and nobles, the proud king of England humbly laid his hand upon the Book of the Gospels, and declared that he was innocent of all intention to murder St. Thomas; then he promised to send two hundred knights to the Holy Land for a whole year at his own expense, to give back all St. Thomas's money and lands to his relations, and finally to abolish the Customs of Clarendon. And having so done, he knelt down before the altar, and the Pope's legate absolved him from all the censures that had been put upon him.

You see that the blood of the Martyr had not been shed in vain.

Chapter XX.

Henry's Wars, Troubles, and End

From 1171 to 1189

YOU must now hear about King Henry's wars; and first of all, about the Conquest of Ireland, which never seems to have brought much blessing on Ireland, or England either. You know that Ireland had been converted by St. Patrick to the true faith many hundred years ago, in the fourth century, and had become a land of Saints. It had become a land of learning, too; for there were a great many monasteries built, and Irish scholars went out to all the cities of Europe to teach; so that if any young man was cleverer or more learned than his companions, it became a proverb to say jestingly, "You must have learning in Ireland." But after many years of fame, Ireland became wild and savage again, and it was divided into a great many little kingdoms, or provinces, governed by petty princes, who were always quarrelling and fighting with one another. In the reign of Henry II, one of these chiefs, named Dermot, carried away the wife of another chief, named O'Ruarc; and O'Ruarc asked several chiefs to help him to get back his wife, and punish Dermot for his wickedness. They turned Dermot at last out of his kingdom of Leinster; and he went in revenge to England, and asked some of the great English barons to help him to conquer it back again. The Earl of Pembroke, who is sometimes called Lord Strigul, and sometimes Strongbow, said he would help Dermot, and two Welsh gentlemen promised to join him. They took their own soldiers over to Ireland, and beat the Prince of Ossory in battle, and gave Dermot his kingdom of Leinster again. As soon as the battle was over, Dermot made a pile of the heads of the men of Ossory, and, as he was turning them over with savage delight, he found the head of a man who had been his enemy. He instinctively seized it like a wild beast, and tore off the nose with his teeth.

I cannot stop to tell you of all the battles which were fought and the cruelties which were committed in Ireland after this. King Henry thought that as Earl Strongbow had made a beginning of conquering the island, he might as well finish it, and take it for himself; so he sent an army and generals to Ireland, who burned and destroyed every thing they could, and took possession of the country by force of arms.

At last the Irish Bishops met together in council, and agreed to obey King Henry as their "lord," and that the Irish princes should do him homage. A great many good and useful changes were made in the Irish Church by the Archbishop of Canterbury; so that some good was done, at least for a while.

Besides his wars in Ireland, Henry was obliged to fight with his own sons. He had married a very rich and beautiful lady, named Eleanor of Aquitaine, which was the name given to some of the most beautiful provinces in the south of

Henry's Wars, Troubles, and End

France. Eleanor had been married to the King of France; but she behaved so wickedly that he sent her away, and would not have her for his wife any longer. After this, it was very foolish of Henry to marry her; but he wished very much to get her money and lands; and as he married her chiefly from this bad motive, we cannot wonder that they were not happy. He grew tired of her, and spent his time with other people, and especially with a beautiful lady named Rosamond Clifford, who was called Fair Rosamond. Fair Rosamond afterwards repented of her bad actions, and became a nun at Godstow, near Woodstock.

Eleanor was very proud and revengeful, and she encouraged her sons to rebel against their father. They were named Henry, Richard, Geoffrey, and John. They were quite spoilt, and very badly brought up altogether. Henry, the eldest, had been crowned king of England when he was quite a boy, and he asked his father to give him either England or Normandy for his own; for he was so proud and full of himself that he could not bear to be dependant on the king. King Henry refused to give up his dominions before he died, which made the queen and her son so angry that they left him and went to France, where they tried to raise an army against him. The king of France had very often been deceived by Henry, and he was glad of the opportunity of fighting against him. Richard joined his mother and brother; for his father had behaved very badly to him, and had taken away the wife to whom he was betrothed, Princess Alice of France, and kept her in a kind of imprisonment at Woodstock. After this Richard and his father were never friends together.

The king was very unhappy; and I am glad to say that his unhappiness softened his proud heart; and he now saw that these were the temporal punishments of his crimes.

He came back from Normandy, where he had gone to fight with his rebellious children, and rode from Southampton to Canterbury without stopping. He walked into Canterbury barefoot and dressed like a pilgrim, and went into the cathedral where, through his fault, the holy blood of St. Thomas had flowed; and there, before the shrine in which his relics were placed, he fell prostrate and prayed. He then went into the chapter-house, when all the assembled monks gave him some strokes on the shoulders with a knotted cord or discipline, after which he prayed all night in the crypt, and heard Mass the next morning, always begging the intercession of St. Thomas.

A few days afterwards news was brought that his greatest enemy, the king of Scotland, was taken prisoner. In a little while one enemy after another was beaten or submitted; and the proud king acknowledged, with a changed heart, that the intercession of the martyred St. Thomas was more powerful than all his armies.

King Henry went to France; and, after several battles, both the French king and his own sons were glad to make peace, and they came back to England. Henry brought Queen Eleanor back too; and to prevent her from doing so much mischief again, he sent her to the palace at Winchester, where she could walk and ride about as she pleased, but was not allowed to go to any other place.

After this, the sad news was brought that the Saracens had taken Jerusalem; and that the Pope, who was very old, had died of a broken heart. Most of the kings of Europe said they would take the Cross, and begin another crusade; and Henry went to meet the new king, Philip of France, at Gisors, and they agreed to go together to the Holy Land.

But when King Henry came back to England, his sons

Henry's Wars, Troubles, and End

began again to rebel against him; and he found so much to do in quieting them, that he never went to the Crusade. Perhaps he never heartily wished to go; for he was too calculating and crafty to be generous. His second son, Richard, began to fight with his eldest brother; and young Henry persuaded Geoffrey to join him in raising an army against Richard. In short, they all behaved so wickedly, that they more than once tried to murder their own father. At last young Henry fell very sick, and was soon told that he had only a few hours to live. When he knew this, all his wicked behaviour to his father rushed upon his mind, and he sent a messenger to him begging of him to come and give him his blessing before he died.

Poor King Henry wished very much to go, for he loved his rebellious sons very much; but his nobles would not allow him, for they were afraid that Henry was not really sick, but that the princes wished to murder him; so the king took a ring from his finger, and, giving it to the Bishop of Bordeaux, bade him tell the prince that he forgave him with all his heart. When young Henry saw the ring, he kissed it in a transport of sorrow; and begging to be laid in the middle of the room upon ashes, he received the last Sacraments, and died.

I am sorry to say that Geoffrey was not the least touched by his brother's contrition. He went to the French court, where he made all kinds of plots against his father; but died before he could do any more mischief.

Richard left his father too, and went to France, when King Philip gave him all the French castles that belonged to his father. The French king and Richard raised an army, and drove King Henry from one place to another, till at last he was obliged to offer to make peace. When he met them at Tours, King Henry found that his darling son John, whom at least he had thought to be faithful and affectionate, had been secretly helping the others to plot against him. He could not speak a single word, but returned the paper, on which John's name, with the other conspirators, was written, with a heart quite broken with grief. He went from Tours to Chinon, and there was attacked by such a raging fever, that his life was soon despaired of. He asked to be carried into the church and laid at the foot of the altar, where he received the last Sacraments, and soon after died. As soon as his soul had left his body, the Bishops and barons who were there then went away; and the servants who remained stripped the body of its rings and jewels, and left it nearly naked and alone. At last Richard came to be present at his father's funeral; and when he came into the church of Fontevraud, where it was to be buried, and looked at the stern convulsed face of his dead father, he burst into a passion of tears. And, while he was standing there, a dark stream of blood gushed from the nostrils of the corpse, as if to bear witness that his own sons had been the cause of his death. It is said that at this awful sign Richard swooned away.

This was the mournful end of Henry Plantagenet, one of the richest, bravest, most learned, and most powerful kings that ever reigned in Europe; and this will show you, my dear children, in some degree, the true value of those things which are most prized and esteemed by the world.

Chapter XXI.

The Lion-Heart
From 1189 to 1199

Coronation Procession of Richard I, the Lion Heart

YOUNG Henry, you know, had died, and Geoffrey was dead too; so that Richard became king of England after Henry the Second, his father. He was certainly by far the best of the young princes; and I am glad to tell you that, when he first saw his father's body lying in the coffin, he burst into tears. I am sure he was very sorry for his rebellious conduct towards him.

Richard was crowned in Westminster Abbey. He was very tall and handsome, and stronger and braver than any man then living in the world. He was so brave, that he could not even fancy what it was to be afraid in any danger. This made the people love him very much. Besides being so brave and handsome, Richard had very pleasant manners; and, when he was not angry, none could help loving him. But when he was angry, his eyes flashed so terribly, and his hair stood upright like a lion's mane, that even his bravest generals and nobles were frightened. I am sorry to say, that Richard was often angry; for he was very impatient, and could not bear that any one should be before him, or be thought braver than him.

You would like to have seen Richard's coronation. All the bishops and abbots went first, with the clergy; and after them came the nobles in their robes. The king walked under a canopy stretched upon four spears. The Archbishop of Canterbury received him at the high altar; and when Richard had taken off his robes, and put on some golden sandals, he was anointed on the head, shoulders, and breasts with holy oil; and had the tunic, cap, dalmatic, swords, spurs, and mantle given to him, one after another. These things were all emblems of the royal power, just as the mitre and pastoral staff are emblems of the power which is given to Bishops.

As soon as Richard was crowned, he began to get ready to go to the Holy Land. He got as much money as he could from his people, and I am sorry to say he treated some of his subjects very badly to get money from them. These were the Jews, who were very much disliked on account of their religion, but who were encouraged because they understood

The Lion-Heart

a great many useful trades better than the English did then, and were better physicians.

On his way to Palestine Richard married Berengaria, the daughter of the King of Navarre; and made the King of Cyprus do him homage for his kingdom. He was visited at Cyprus by Guy de Lusignan, the poor king of Jerusalem, whom the Saracens had driven away; and Richard promised to help him to get his kingdom back again. He was so brave and so generous, that every one who wanted help went to him.

All this time the Crusaders were besieging Acre, where they had been for nearly two years, and yet could not take it. Famine, pestilence, and fighting had killed 120,000 men in one year alone; and among those who died were six Archbishops, twelve Bishops, and a great many noblemen. Philip had taken his army there, and was fighting, himself, with great bravery; but still Acre was not taken. At last they sent some envoys to look for Richard; and begged of him to come as soon as he could to help them; and they even scolded him soundly, for wasting so much time at Cyprus, and leaving them to carry on the war alone. Richard was so angry at what they said, and spoke so loudly and sharply, that they were all frightened; but he went with them as fast as he could to Acre, where he was welcomed with loud shouts of joy by all the Crusaders; for, as I told you, no one could help loving the great soldier, whom they called the Lion-heart. Although he was very sick with a dangerous fever, Richard would be carried to the walls upon a silk mattress, and shot the arrows, or *quarrels*,[9] with his own hands. When he got well, he performed the most wonderful deeds of valour. And at last the brave Saladin consented to give up Acre; and what was still better, the Holy Cross, which

[9] *Quarrel*, from the French *carré*. So called from the square head of the engine.

he had in his possession.

But, just as the Crusaders thought they were going to take Jerusalem, and to free Jerusalem from the infidels, King Philip said he should go back to France, and take his army with him. He was angry with Richard, who was never satisfied unless he had the first place; and he was worn out, too, by a bad illness; but I am afraid Richard's passionate temper was the chief cause of Philip's leaving the holy war unfinished. Richard led the army to Bethany; but, after many consultations, the princes decided to go back to Acre instead of besieging Jerusalem. A great deal of time was wasted by all these consultations; and, after performing deeds of bravery which are more like fairy-tales than real facts, Richard found that he must go back to England, where every thing was going wrong owing to his brother John's treachery.

Richard's lion heart was in the Holy Land, though he was obliged to go. There was a generous faith and enthusiasm in those times, which, though mixed and stained with great cruelties, was far more noble than the hesitating, calculating spirit of our own day. Besides the natural love of distinguishing themselves, as brave knights, in the field of battle, the Crusaders felt a child-like love for the land of Bethlehem and Nazareth, of Calvary and Gethsemane; and they burned with an ardent desire to rescue these holy places from infidel rulers, not with the lust of power, but to save them from desecration.

As Richard sailed away from Acre, he looked back at the shore with longing eyes; and, stretching out his arms, he cried, "Most holy land, I commend thee to the care of the Almighty; may He grant me life to return and rescue thee from the yoke of the infidels!"

Richard thought it was very likely that some of his enemies

would be watching for him; for he had offended Leopold, the Archduke of Austria, and some other princes, while he was at the holy war; so he dressed up as a pilgrim, with one of his friends, and asked leave to pass through Germany. But, as the Archduke was watching for Richard, the pilgrims were expected; and a faithful Norman knight, who was at Freisach, told him of his danger. The king escaped, with one of his knights and a boy, and they rode for three days without daring to buy any thing to eat, and sleeping in the woods. Richard fell very ill after this, and the boy was sent to market to buy some food. The people saw in his belt some worked gloves, which were only worn then by princes and nobles, and he was seized and tortured to make him tell where Richard was. The pain made the boy confess that he knew where he was hidden; and they sent soldiers to surround the house.

When he saw the soldiers, Richard drew his sword, and would not give it up to any but their leader, who turned out to be liis old enemy, Leopold himself. Leopold was not a generous enemy; and, as he wanted money, he sold Richard to Henry the Sixth, the Emperor of Germany, who carried him to the Tyrol, and shut him up in the Castle of Tiernstein, where the Emperor's guards watched him day and night, with their swords drawn.

All this time every thing had been going wrong in England. The chancellor, Longchamp, a bad, ambitious man, had seized all the power he could, and ruled the country almost like the king himself. Prince John had got a great many of the royal castles into his hands, and was trying all he could to persuade the people to make him king instead of Richard, whom he pretended to think would never come back. Some of the wicked and foolish barons said they would have John for their king; but the good ones and the Bishops defended

Richard, and would have nothing to do with John. All these divisions and quarrels were very bad for the country; for a great many of the lesser barons began to rob the people and treat them ill, and there was no one to see that justice was done, because the king was away, and Longchamp only cared about getting money and offices for himself. Many of the men, too, were gone to be soldiers, so that the farms could not be properly ploughed and sown; and there was great distress among the people; and they all cried out very loudly for Richard to come home again.

It is not easy to say what every one felt, not only in England but in all Europe, when they heard that the King of England had been sold like an ox or a sheep, and was shut up in a castle somewhere in the Tyrol. The clergy and nobles sent messages to the Pope to ask him to excommunicate Henry and Leopold; and every body except John was full of sorrow and indignation. John was very glad, for he thought he was now sure of the crown. He went to France, and did homage to King Philip for Normandy; and Philip was base enough to accept his homage and to help him,

A very pretty story is told of the wray in which Richard was discovered at last; for the Emperor would never tell where he was. I cannot say if the story is true or not; but, as it agrees so well with all the rest of Richard's life and adventures, I should think that it is most likely to be true. Richard had a favorite minstrel, named Blondel, who went with him to the Holy Land, and whom he loved very much. Blondel thought that Leopold had something to do with his master's disappearance; and he set out, and went from one castle to another in Germany, to try and find him. At last he came to the Castle of Tiernstein, and sat down under the walls to rest; and, as he was resting, he heard a voice singing a song that he knew very well. It was one that Richard had made; and Blondel was certain that it was Richard's voice that was singing it. When he stopped, Blondel sung the next verse; and so Richard knew that at last his faithful minstrel had found him out, and that there was a chance of his being set free.

The Chancellor Longchamp then went to Germany, and persuaded the Emperor to bring Richard to his Council at Hagenau, and to let him defend himself there against the charges made against him.

And at the council, when they accused him of making a disgraceful peace with the generous Saladin, and many other such foolish things, Richard defended himself with such manly courage and eloquence, that even Henry was obliged to give way; and he said that, if the English would pay him a great deal of money, he would send their king back to England. The English were already become very poor, as I told you; but they were determined to get together the money for the greedy Emperor. The ladies gave their gold necklaces and jewels; and every body sent what they had; and at last Richard came back to Old England.

When the Germans who came with him saw the magnificent show the people made in London to welcome their king, with carpets, and tapestry, and feasting, and music, they said to Richard: "Ah, if our master had seen all this, he would not have let you off so easily!"

Richard could not rest quiet, even now. He went to France as soon as he could get together an army, to punish Philip and John; for Philip had written to John a curious little letter, when he knew that Richard was on his way home. It had in it only these words: "*Take heed to yourself, for the devil is unchained!*" and when John got it he fled to France. But as soon as Richard landed in Normandy with his army, John invited all of Philip's officers who were in the same town with him to dinner, and had them all killed; and then he went to Richard, and fell on his knees to beg his pardon. He thought that this cowardly and detestable murder would please Richard, but I am sure that it was as hateful to him as it is to us. Richard perhaps thought that punishment could not do such a wretch as John any good, and he was so generous that he did not wish to punish him. He only said to him, "I wish I could forget all your injuries as quickly as you will my pardon."

One day soon after this, as Richard was besieging the Castle of Chaluz, an archer shot him with a poisoned arrow, and the wound mortified, so that he knew he should soon die. He ordered that his body should be buried at his father's feet at Fontevraud, and that his lion-heart should be sent to Rouen, which had always been remarkable for its faithfulness to him. For more than a hundred years after his death, if a Saracen's horse started, he used to say to him, "Dost thou think King Richard is in that bush?" and when the Syrian babies cried, their mothers said, "If you are not quiet, I will take you to King Richard!"

We cannot help loving and admiring Richard for many things, especially for his zeal for the Holy Sepulchre and Jerusalem, and his charity towards the weak and oppressed. But the Lion-heart would have been a better king if he had governed his kingdom himself, or seen that it was well governed by good ministers, instead of leaving it at the mercy of bad ones; and if he had thought more about the solid good of his people, and less about winning fame as a brave knight.

There are several things in the history of Coeur-de-lion which you should know about, and for which we have not yet had time. You remember that his chief enemy in the holy wars was Saladin, the Sultan or Soldan of Egypt. This prince, although he was an infidel, was of so noble and generous a character, that you must hear some stories about him. He was a most zealous Mahometan, and never failed to perform all his prayers and devotions at the exact time; so that when he was on horseback, he got down and knelt on the ground till he had finished them. He heard all the complaints of his people himself on Mondays and Thursdays, and never allowed any poor person to go away without an answer, and without justice having been done him.

He was very brave too, as well as just. He was not so fiery and reckless as Richard, but he had much more patient fortitude. Once when he was very ill, he heard that the Christians were coming, and he got out, of bed directly, and mounted his horse, though he could scarcely sit upon it for the pain he suffered. At night he would not let them set up a tent for him, lest the enemy should find out that he was ill, and he lay down under the trees. The next morning, he was on horseback again, reviewing his troops, and trying to find out the best plan for conquering the enemy.

Once he sent Richard some beautiful Arabian horses; and when he was ill he sent him every day peaches and plums, and snow to cool his burning fever. He loved and respected Richard very much for his bravery and manly courtesy; and Richard always called Saladin *his generous enemy.* Indeed, the whole history of these two princes is a beautiful exception to the wild, fierce cruelty of those times.

There was another lesser enemy of Richard's, about whom there is a story that will make you laugh. This was the Bishop of Beauvais, who was so fond of fighting that he never could keep from battle, and who offended Richard by taking Philip's part in the quarrels with France. At last Richard caught the warlike Bishop and shut him up in prison; and when the Pope heard of it, he sent to Richard, and begged of him to set free *his dear son the Bishop of Beauvais*. Richard, who was very clever and witty, sent back the Bishop's bloody coat-of-mail to the Pope, with this message: "*See if this be thy son's coat or no.*" The Pope could not help laughing, and he said, "Indeed he is more like a son of Mars than a son of the Church."

It was in Richard's reign that the famous Robin Hood lived. He was said to be the Earl of Huntingdon, who was *outlawed*—that is, who was declared to be under punishment by law—for his wild life. Robin Hood was very merry, although he was outlawed, and he and his friends lived in Sherwood Forest in Nottinghamshire, where they fed upon the deer and game, and robbed all the rich folks who passed through the forest. They dressed in green, and shot with bows and arrows; and they were so clever at shooting, that Robin Hood could split a willow-wand in two at a hundred yards from it. Robin's friends were called his "merry men and their names, Little-John, Allan-a-Dale, Friar Tuck, and Mutch-the-Miller, are as well known as Robin Hood's own. They never robbed the poor, and, they gave most of what they got to people in want and distress; so that all the people round Sherwood loved them, and defended them against the sheriff of Nottingham.

A great many droll stories are told of their adventures; and once it is said that Robin dressed up as a Bishop, and went and asked the sheriff to dine with him. The sheriff rode along with the sham Bishop to the Forest of Sherwood: and when they were in it, Robin Hood whistled loudly, and the merry men started out from the trees and took the sheriff prisoner. Robin Hood took him to their haunts, and gave him a very good dinner, after which they sung songs, and played at all kinds of games; and after they had taken all the sheriffs money, with great politeness they sent him home again.

There is a pretty ballad which speaks of Robin Hood's piety, and that the only sorrow he had was not being able to go to Mass always on Sundays.

FRAGMENT OF ONE OF THE POEMS OF THAT TIME.

In summer, when the shaws[10] be sheen,
   And leaves be large and long,
It is full merrie in faire forest
   To hear the blackbird's song;

To see the deer draw to the lea,
   And leave their own hills high,
And shadow them in leaves green
   Under the greenwood tree.

It befel on Whit-Sunday,
   In a May-morning early,
The sun up fair did spring that day,
   And the birds sing merrily.

" It is a merry morning," said Little-John,
   "By Him who died on tree ;
And more merry man than I am one
   Is not in Christiantie.[11]

Pluck up thy heart, my dear master,
   Now Little-John can say;
And think it is a full fair time,
   In a morning of May."

---

[10] A bank covered with trees.
[11] Christendom

> *" The one thing that grieves me," said Robin,*
> *"And does my heart much woe,*
> *That I may not, no solemn day,*
> *To Mass nor Matins go.*

There were other heroes in the north of England, named Adam Bell, Clym of the Clough, and William of Cloudesley, who were all nearly as famous, in their way, as Robin Earl of Huntingdon; and these all show that same bold, frank, sturdy character which so strongly marks the Anglo-Saxon race, and which, when England was *really* "merry England," that is, when it was *Catholic* England, was as widely opposite to the cold, sullen, gloomy disposition we now see in our poor faithless countrymen, as the skulking poacher and the savage smuggler of our times are unlike the merry outlaws Robin Hood and Little-John.

The Passing of Robin Hood by N.C. Wyeth

Chapter XXII.

The Church of the People

From 1199 to 1216

THE last was a very long chapter. I think this will be a long one too, and I am afraid you will not find it so amusing as the last. But as it is a very important one, you must try and attend to it, and you will find that there is a great deal that you ought to take an interest in.

You know that English history is not intended only to tell us the adventures of our kings and brave men. It teaches us too about the government of our country and its constitutional laws.

It is a very important matter that the constitution of our country should be a good one, and although you have nothing to do with the making of it, it is right that you should understand it; and you must always keep in mind that though you are now a child, you will grow up some day, and will be required to have just and intelligent ideas about the country in which God has placed you.

You will remember that you were told at the beginning of this history, that our Saxon forefathers loved justice and freedom; and by freedom is meant, *the clear understanding and possession of certain rights, and the just observance of them.* For instance, Caesar had a right to the tribute-money, and our Lord commanded that it should be paid him; laborers have a right to their wages, and the Church has, by Divine authority, declared it to be a grievous sin to defraud them of them. The poor have a right to the gleaning of our corn-fields; and in the Old Scripture, Almighty God commands that some handfuls of corn and olives should be scattered for them. When any one does not pay the lawful taxes, or deprives his workmen of their wages, or forbids the poor to glean in his fields, he is *unjust;* he is depriving people of their *rights.*

On the other hand, if the tax-gatherers ask more than is due to the king, as the publicans did in Judea, and as many tax-gatherers have done in English history; or if workmen waste their master's goods, or clamour for higher wages than are just, or take them by force; or the poor steal corn from the sheaves in the fields in which they are gleaning, *they* become unjust, and are depriving others of their rights in their turn. Every state and condition of life has its rights, and has to respect the rights of others.

The Saxons understood this very welt; and when they came to England and drove away the Britons, they brought with them their own laws and customs and ways of thinking, and planted them so firmly in this country, that nothing has ever been able to root them out; and most likely nothing ever will do so, so long as England is a nation at all.

One of the Saxon kings named Cerdic, and King Ilia, whom you recollect very well, were the first kings who collected the Saxon habits and customs, and made them laws. One of

Cerdic's descendants made these laws larger and better, and explained them, and wrote them down, so that every judge could tell exactly what to do. This was the great and wise King Alfred, to whom we owe so much, and whom all Englishmen ought to venerate as one of their best friends, as well as the greatest of their kings. It was Alfred who, after his father, established the Witan, or English Parliament, which has always been a prudent check to the power of our kings; and he also, as far as he could, made the life of the serfs or bondsmen easier, and set the example of *making freedmen* of them.

St. Edward the Confessor carried out the work of Alfred, and many additional foundations were laid to the English constitution in his wise and temperate reign; so that these laws and observances were commonly called by the people "the laws and customs of good King Edward."

Henry Beauclerc thought it wise to grant the people a charter, in which he promised to keep these laws; but Henry the Second had done all he could to take away the rights of his people, as he had tried to rob the Church of hers. When Richard was dead, and John became king, the people soon saw that, as he had been a bad son and a bad brother, he intended to be a bad king too. The first thing he did was to get hold of his nephew Arthur of Brittany, who had the fullest right to be king instead of him, because he was Geoffrey's son, who you know was older than John. He shut Arthur up in one of his castles.

Philip of France, who had been watching for an opportunity of getting back all the lands which belonged to the English in France, sent word to John that he acknowledged Arthur to be King of England, and that if John did not give up the crown to him, he should take Anjou, Maine, Tourenne, and Aquitaine, and all those rich lands which belonged to Eleanor. John was in a great fright at this, but he would not give up Arthur. He took him to another castle, where he shut him up, and tried to frighten him into giving up the English crown. But Arthur was a very brave boy, and he said that he would never give up his rights.

John then sent a man named Hubert de Burgh to put out his eyes with red-hot irons; but Arthur begged and prayed so earnestly not to have his eyes put out, and clung round Hubert so affectionately, that Hubert could not do the cruel deed.

John then took Arthur away to Rouen, where he put him into a dark dungeon. One night, when it was quite dark, the poor prince heard a knocking at the door of his prison, and heard his cruel uncle's voice. He was taken out and put into a boat; and when the boat got into the middle of the river, John stabbed him with his dagger, and threw his body into the Seine. Some people say that John hired a ruffian named Maluc to stab him, while he stood by to see that it was done, but it is most likely that John did the wicked deed himself.

Everybody was very angry, and sorry for poor Arthur; and Philip got all the soldiers he could, and took possession of John's French lands, so that the English had nothing left in France but Guienne; and the French laughed at John, and nicknamed him *Sans Terre*, or Lackland.

This was a very disgraceful war for England, and the English barons felt it very much. But John went on to do other wicked actions. He quarrelled with the monks of St. Augustin's Abbey at Canterbury, because they had chosen an Archbishop who did not please him. He chose another whom he thought would let him rob the Church as much as he liked. The Archbishop whom the monks chose was named Reginald, and the one John chose was John de Gray, who was a kind of lawyer as well, and a great friend of his.

There was at that time a very great and wise Pope. He was named Innocent the Third, and he was one of the very best and greatest men that ever lived. Besides being holy and zealous, he was very clever and learned, and was a great statesman, and governed the Church in such a wonderful manner that all the kings of Europe were glad to ask him to settle their quarrels, and to put the affairs of their kingdoms in order. He had a very sweet and gracious countenance, and

Vision of Pope Innocent III regarding St. Francis by Manual de la Cruz

could speak and write beautifully. But the greatest and best thing was, that if any one was oppressed, he was sure to find a friend in the Pope, who never rested till the oppressor was either punished or left off oppressing. I cannot stop now to tell you of all the good that he did; but he forced Philip of France, who was one of the craftiest and most powerful kings of the time, to send away Agnes de Meranie, whom he had married, and to take back his own good and beautiful Queen

Ingeburga, whom he had unjustly divorced to marry Agnes.

When Pope Innocent heard what John was doing at Canterbury, he sent to him, and said that he would not allow either Reginald or John de Gray to be Archbishop, and that he should choose an Archbishop himself, whom he hoped John would approve of. This was Cardinal Stephen Langton, to whom all Englishmen are grateful for the benefits he so greatly helped to obtain for their country.

John was so angry with the Pope, that he would not say whether he agreed to Cardinal Langton being Archbishop, or not; and the Pope had him consecrated, and sent to England. However, John would not allow him to come, and, to punish John for his disobedience, the Pope laid the kingdom under an interdict, which means, that no one but the priests are allowed to hear Mass; no one might receive communion or go to confession, unless they were dying; and those who died were buried any how, without any of the ceremonies of religion. The bells were taken down and covered up, and the crucifixes and images were covered up too.

The poor people were obliged to suffer this dreadful punishment together with their wicked king; and the barons were very angry, and began to write letters to Langton and some other Bishops whom John had banished; but still John would not give up. The next year, the Pope excommunicated him; and, as he still refused to let Langton come to England, Innocent told the English barons and people that they need not obey him any longer as king, for that he was deposed.

The barons and people who had sent to beg the Pope to help them, were rejoiced that the wicked cowardly John was king no longer; and the Pope offered the English crown to Philip for his eldest son Louis. He did not, however, mean to make Louis king, unless there was nothing better to be done;

Stephen Langton, Archbishop of Canterbury on Canterbury Cathedral

and he sent messengers with his legate Pandollo to England, to beg of John to be reconciled to the Church. John was now so frightened, that he was very glad to get his kingdom again on any terms; and he agreed with Pandolfo to let Langton be Archbishop, to recall all the Bishops and clergy he had banished, and to swear fealty to the Pope, as his liege or feudal lord. He knelt before Pandolfo, saying that he had, with the unanimous consent of his barons, granted to God, the holy Apostles Peter and Paul, to Pope Innocent and his successors, the kingdoms of England and Ireland; and that he swore to defend against all men the patrimony of St. Peter, and especially England and Ireland. Pandolfo then, in the Pope's name, as John's liege lord, gave him back the crown of England, to hold as the Pope's vassal.

You will perhaps read in some histories a great deal of abuse of the Pope and of John for this giving up and making over the English crown; and you must recollect, and firmly fix in your mind what you have been told, and remember that the chief English historian was a Protestant and an infidel,[12] who did not like to acknowledge that the authority exerted by Innocent the Third was not only lawful and just, but that it was also most beneficial to all Christendom.

People are now beginning to see how blinded they have been, and that Rome has always been in these extraordinary cases the Mediator and Peacemaker of Europe.

It was certainly disgraceful that John should have been excommunicated and his kingdom laid under an interdict, and that he should have done so many wicked and cowardly actions; but the one for which he is most blamed is the very one in which he acted wisely and rightly, and perhaps the only time that he did so in his life.

Cardinal Langton at last came to England, and the other Bishops with him; and as soon as he was come, this great and wise prelate spoke with the barons who had written to him, and many of the others who really wished for the good of their country; and one day, when the barons were all in council together, considering how they should keep John from doing any more mischief, Langton came in with a large parchment in his hands, and said: "I have found the charter of Henry the First, by which, if you choose, you may recall the lost liberties to their former state." He read it to them; and the barons all declared, in great joy, that now was the time to defend these liberties. The Archbishop promised to help them, and the council broke up.

The Archbishop kept his word. He called the barons together; and they asked John to put his name to a Charter, in which they had written down the old laws of Edward and Alfred, and some others. The chief of some of them are put down here, which you can easily understand. When you are

---

[12] Hume

older, you can go to the British Museum and see the Charter itself, which has been kept ever since with the greatest care.

1. No taxes were to be made except by Parliament, unless the king was taken prisoner in battle, his eldest son was made a knight, or his eldest daughter married.
2. The king was not to sell justice, or deny it to any one.
3. One weight and measure were to be used through all England.
4. All merchants might come and go freely through the country, buying and selling; but if they came from a country with which England was at war, they might be arrested, till it was known how English merchants were treated in their country.
5. That London, and all the cities and ports, were to have their full liberties and customs.
6. Lastly, every body in the kingdom was to have the full and free possession of his own life, liberty, and property, unless it was forfeited as a just punishment for some crime, by the judgment of his peers, which means a jury.

When Langton and the barons sent this Charter to John, he said they might as well ask for his kingdom. They saw that it would be impossible to persuade him to sign it; so they got an army together, which they called "The Array of God and His Church," and took possession of London. John did not like to lose his capital; and he sent word to the Archbishop and barons to meet him at Runnymead, which is a large meadow between Staines and Windsor. There came all the army of God and the Church, and John and his friends; and then, after some consulting, John signed Magna Charta, as it is called, and swore to keep faithfully all laws written in it.

It is too long to tell you now of all the difficulties Langton and the barons had, before they could make the faithless king keep his promises. As he was going in a great hurry from Wisbeach to Fosdike in Lincolnshire, the Wash carried away part of his army, and all his jewels and money; and this misfortune grieved him so much, that he fell sick, and died at Newark soon after. He ordered his body to be buried near St. Wulstan's shrine, in Worcester Cathedral; so that even this most miserable king upon his deathbed turned with reverence to the relics of the blessed Saints; and thus we see that the great and mighty of this world are forced to recognise and bear witness to God's chosen Friends and Servants.

And now we will end this long chapter; but before doing so, one thing must be said, that it is to be hoped you will always remember with veneration the great and wise Pope Innocent the Third, and love and be grateful to Cardinal Langton, the just Archbishop of Canterbury.

King John signs the Magna Carta at Runnymead

Chapter XXIII.

Peace In England
From 1216 to 1253

It is certain you will not be sorry that we have done with the very worst king that ever reigned in England. As soon as John was dead, his little son Henry the Third was crowned. He was only nine years old; and as the crown and all the royal jewels had been washed away at Wisbeach, little Henry had only a golden ring or circle put on his head for a crown. The poor little king was not very wise; but he had good friends in Cardinal Langton and Earl Pembroke, who had been at the head of the barons at Runnymead, and they fought his battles, and drove Louis of France out of England; for he had thought, as John was dead and as Henry was only a boy, he could take England for himself.

When Henry grew up, and the good Earl Pembroke was dead, he made a number of foolish friends, and gave them every thing they wanted, and offended the wise barons and the people by giving these foreign lords and soldiers so much money. They tried to make him sign the Charter; and one

King Henry III with his Parliament, *A Chronicle of English History*

day, as Cardinal Langton was asking him to do it, one of the foolish young gentlemen whom Henry was so fond of said, that he need not do it, and that he ought not to be forced to do it. The noble Archbishop, indignant at their folly, said to him, "If you really loved the king, sir, you would not prevent the peace of his country!"

The king, soon after, lost this good and wise friend. He died when Henry was twenty-one; but the Pope was very kind to him, and had sent a legate for many years to take care of him. Henry was always mild, gentle, affectionate, and fond of the exercises of religion, but he had nothing great or generous in his character; and although he was a good man, he can never be called a good king. He died with great piety, after a reign of fifty-six years; and his body was laid in the old shrine of St. Edward.

Though there is so little to tell you about Henry himself,

there are some very important things to be remembered in his long reign.

In the first place, the great Earl of Leicester, Simon de Montfort, who at one time ruled England completely, was the chief cause of calling the English Parliament regularly, and of dividing it into the two Houses of Lords and Commons, as it is now. And as the king was so weak and changeable, the barons and people began to see that their great hope lay in the Parliament, and that by its means they might check the injustice of their kings, without the misery of rebellion and civil wars.

This was the *end* or *consequence* of the laws of good King Edward and Alfred, and of Magna Charta, and it was very useful for our country.

Henry's cowardice and love of peace, too, were useful. During all the wars of Richard and John, England had been robbed and plundered from one end to the other; and the quantities of foreigners John brought in did not care for the English laws, and laughed at the judges. But in Henry's reign there was time to put every thing in order; the foreign soldiers were all sent away; and the judges went regularly through the country every year, so that every crime was punished, and justice was done to all. This was a very great blessing; for you know, my dear children, that where there is no *order*, the spirit of God cannot be.

Henry's love of foreigners also turned to good in many ways. The merchants who came from France and Italy taught the people how to make many things better than they could themselves; and a number of new manufactures were brought into England. Trade and commerce increased, and there were better shops. This was a very good and useful thing.

I have spoken of Henry's cowardice, and I will tell you a

story about it which will make you laugh. He was one day going down the river in his barge, and a great storm of thunder and lightning came on, and as the king was very much afraid of it, he got on shore near the Tower. Just as he landed he met Simon de Montfort, who tried to console him by saying that the storm was passing over. The king, who was shaking with fear, said to him, "I fear *thee* more than the worst storm in the universe!"

There were two great bishops in Henry's reign, about whom I must tell you something. When Langton died, the next archbishop was called Dr. Rich. He was very learned and wise, but he was much more holy. He used always to consult our Lady about his studies, and she taught him to be both holy and learned. When he had been archbishop a good many years, he could not bear to live any longer in the world, and so he went to Pontigny, where St. Thomas had gone before him, and there he died. He was, as it were, quite buried and forgotten at Pontigny; but as soon as he died he was known to be a Saint, and the gentle, holy Dr. Rich became the blessed St. Edmund.

The other bishop's name was Robert Grostete, bishop of Lincoln. He was as stern and determined as St. Edmund was mild and gentle; and he was always busied in reforming the Church, especially in hindering abbots or clergymen from having more than one living or benefice. He was so active, indeed, that he had a great many enemies, and so determined, that he sometimes argued with the Pope himself. He was the first bishop who asked the Dominicans to come to England, where they became very celebrated for their preaching and learning.

Chapter XXIV.

The Good Queen
From 1253 to 1307

The next king of England was very unlike his father. Edward the First was as brave and warlike as Henry the Third was mild and cowardly. Indeed, he was as brave and fond of fighting as Richard the Lionheart. He had gone to the Holy Land to fight for the Holy Sepulchre, while his father lived; and on his way there, he had gone through France and Spain, and he observed all that he saw in these countries, and brought back with him some very useful things to England. He learnt how to feed cows and sheep better, and to grow different kinds of grass; and he brought some Spanish sheep to England, which made the English wool a great deal better than it was before. It was in Spain that Edward married his dear good wife, Eleanor of Castile. She was not at all like Eleanor of Aquitane; for she was very pious, and beloved by every body.

Eleanor went with her husband to the Holy Land; and while he was there, he was resting in his tent on the evening of one very hot day, and a Saracen came up suddenly, and struck at him with a poisoned dagger. Edward caught the blow upon his arm, and killed the assassin, but as the dagger was poisoned, the wound was dangerous. Eleanor, however, at the risk of her own life, sucked it, and cured him. When Edward was coming back to England, he was invited to Rome by the pope, Gregory the Tenth; and he went to pay him a visit. He went to Sicily too; and there he first heard of the death of his father and of his little son. He shed a great many more tears for his father than for his son, at which Charles of Anjou was surprised; but Edward said to him, "I may have another son, but I can never have another good father."

Edward was so much loved and respected in Europe, that as he went along, on his way to England, he was received like a conqueror. The Milanese gave him great pieces of scarlet cloth, and beautiful horses; and the people in all the towns came out to meet him, and made processions to do him honor. This was because they looked upon him as the champion and brave defender of the Cross and of the Holy Sepulchre.

When he got to London, the people were so glad, that they hung out carpets and tapestry from their windows, and made arches of flags and flowers for him to pass under, and threw handfuls of gold and silver pieces upon him as he went along. He and his dear Queen Eleanor were crowned in Westminster Abbey, where the king of Scotland came to do him homage. The people were delighted with him. He was so tall that very few men came up to his shoulders, and was very strong and active. His legs were so long, that he never could be thrown from his horse, which was very useful in those warlike days. He was passionate and cruel, but not revengeful; and he was very prudent and wise.

The Good Queen

John, King of Scotland being brought before King Edward I.

Though Edward was so fond of fighting, he found time to do a great many useful things in England. He altered the Parliament, and improved it a great deal, by having citizens sent from the towns to answer for the shopkeepers and merchants, who were called Burgesses, besides the knights or gentlemen who were sent from the counties. There were now, the King, to say what he wished to be done; the Bishops and Nobles, to say what they wished to be done; and the Gentlemen and Citizens from the counties (or *shirts*) and towns, to say what they wished to be done; so that every class of people in the country might know what laws were going to be made, and what to object to. The king intended to use the Parliament mostly to get grants of money for him; but the nobles and people found out what a good thing it was to be able to speak their minds about the laws; and by degrees they got the kings to agree to what they wished, and to settle the

Houses of Parliament as they are now.

Besides this, Edward sent people round the country to find out which judges were good and which were bad; for some of them were very bad. He either sent them all away or punished them, and made the gentlemen magistrates, that they might find out and punish robbers and bad men; so that the thieves and idlers were frightened, and the country became quiet and orderly from one end to the other.

It was for making these good laws, and many others, that Edward is called the English Justinian; because Justinian was a Roman Emperor who established the best laws that ever were known at Rome.

Edward sent for some foreign merchants too, who made better cloth than the English; and he brought with him from Spain some sheep whose wool was very fine, and who improved the English sheep. A great many useful laws were made about the wool-trade, which you know is one cf the chief trades of England.

And now I will tell you about Edward's wars.

You know that the Saxons had driven the Britons into the mountains in the west of Britain; and these British are now called Welsh, and their country is called Wales. The Welsh were always quarrelling and fighting with the English, and they hated them very much because they had taken their country from them. Most of the Welsh princes were bad men, and fought and killed one another as well as the English. They were so troublesome and revengeful, that Edward thought it would be best to conquer Wales, and to make it part of England.

The name of the Welsh king then was Llewellyn, whom Edward had conquered, and whom he had been very kind to, as well as his brother David; and Llewellyn promised never to fight against Edward any more. I am sorry to say that he broke his promise, and took some English castles. Edward could scarcely believe that he had really been so treacherous; but when he found that it was true, he was very angry indeed, and got an army to fight against him. As he was hiding in a barn, a knight named Adam Frankton found him and killed him, without knowing that it was Llewellyn. Edward ordered his head to be sent to London; and as Merlin, a Welsh bard, had prophesied that a Welsh king should reign over England,[13] he had a wreath of silver put round it in mockery. This was very cruel and savage, and you will be sorry for it.

A very pretty story is told about Edward's treatment of the Welsh bards or minstrels, who had great influence over the people by their songs and tales of the chiefs and their deeds.

This legend says that he had killed them all but one; and this one had been hunted a long time with bloodhounds, and was at last found sitting on a high crag or rock overhanging the sea. The English soldiers begged of him to come down, and give himself up to them; but he went on singing a wild song about their cruelty, and the greatness of the old kings of Wales, and then throwing his harp into the sea, he leaped after it, and was drowned.

When he had conquered Wales, Edward thought he would get Scotland too. Alexander the king of Scotland died suddenly; and as he had no children, the crown went to his granddaughter Margaret, the daughter of the king of Norway. Edward thought it would be a very good thing for his son to be betrothed to this little princess, who was only three years old, and that she should come and live in England, and

---

[13] Merlin's prophecy was, "When England's coin becomes round, a Welsh king shall rule." And in Edward's time round money was first coined in this country. Before this time it had been of a square shape.

marry the prince when she grew up. Every body agreed to this plan, which would have saved a great many more, battles and bloodshed than can easily be imagined.

But as the little Maid of Norway (as she was called) was coming to England, she sickened and died; and there was an end of all Edward's plans.

Her two cousins, John Baliol and Robert Bruce, both wished to be king; and they agreed to ask Edward to settle between them. Edward was very much pleased at being acknowledged the feudal lord of Scotland, and he said that John Baliol had the best right to the crown, but that he must do homage for it to him. Baliol agreed to this; and Edward was very kind and generous to the Scots, and allowed Baliol a great many privileges.

But a feudal lord might always summon his vassals to his court to answer for themselves, if any of their subjects complained of them; so that they were kings, and not kings, as it were, at the same time; that is, they had not the authority of kings.

Baliol was summoned by Edward several times, to defend himself for showing contempt of his feudal lord. This was wrong of him; because if he agreed to be Edward's vassal, he ought to have done as vassals always did. Instead of obeying he raised an army, and openly rebelled. When Edward heard of this he was very angry, and cried out, "Felon fool! we must go and find him out." And he took a large army into Scotland, and beat Baliol, and took him prisoner.

He treated him very kindly, and sent him to his fort in the Tower in London, and then in Normandy, where he died. No one either loved or esteemed him, for he was a sad coward; and no one ever thought about him after he lost his crown.

Edward thought now that Scotland was quite his own;

but the Scots would not submit, and Sir William Wallace, a very brave gentleman, helped them, and fought a great many battles with the English; but he was beaten, and at last he was betrayed by one of his own friends, Sir John Monteith, and was taken prisoner. I am sorry to say that Edward had his head cut off, and stuck up in London, just as Llewellyn's had been.

You remember that Robert Bruce had disputed the crown with John Baliol. He had afterwards submitted to Edward, as well as another great nobleman called John Comyn, but more commonly the Red Comyn, who was a cousin of Baliol. Bruce asked Red Comyn to help him to fight against Edward, and to make his country independent. Red Comyn promised to help him, but went and told Edward of Bruce's plans, who was obliged to escape as fast as he could from London to Scotland.

When he got there he raised the whole country against Edward; and finding that Red Comyn was always opposing him and helping the English, he asked him to meet him in the church of the Friars Minors at Dumfries.

They talked there a long time, and at last quarrelled. Bruce said that Comyn was a traitor to Scotland, and Comyn said that Bruce was a traitor to his liege lord Edward; and Bruce drew his dagger and plunged it into Red Comyn's side. He rushed out of the church, and met two of his friends at the door. "What news?" they asked him, eagerly.

"News?" he answered; "I doubt I have slain Red Comyn!"

"Doubt I" repeated Sir James Lindsay, who was one of them, "I will make it certain;" and he ran into the church, and stabbed Comyn several times, till he was quite dead.

This was a wicked beginning; and Bruce felt the greatest remorse for his crime all his life. But after a great many adventures, which I cannot stop to tell you now, he became king of Scotland.

Edward hunted him about from place to place, together with his queen, her ladies, and a few nobles. At last Neil Bruce, King Robert's brother, and some others, were taken; and Edward ordered them to be hanged. The Countess of Buchan, who had crowned Bruce, was also taken; and Edward said, that as she had not struck with the sword, she should not be punished with the sword, but that she should have a round chamber, like the crown she gave.

She was put into a *cage,* or round stone cell, in Berwick Castle. This was very cruel; but it is not quite just to accuse Edward of cruelty in putting the Scottish nobles to death. He had pardoned them many times; and he knew that as long as they lived, he could never conquer Scotland.

He was very ill during all these last Scottish wars, and was obliged to be carried about in a horse-litter. He tried once to ride forward, and even made an offering of his litter in Carlisle Cathedral; but he was too weak, and he died in his tent at Burgh-on-the-Sands, on the 7th of July.

Before he died he did a very strange thing. He called his son to his bedside, and made him swear that as soon as he was dead he would have his body put into a large cauldron, and boiled till the flesh was off the bones; that the flesh should be buried, and the bones wrapped in a bullock's skin, and carried before the army; for he was sure that the Scots would always be afraid when they knew his bones were coming.

If Edward had not been so full of pride and ambition, he would not have asked, with his last breath, so savage and heathen a thing as this. He would have been thinking of preparing his soul to meet his God, and of forgiving all his enemies.

Chapter XXV.

The Wicked Queen and Bad Company

From 1307 to 1327

PRINCE EDWARD succeeded his father. He was not brave, or strong, or active. He liked eating and drinking, and dancing, and amusing himself; and above all, he liked to have his own way. He always had some bad, foolish young men with him, who amused him by their laughing and silly talk; and he neglected all his wise and prudent barons, and all the affairs of his kingdom, to be with these bad companions.

One of them had been brought up with him; and as he was very handsome, and graceful, and merry, Edward loved him the best of all. His name was Piers Gaveston, and he was a French gentleman from Guienne. The grave old English barons did not like to see this foolish young Frenchman always with Edward, especially as Edward was so wrong as to put him always above them at the tournaments and royal banquets, and always talked to him and not to them; and

King Edward II

Gaveston laughed at the barons, and called them nicknames. One he named 'the Old Hog;' and the great Earl of Warwick he called 'the Black Dog of the Wood.'

Edward married a French princess, Isabella, who was one of the most beautiful ladies of the time; but though she was beautiful, she was very wicked, and so cruel and passionate that she was called 'the She-Wolf of France.'

The old king had ordered his son to banish Gaveston, and never to let him come to England, and the barons often reminded Edward of this, and persuaded him to banish him several times. But as soon as he was gone, the foolish king was so unhappy that he shed a great many tears, and said he could not live without Piers Gaveston; so he came back again; and Edward gave him more lands and money every time he came back.

The barons would not bear this, at last, any longer. They got a large army, and marched against Gaveston, and shut up him in a castle, and then took him prisoner. The Earl of Warwick was foremost in doing this, and said *he should feel the Black Dog's bite*. One morning they carried out Gaveston, and beheaded him.

Edward was very angry at this; but it was of no use, for the barons were determined not to let him have his own way any longer, and the queen helped them. She was so wicked as to go away with her little son, and choose a bad man named Mortimer to help her to fight against her husband, who, though he was so foolish, had always been kind and good to her.

She went to France, and raised a large army against Edward, who had now got another favorite named Hugh Spenser. The barons and the queen fought the king and Spenser, and at last took the king prisoner, and shut him up in Berkeley Castle. They treated him very cruelly. They gave him dirty water to wash and shave with, and never let him see any of his friends. One day, when he asked for some warm water to shave with, they sent him to a dirty ditch, and told him to get water for himself. The poor king burst into tears, and said, "See, here is plenty of clean warm water!" One night two cruel ruffians went into his room, and put him to death with red-hot irons. His shrieks were heard all over the castle, so that their wickedness was discovered; for they had hoped to make people believe that he had died naturally. This poor king reigned twenty years; and he never had a day's happiness all that time, because he liked pleasure and doing his own will better than doing his duty.

HISTORY OF ENGLAND

Robert de Bruce strikes and kills Sir Henry de Bohun with his axe in single combat before the Battle of Bannockburn on 23rd June 1314: picture by Ambrose de Walton. The Scottish army defeats King Edward II and he flees after losing many of his knights.

Chapter XXVI.

The Glory of England

From 1327 to 1364

POOR Edward the Second's son was named Edward too; and when his father was dead, he became King Edward the Third. But the wicked Queen Isabella and Mortimer thought it was a good opportunity to get all the power into their own hands; and they carried Edward about with them, and tried to keep him with them, to help them in their wicked plans.

Isabella took him with her to Flanders, where she married him to Philippa, a daughter of the Count of Hainault, about whom we shall hear more by and by. Philippa was very beautiful and clever; but she was something better than either, besides: she was very pious, and had great good sense and judgment.

Mortimer tried to make Edward like him by teaching him all kinds of warlike exercises, and by taking him to tilts and tournaments. He instituted a set of knights, who sat at a round table, in imitation of King Arthurs Round Table, to amuse Edward, and to prevent him from occupying himself with the affairs of the kingdom.

For some time Edward did not think about any thing but these fights and amusements, for he was only fourteen when his father died; but when his little son was born, he began to think it was time for him to govern by himself.

He had a brave friend named Lord Montacute, to whom he told his thoughts, and his dislike of Mortimer. Only a little time before, Mortimer had one of his uncles, the Earl of Kent, put to death; and Edward began to see that his mother was wicked, and that this bad man ought to be punished for his crimes.

It happened that Parliament was going to be held at Northampton, and the queen and Mortimer took Edward with them there. Lord Montacute went to the governor of the castle, and asked him if Mortimer could be surprised there. The governor said that there was a subterranean passage under the castle; and that he would send a number of soldiers through it to take Mortimer prisoner, if Edward would wait for them at the inner door.

In the night the soldiers came in, and Edward took them to Mortimer's room, where he was talking to the Bishop of Lincoln. The queen heard the noise, and rushing in from the next room, she cried out, "Oh, spare my gentle Mortimer!" But he was soon killed, and the queen was taken prisoner.

Every body was very glad that these two wicked people were punished. The Pope asked Edward not to let his mother be publicly tried for her husband's murder, because as she was the queen, it would be a greater scandal. She was allowed to have a house to live in, and some money to live upon. Edward went to see her every year, because she was his mother; but she was never allowed to go out of her own park again as long as she lived.

Edward now began to reign by himself. He was eighteen years old, very handsome and agreeable, as well as noble in his conversation and manners. He had been extremely well educated, and could speak French, Italian, German, and Latin, which was very uncommon in England in those days.

The first thing he did was to set out, with a strong army, to Scotland, to try to conquer Robert Bruce, who was still alive. As the expedition is very amusing to read, I will tell you some particulars of it; and it will show you how brave and hardy men were in those times.

The Scottish army consisted of about 4000 men mounted upon large bay horses, and 20,000 mounted upon little Scotch ponies, who were rough and shaggy, and were never dressed, or fed upon corn, but were turned out every night to feed in the bogs and mountains. Every man carried an iron plate and a bag of oatmeal. When they stopped they made a fire, put the iron plate upon it, and mixed the oatmeal with water upon the plate. This made the thin oat-cake the Scotch are so fond of at this day. Sometimes they killed some sheep or oxen, and boiled them in their own skins, or stuck them on a stake and roasted them.

The English army were all horsemen, too. Every man carried one loaf slung behind him, and nothing more. When the trumpet sounded the first time, they were to saddle their horses. When it sounded again, they were to arm themselves; and when it sounded the third time, they were to mount and join their banners. They rode full gallop all day long, only stopping to put their saddles straight, and to give drink to their poor horses. In this way they went over the mountains and bogs, looking for the Scottish army.

They suffered great hardships, for it rained very fast; and as they could not catch the Scots, they never could fight a battle, and go home again, but had to go wandering about; sometimes hearing that they had just been seen, and sometimes not hearing any news of them.

At last they heard of them, and found them posted on a high steep hill, where it was impossible to reach them, because it was surrounded by bogs. The English tied up their horses, and lay down to rest; they could not sleep, for the Scots blew great horns all night. Froissart says, "like so many devils, to keep them awake." In the night the brave Earl Douglas gallopped into the English camp, cut the cords of the king's tent, and shouting out, 'A Douglas! a Douglas! Die, ye English thieves!' killed about 300 men, and went off without being taken.

When the English got up next morning, expecting to fight a battle, and take revenge for the last night's disgrace, they found, to their great disappointment, that the Scots had ridden off in the night; and no one knew where they had gone.

Edward was forced to make peace with Robert Bruce, after all his hard labor; and the English people were very angry.

The next thing Edward did was to declare war against France. The French king, Charles IV, was dead, and he had no son; and in France there can be no queens—owing to a law called the Salic law, which says that women are not fit to govern a kingdom.

Two people claimed the crown of France. Edward, who was grandson to Philip the Hardy, and Philip of Valois, who was his cousin. The French chose Philip of Valois; because, as they truly said, Edward's mother could not give him a right to the crown, when she had none herself.

Edward had to get a great deal of money from the people for the French war. He took all the wool that was shorn that year; and raised a great deal from the clergy. Philip seized all the salt from his subjects; and a great many jokes were made by the two kings about these ways of raising money. Edward said that Philip ruled by the *Salic* law, *(sal, sel,* salt); and Philip called Edward 'the Wool-merchant.'

The first battle Edward gained over the French was a sea-battle. The English are some of the best sailors in the world; partly because they are very active, hardy, and silent; and partly because they live in an island, and are accustomed to the sea. But this battle of Slings was the first sea-battle the English had gained since the time when Alfred fought with the Danes.

They did not fight with guns, as they do now; but each ship had a turret built upon the deck, from which the sailors threw stones at the enemy; and then hooked their ship on to one of the enemy's ships, and fought with their swords, just as they would on land.

Edward went to the church at Ardenbourg to return solemn thanks to Almighty God for this victory; and the Pope asked him to be satisfied now, and to make peace. Edward agreed to do so, if Philip would let him be king of Guienne; but Philip was proud, and said he would not let him have even Guienne, and refused. So Edward marched an army into France to fight for the crown.

Philip had a much larger army. It was eight times as large as Edward's; and he made sure of driving the English into the sea. The two kings met near the little village of Crecy in Normandy; and Edward said, that though his army was so small, he would fight, and trust in God.

He asked his officers to supper; and after he had animated

them with his piety and courage, he told them to go to rest, for tomorrow would be a great victory. He did not go to sleep himself, but knelt down in his oratory, where he prayed most fervently. In the morning he called up his son, the Black Prince, who was only fifteen years old; and they heard Mass, and went to Holy Communion together, while the rest of the army did so too.

This was a good beginning, as you will think; and God rewarded their piety, or the whole army must have been destroyed.

The Battle of Crecy
From Chapter CXXIX of Jean Froissart's Chronicles

Philip had been marching from Abbeville that morning, and his troops were straggling in great disorder. He would not stop to arrange them, but attacked the English as soon as he saw them, in great haste and anger. He had a large body of

Genoese archers, whom he ordered to begin the battle.

It was a very awful sight. The sun was nearly eclipsed, so that a strange darkness came over the earth; great flocks of birds flew screaming over the armies; and it rained in torrents, with thunder and lightning. Amidst all this, the little handful of English stood firm; feeling sure that God would fight for them.

The Genoese set up great shouts, and discharged their cross-bows. It is amusing to see that though it was so long ago, the English showed the same character as they do now. *They stood quite silent,* and returned a volley of long arrows with such force, that the Genoese gave way.

The Welshmen cut down as many as they could with long knives, and they were forced to fly.

The Black Prince was in the thickest part of the battle. Lord Warwick and Lord Oxford were taking care of him; and they sent to the king to ask for some help. The king asked if the prince complained. They said "No."

"Then," said Edward, "he shall have no help from me. Let the boy win his spurs. He shall have the whole glory of the day."

Philip fought with the greatest bravery. His brother and the Earl of Flanders were killed; and John of Hainault at last took his horse by the bridle, and led him off the field of battle by force. He escaped to Amiens with only a few soldiers and friends.

It was now quite dark. Edward ordered fires to be lighted, and his men to stand firm at their posts; for he did not know that Philip had fled. At last he met his son; and going forward to meet him, he cried: "Fair son, go on as you have begun, you have shown yourself worthy of me, and of the crown!" But the Black Prince knelt down for his father's blessing; and said, very modestly, that all the merit he had was owing to his father, who had taught him so well.

It gave Edward much more pleasure to see his son so pious and modest, than it would have done to have gained all France.

The number of French who were killed was frightful. Eleven princes, 1200 knights, and 30,000 men were left upon the field of battle: and Edward went himself to hear Mass, and pray for the dead.

The king of Bohemia was one of the princes killed. He was quite blind; yet he would go into the battle, as he said, "to have a stroke at the English." He had his horse's bridle hooked to the bridles of four knights, who took care of him; and they all rode together into the thickest part of the battle, and were killed. The Black Prince admired his courage and devotion so much, that he took his crest and motto for his own. It was three ostrich feathers, with the words, '*Ich dien*' (I serve), written under them. Did you never see this crest?

About the same time Edward gained a great victory over the Scots at Neville's Cross. The English archers chiefly won this battle, as well as Crecy. David, the king of Scotland, was taken prisoner in this battle, and carried to the Tower in London. Indeed, there were nothing but victories. Calais was taken next. Edward had been besieging it for a year, and could not take it. At last the people began to be very hungry; for, as the English soldiers were posted all round the town, the market-people could not get in to sell any thing;

and the citizens were obliged to say they would surrender. Edward said he would hang them all; but the Black Prince and his nobles begged him to have pity upon these brave men, who were only fighting for their king. Then he said that if six gentlemen would give themselves up to be hanged, he would spare the rest. After a little while a brave gentleman named Eustace de St. Pierre stepped forward, and said he would give his life to save his countrymen; and his son did the same. Four other gentlemen joined them; and though all the citizens cried and sobbed, and begged of them not to go, and said they would rather starve, they went out, bareheaded and barefooted, with their shirts on, and ropes round their necks, to Edward's camp.

Edward III and the Burghers of Calais, Anonymous, 1347; St. Alban's Chronicles

He received them very sternly, called them traitors and rebels, and sent for the hangman to put them to death. Then his good Queen Philippa rushed out of her tent with her ladies, and kneeling down before Edward, begged of him to let these brave gentlemen go. For a long time he said nothing; but at last he smiled, and said, "Dame, I can deny you nothing." It is most likely he never really intended to be so cruel.

The queen took them to her tent, gave them rich robes, invited them to a banquet, and sent them home with a present of gold pieces.

Very generous and noble deeds were done in those days as well as cruel ones. It was then thought very disgraceful to be cowardly and mean; and when once a gentleman was made a knight, he was obliged to obey certain laws, which were called the laws of Chivalry, from *chevalier,* a knight.

A knight might never break his word, or say anything unworthy of another knight. He might never attack a weaker enemy than himself, or injure any woman, or rob an orphan of his portion. On all occasions, he was bound to be more attentive to his religious duties, more charitable and kind to the oppressed, more brave and zealous in the service of his king, than another man. Boys were sent when they were quite young to be trained up in the castles of those knights who observed these laws the most strictly, and even kings' sons were given into their hands to be taught the spirit and laws of chivalry, that they might become true and brave knights too.

Edward the Third did not carry his love of chivalrous adventure so far as Richard Coeur-de-lion, but there are some stories told of his bravery which show that his wisdom and prudence did not stifle his love of it.

Once during the French wars, he dressed like a common

soldier, and fought under Sir Walter Manny. He chose out the tallest and strongest French knight to fight with, and was struck down upon his knees. At last, however, he mastered him, and took him prisoner, together with a great many others. While these prisoner-guests were at supper, Edward the Black Prince and Sir Walter Manny waited upon them as their servants. Afterwards the king made himself known to them; and taking a chaplet or coronet of pearls from his head, he put it upon the head of the French knight whom he had conquered, and said, "Wherever you go, say that this chaplet was given by the King of England to the bravest of knights."

Sir Walter Manny was one of the very best and bravest of all the brave knights at that time. When he was quite young, he had come with Queen Philippa from Hainault to wait upon her, and she and Edward always loved him very much for his piety and faithful services. I will tell you a story about him, which will show you what the laws of chivalry were, better than a long description.

Once when Sir Walter was fighting in France, he took a brave knight prisoner, and, as the custom of the time was, he asked him what ransom he would pay. The knight said he would pay 3000 crowns. Sir Walter told him, that if he would get him a passport to ride through France to Calais, to see the King of England, he would let him go free, without any ransom. The knight gave his word of honor, and Sir Walter set him free.

Very soon afterwards, the knight got the passport from his friend the Duke of Normandy, and sent it to Sir Walter, who set out on his way to Calais. He rode through France; and when he showed his passport, he was treated courteously wherever he went, till he came to Orleans, where he was seized and put into a dungeon. When the Duke of Normandy heard this, he was very angry indeed, and begged of Philip to let Sir Walter go, because he had given his word of honor that he should be safe and well treated. The king answered coolly, that Sir Walter Manny was one of his greatest enemies, and that he was going to put him to death. The Duke of Normandy then went away, saying that he would never again serve in the king's armies until Sir Walter Manny was set free, according to the promise he had given.

Philip soon after repented of his treachery, and set Sir Walter free. To show that he was sorry for what he had done, he invited him to dinner, and gave him a quantity of beautiful jewels. Sir Walter thanked him with great courtesy, but said that he could not accept the jewels until he had asked leave from his master, the King of England, to do so. Philip said that he acted like a loyal and true knight, and sent him on his way.

Sir Walter rode on to Calais, and told Edward all that had happened. Edward said to him : "Sir Walter, you have hitherto most loyally served us, and we hope you will continue to do so. Send back to King Philip his jewels, for you have no right to keep them. We have enough for ourselves and you."

Sir Walter took out all the jewels directly, and gave them to his cousin, the Lord of Mansac, saying, "Ride into France quickly, and commend me to King Philip: tell him I thank him for the fine jewels, but it is not agreeable to the King of England that I should keep them."

King Philip was delighted with the loyalty and obedience of Sir Walter Manny; and as he would not take back what he had once given, he told the Lord of Mansac to keep the jewels.

Ten years after the battle of Crecy, Edward won another

great battle over the French. The proud and ambitious Philip of Valois was dead, and the name of the new king was John. The French as usual had a much larger army than the English, but the French were very badly placed for fighting. Just as they were going to begin the battle, Cardinal Talleyrand-Perigord rode into the field, and begged of John to spare the blood of his troops. He rode from John to the Black Prince, who was quite willing to make peace; but John would not agree, unless the prince would give himself up as his prisoner. The Black Prince said he would not do this; and when the Cardinal reminded him how small his army was, he replied only: "God defend the right." The battle of Poitiers was very like the battle of Crecy. Most of the French ran away from the terrible fire of the English arrows, and a great many of their nobles and soldiers were killed. The King of France was taken prisoner. He fought with the greatest bravery; and at last surrendered to a French gentleman named Denis de Morbreque, who served in Edward's army. John's son, Philip, was made prisoner at the same time.

The Black Prince treated John with great kindness. He waited on him at supper; gave him his own plate, and told him that by his valour he had that day won the prize of chivalry.

He was brought to England; and great preparations were made by Edward for his brave son's triumphal entry into London. Arches were built across the streets, made of flowers and greens; rich carpets and tapestry, with gold and silver plate and arms, were hung out of the windows; and every street was lined with crowds of people, who welcomed their brave and dear Black Prince with shouts and cries of joy.

He was not thinking of himself at all. He gave King John

the beautiful white charger[14] to ride upon which had been taken with him at Crecy, while he had only a little black pony, and a very plain and simple dress. When the procession stopped at Westminster Hall, they found the King there with his court, and all the bishops and barons of England.

Edward received the King of France very kindly, and gave him the Savoy Palace to live in. It stood in the Strand; but it has been pulled down now some years.

King John died in England. He made a treaty with Edward by which he engaged to pay a good deal of money for his ransom; and they heard Mass together at Calais, and swore upon the Gospels to keep the treaty. Edward had taken four French princes prisoners as well as John and his son. They were the Dukes of Orleans, Anjou, Berri, and Bourbon; and because they were of royal blood, they were called " the Lords of the *Fleur de Lys*. One of them, the Duke of Anjou, broke his *parole*,[15] and escaped to Paris; and when his father, King John, heard of it, he said he would go back and give himself up to Edward as a prisoner instead of his faithless son. For, he said, "If honor is banished from every other place, it ought to be found in the breast of kings."

John put his generous plan into execution. He came back to England with the three faithful Lords of the *Fleur de Lys*, and lived in the Savoy Palace for a little while; but he soon caught a dangerous illness, and died. Edward ordered his body to be carried, with royal magnificence, to France, where it was buried in the Abbey of St. Denis.

---

[14] This famous white, or rather cream-colored, warhorse became afterwards as well known in history as the Black Prince himself.

[15] When a solider is taken prisoner, he is sometimes set free after promising to come back at a certain time. If he does not keep is promise, he breaks his *parole* or word.

Chapter XXVII.

The Sad End
From 1364 to 1376

WHEN Croesus, the great and rich king of Lydia, asked Solon if he did not think him the happiest man he had ever seen, the wise Greek replied: *"What man can be pronounced happy till he dies?"* and when he was about to be burnt alive by Cyrus, who had stripped him of all his glory, he called to mind Solon's words.

These wise words were spoken by a Pagan philosopher. We, dear children, know far better than he could do, how quickly human glory fades away and human happiness comes to an end; and one of the saddest and most striking of all the instances of this is the history of the last days of the great and good king Edward.

You know that his dear queen, Philippa, was very good, and clever, and beautiful. She had always governed the kingdom while Edward was away; and she governed it so wisely, that no harm came of the king's long absences during the French and Scottish wars. The people all loved her just as much as if she had been their own mother; and she was like a mother to England. She was always doing something for the good of the country.

Queen Philippa, consort of Edward III

I told you that she brought the brave Sir Walter Manny to England. Another gentleman whom she brought from France was named Sir John Froissart. He wrote a beautiful history of those times, called Froissart's Chronicles, which I hope you will read by and by. It is full of beautiful and pious stories about all the people who lived then; and it is he who tells us about Queen Philippa, the Black Prince, and the battles with France. Amongst other things, he remarks with great astonishment that the English people treat their children more cruelly, and bring them up worse, than any nation he ever saw.

Queen Philippa had a great many sons and daughters besides the Black Prince. One of them was John of Gaunt, the Duke of Lancaster, who was very clever and learned;—and all of them were better brought up and better educated than any other princes and princesses of the time.

The Sad End

One of the princesses, Joanna, went to Spain to be married to the Infant, or eldest son of the king, who was afterwards, from his fierce and cruel deeds, called Peter the Cruel. This sweet and good princess was saved from such an unhappy lot by a plague which was called the Black Death. It raged in England as well as in other countries; and Sir Walter Manny bought a large burial-ground near London, to save the city from the danger of burying in the crowded churchyards.

On the very day and hour fixed for the marriage of the young Joanna and Pedro, she was carried to the Cathedral at Bayonne, and buried.

Philippa sent for some good architects to come to England to build churches, and to show the people how to build better ones than they could build themselves. She greatly improved the woollen manufacture, which Edward the First had brought into England; and she had large and new coal-pits dug near Newcastle, where she had some estates.

All the brave sons of this great and good queen except one, were away when she died. The Black Prince was ill in Gascon after fighting for his Spanish friends; John of Gaunt was fighting in Burgundy; and Lionel, Duke of Clarence, was on his deathbed in Italy; Thomas of Woodstock, the youngest, was with her when she lay sick at Windsor.

When Philippa saw that she must die, she called her husband to her bedside, and said to him: "We have long enjoyed happiness, peace, and prosperity together, my husband. Promise me, before I depart, that you will grant me three requests." Edward promised with sighs and tears. "I beg, then," said Philippa, "that you will fulfill whatever engagements I have entered into with merchants; that all the gifts I have made to churches and to my servants shall be confirmed; and that you will choose no other sepulchre than mine in the cloisters of Westminster." The king, in tears, replied, "Lady, all this shall be done."

And "soon after," says Froissart, "this most excellent lady made the sign of the Cross on her breast, and, recommending her soul to God, she gave up her spirit; which I firmly believe was caught up by holy Angels, and carried to the glory of Heaven." This great queen died on the Eve of the Assumption; and all the people of England mourned for her as if they had lost their only friend.

With her all Edward the Third's glory and prosperity departed. The Black Prince, who had been so good and gentle, was so changed by his long and wasting sickness that no one knew him. He became fierce, revengeful, and gloomy. I am afraid that he had committed many cruel deeds in France and Spain, for which he was punished by this sickness; and if so, how glad he must have felt on his deathbed for this purgatory! Certainly it must have been a bitter penance to him to have seen one English possession after another in France conquered back again by the French king, while he, who won Crecy and Poitiers, was as weak and powerless as a woman.

He died at Canterbury on Trinity Sunday, and was buried with great pomp very near to St. Thomas's shrine. Notwithstanding the change in his latter years, the Black Prince was so beloved by all the people that they said, "the prosperity of England flourished in his health, and faded in his decline," and they mourned for him with a long and sincere sorrow.

The king was now left alone, and his end was the saddest of all. A wicked woman, who had been one of his dear queen Philippa's ladies, gained such power over him that he did whatever she asked him, for he was very old and almost

The death of Edward III (1312–1377). De Luan / Alamy Stock Photo

childish. When he was lying on his deathbed, this woman, who was called Alice Ferrars, stole a beautiful ring from his finger, and then went away and left him to die alone. The servants went away too, to rob the house. A good old priest happened to come in to see the king, and found him quite deserted. He knelt down and prayed by him, and held the Crucifix before his eyes. The tears streamed down the old king's cheeks. He had just power enough to kiss the Crucifix, and then he died.

This was the most sad end of the great Conqueror of France. When we read of it, we cannot help observing two things particularly: first, that all glory and splendour that has not Almighty God for its object, but only human pride and ambition, comes quickly to an end, and generally to a very sad end. Secondly, how necessary, and of how much use holiness and piety are in kings and queens, and all great people. As long as Queen Philippa lived, Edward prospered; her example caused him to do what was right, and her good deeds made reparation for his cruel ones. And this shows us that we ought to pray for our rulers and all in authority, with great faith and constancy.

Chapter XXVIII.

Richard of Bordeaux
From 1376 to 1399

THE Black Prince's son became King of England. He was born at Bordeaux, and was generally called Richard of Bordeaux. Richard the Second was a handsome, affectionate boy, but he was weak and effeminate. He was born in a southern climate, and was brought up in the greatest luxury and pleasure. He was taught music and dancing, and loved fine shows and processions, and every thing that was pleasant and grand, much better than doing his duty and attending to the affairs of his kingdom, as a good king ought to do.

When he was very young, there was a dangerous insurrection in England. The wars with France had made the country very poor, and Richard wanted a great deal of money for his court, because he liked to have great feasts, and banquets, and games, and he kept a great many noblemen, and ladies, and fine horses, which cost a great deal of money. He sent his tax-gatherers to ask for a new tax upon the head of every one above fifteen in the kingdom. It was called the poll-tax.

The tax-gatherers behaved so cruelly in the house of a poor man named Wat Tyler, that Tyler hit one of them on the head with his hammer, and struck him dead. All the people around who heard the noise came out of their houses, and said they would help Wat Tyler; and a rude madman called Jack Straw began to preach and to say seditious words against the king.

The end of this was that a very large mob of rioters gathered together, and they went to Smithfield in London, and asked the king to meet them there and hear all their grievances. Richard went, and a great many gentlemen went with him. One of these gentlemen was named William Walworth; he was the mayor of London; and when Wat Tyler began to speak rudely to the king, and to take hold of the bridle of his horse, Walworth struck him down with his dagger, for he was afraid he was going to hurt the king.

When the people saw that their leader was dead, they were very angry indeed, and would have shot Richard with their arrows; but he had the courage to gallop up to them and say, "Well, my friends, do you want a leader? Come, follow me, and I will be your leader." The people, who are always struck with what is brave and generous, followed him directly, and Richard's soldiers disarmed them, and sent them home.

There was a long dispute then between the king and his Parliament. The king wanted money, and the Parliament wanted the taxes to be remitted, and Richard said he would not pardon the offences till the money he asked for was paid.

At last, when he was going to be married, the Commons granted him a tax on wool, fleeces, and leather, for five years. The good Queen Anne, whom Richard married, begged a pardon for all offenders, and Richard, who loved her very

Queen Anne pleads for Sir Simon Burley by James Doyle, in A Chronicle of England, Longman, Green, Longman, Roberts & Green.

dearly, granted it. Queen Anne came from Bohemia. She was very gentle and good, and was so beloved by the people that they always called her 'Good Queen Anne.'

I told you that one of Wat Tyler's friends preached and spoke seditiously. It was about this time that the English people began to show a rebellious and untractable spirit both towards their rulers and towards the Church. A priest, who was rector of Lutterworth, named Wycliffe, began to teach all kinds of errors, and to condemn nearly all the clergy of England.

I dare say a great many of them were very rich and very proud, for many of them were of noble blood, and sat in Parliament, and were sent as ambassadors by the kings. This is the office of those clergy who are high in rank and dignity in the Church; and this, as you have heard many times in this history, is a very dangerous position.

But it is very unreasonable, as well as very wrong, to blame the whole Church, and her doctrines and practices, because some of her children do not do every thing they ought to do. This is what Wycliffe did, and what every heretic begins by doing.

A great many of the common people went to hear Wycliffe preach. He and his friends, whom he called his 'poor priests,' because they went on foot, in imitation of our Lord, went about to preach their heresy, and to abuse the Pope, and find fault with better and wiser men than themselves. Among other falsehoods believed about Wycliffe, it is said that he has the merit of first making the Bible knowm to the people in their native tongue. This, you know, is not true, because it had been translated more than 500 years before by Alfred and his grandson Athelstan; and the great and good Cardinal Langton had improved it, and first divided it into verses.

Wycliffe's friends were called the Lollards, and they made riots all over England, so that the king had to send troops against them. These troubles brought about very strange things; for, as many of the nobles and gentlemen were afraid, and went and shut themselves up in their castles, the Bishops and clergy were obliged to do all they could to put down the heretics.

The foremost and most active among them was Henry Spenser, the young Bishop of Norwich. He led the troops, in complete armor, against the Lollards, judged them when they were taken, and confessed them before they were executed; and his zeal and energy in this holy cause were so great, that he was more feared by them than all the king's officers.

Wycliffe's death might have struck terror into his followers, if they had not been blinded by the love of singularity. One day, as his curate was saying Mass, just as he had raised the

Sacred Host at the Elevation, Wycliffe was seized with an apoplectic stroke, which took from him the use of his limbs and of his speech. In this miserable condition, deprived, by the judgment of God, of the sacraments he had blasphemed, the unhappy man expired.

Richard and good Queen Anne had no children; and this caused a great many quarrels and a great many crimes. All his reign, after Anne died, was very miserable. His uncle, John of Gaunt, was accused of trying to make himself king; and though he was the very best friend Richard had, the foolish king was always suspecting him. At last John of Gaunt was tired of being always accused and suspected, and he went away to Spain; for he had married a Spanish wife, and, like his brother the Black Prince, he went to help one of his Spanish friends to get his crown back again from some princes who had taken it from him.

When the Duke of Lancaster was gone, Richard found that he had lost a good friend. Another of his uncles, the Duke of Gloucester, was a very clever and bad man; and he was always raising difficulties and quarrels between the king, the nobles, and the people.

Richard married the daughter of the king of France, after Anne died. She was only eight years old when he married her, and was called 'La Petite Reine.' It is said, however, that the little queen spoke and acted like a grown-up woman, and that she showed a wonderful prudence in her conduct and answers. She could not, however, have been any help to Richard, or any stay in the turbulent state of England; and this was a great misfortune to him.

The bold and bad Duke of Gloucester quarrelled with all Richard's ministers, and most of them were *impeached*, that is, accused of behaving badly to the king, and deceiving and robbing the people. Gloucester did this to make friends with the people, who had long been angry with Richard. Richard went to war with Ireland; but he did not do any thing but spend money, which he had a great talent for; and this made the people more angry still.

Richard was so foolish as not to listen to the people. It is not right for a king to be governed by his people; on the contrary, it is the people's duty to submit to their king, and to be peaceable and obedient subjects; neither will a good and religious king ever care for being liked or disliked for doing what he knows to be his duty. But when a king follows only his own will, and attends only to his own pleasure, and becomes unjust, and the people know it and are displeased, the king ought to take warning by their displeasure, and to do what is right, to keep his kingdom in peace, if he will not do it because it is his duty.

At last the Duke of Gloucester was taken prisoner. He begged very hard for his life; but though he was imprisoned privately at Calais, it is not quite certain what became of this turbulent duke. Some say that he was murdered by Richard's orders, to prevent his being publicly tried in England, where the people were very fond of him.

The next thing Richard did was to get rid of his cousin, Henry of Hereford. He was the Duke of Lancaster's son, and was very brave and clever. The people loved him too very much, because he had won a great many battles; and he was kind and good-natured to them, and was a great deal wiser than Richard. Richard was jealous of him, and banished him for ten years, together with another great lord, the Earl of Norfolk, who died of a broken heart at Venice. But Henry of Hereford did not die, as we shall see.

When he thought he had now got rid of his greatest

troubles, Richard went away to fight in Ireland; and while he was gone Henry of Hereford came back to England with a very small army, which soon became a large one, for almost all the nobles joined him. Richard did not hear of his coming for a fortnight; for there were no railroads or telegraphs then, and the sea was very rough between England and Ireland. When he heard that Henry of Hereford was at the head of a large army in England, he said, "Ah, uncle of Lancaster, God reward your soul! If I had taken your advice, this would not have happened. You told me he was worthy of death."

Richard came as quickly as he could to England, expecting to find a large army at his command; but he found his castles empty, and that all the nobles had deserted him. He then sent his two brothers to Henry, who put one of them in prison, and gave the other the Rose to wear instead of the Hart, which was Richard's badge. The *badge* was some figure or letter, which the kings and nobles wore to distinguish one another and their followers in battle and in tournaments.

Henry then rode to Chester, and pretended to be very kind to Richard. He said he was come to help him govern; and he promised a great many things which were written down, and which the Earl of Northumberland swore upon the Host to keep: so that, as an old writer says, "he perjured himself upon the Body of our Lord."

Northumberland rode with Richard from Rhuddlan to Flint; and as they came to the edge of a steep mount and were descending into the valley, Richard stopped his horse and said, "I am betrayed! Ten lances and pennons in the valley!" Northumberland seized the bridle of his horse and forced him on; and Richard could only say to his friends, "We are betrayed; but remember that our Lord also was betrayed and sold into the hands of His enemies."

The next day he got up early, and went up to the top of the castle-tower to see the duke's army come in; and when the long line of 80,000 men wound along the beach and surrounded the castle, the poor king wept, and saw that all was over.

Richard the II resigning the crown to Bolingbroke, by John Gilbert

He was taken to London, and at first he was treated well; but afterwards he was shut up in Pontefract Castle, where he died suddenly; and I am afraid not by a natural death.

His body was carried through London in a litter hung with black, that every one might look once more upon the weak and unfortunate son of the brave Black Prince.

Chapter XXIX.

The Usurper

From 1399 to 1413

ENRY of Hereford was now King Henry the Fourth. He was a *usurper*, as you know; that is, he had taken a crown that belonged to another man. His reign, however, was a very useful one for England just at that time.

In the first place, he punished the Lollards. He caused many of them to be executed for their disturbances and seditious speeches; and when the House of Commons asked him to tax the clergy instead of the people, he sent them word that they ought to be ashamed of themselves, and that he would never again receive such a disgraceful message. When they saw how determined the king was, it stopped the Lollards for a little while from going about and preaching as they had done. And in general Henry was very kind to all the clergy; which was a great help to the Church in her troubles.

He had not many foreign wars to trouble him; but there were some rebellions, about which I must tell you. The great

Earl of Northumberland, Percy, was always fighting against the Scots. He was what was called Warden of the Marches; that is, he took care of that part of England which is next to Scotland; and he had to keep it in order. The Scottish nobleman that gave him the most trouble was named James Douglas. I dare say you recollect that when Edward the Third went to fight in Scotland, it was the Earl of Douglas who cut the cords of his tent, and nearly took him prisoner. This great family was always very terrible to the English; and Northumberland was very glad that he beat Lord Douglas in a great battle at Homildon Hill.

He took a great many Scottish prisoners in this battle; and you know that in those days ransom was taken for prisoners, that is, they were allowed to pay a large sum of money, and then be set free; and the noblemen who took the prisoners looked upon them as their own property, to do what they pleased with.

But when Percy asked King Henry, according to the custom, to let him ransom his prisoners, the king said that he might not, and that he must give them up to the crown.

Percy was very proud: he refused to part with his prisoners, and raised an army to fight against Henry, who, he said, had no right to be king.

There was a Welsh gentleman named Owen Glendower, who had been a friend of poor Richard the Second, and he helped Northumberland with a great many troops, so that Henry's enemies were very powerful and dangerous. Northumberland had a very brave and generous son named Henry; and he was so bold and hot-tempered, that he was called Harry Hotspur.

Henry the Fourth had a very brave son too, named Henry. But he was so mad and wild, that he was nicknamed Madcap

Harry. I will tell you some droll stories about him by and by.

The two armies met at Shrewsbury, where there was a most bloody battle. King Henry had several gentlemen dressed exactly like himself, which was a dangerous honor for them. Harry Hotspur sought them out, and killed several of them; but as he was fighting with the most wonderful bravery, an arrow shot him in the eye, and he was killed.

The Death of Harry Hotspur, in *A Chronicle of England*

I need not tell you what a sad thing it was to have these brave Englishmen killing one another. These two brave Harries ought to have been friends and companions, loving and helping each other, instead of being deadly enemies. God had given them the same country to live in, and had made them of the same race; and yet, you see, they were doing all they could to injure and destroy one another. Civil wars are very shocking.

When you grow older, you must read the beautiful account which Shakspeare gives of this battle. While you are reading it, you can quite fancy that you are there; and that you know Harry Hotspur and Madcap Harry quite well.

Henry the Fourth married a princess named Joanna of Navarre. She was very beautiful, and it is to be hoped she was good; but there were strange stories told at the time of her being a witch; and for many, many years it was said that her ghost haunted her favorite palace of Havering.

It is said that a usurper's crown is a crown of thorns, and certainly Henry found it to be so. His son was a great trouble to him; for he did not live to see him grow good. Madcap Harry was the wildest prince that I ever heard of. He spent all his time with a number of low companions, who went out with him to stop people on the high roads, and to take their money from them. They used to dress in masks, that people might not know who they were and then they went and dined and drank together at some of the taverns in London.

Once, when King Henry was very ill at Windsor, he sent for his son, of whom he had heard stories, and Harry went quickly, dressed just as he was. This was in a blue satin dress, with the sleeves full of eyelet-holes, and at every eyelet-hole a long silk with a tag at the end of it. The king wondered to see him come in such a dress as this; upon which the young prince knelt down, and gave his father a dagger, saying that since he was deprived of his favor, he hoped he would deprive him of life too.

This shows how thoughtless and careless Madcap Harry was, for he knew that if his father had done as he asked him, it would have been a great sin.

King Henry was very often ill after this. He had such dreadful fits, that he lay as if he were dead. He was praying at the shrine of St. Edward in Westminster Abbey when the last fit seized him, and he was carried into the abbot's room and laid before the fire.

When he recovered, he asked where he was; and when they told him "in the Jerusalem Chamber," he said he knew his end was near; for it had been prophesied that he would die at Jerusalem. He seemed to feel that the blood he had shed in winning the crown was still upon his soul; for he asked to have the *Miserere* sung, and he continued every now and then to fall into a trance.

It was while he was in one of these trances that Madcap Harry took the crown from his pillow, and carried it into the next room. When the king recovered a little, he missed his crown, and cried out for it; and when he saw his son bring it back in his hand, he sighed and said, "Couldst not thou wait a while, and it would have been thine own?" Madcap Harry burst into tears when his father said this, and promised never again to follow the wild life he had done.

His father then said, "Alas! son, what right have you to this crown, when your father had none?"

"My liege," replied Harry, "you won it with your sword, and I will keep it with mine." The king then gave his son some beautiful and touching advice about his manner of ruling England, which you will one day read in Shakspeare just as he said it, and then he died.

A gorgeous and beautiful tomb was prepared for Henry and Joanna in Canterbury Cathedral, near that of the Black Prince, which you must go and see some day. But it is said that the body of the usurper does not rest near the father of the king whom he had so deeply injured, and never lay in that royal tomb. Whether this is true or not, it is very certain that a man named Maydestone took a solemn oath that when he was bringing the body of the king from London to Canterbury, a violent storm arose suddenly; and to quiet the storm (according to a very common superstition among sailors), he and his companion threw the body overboard, and brought only the empty coffin with its trappings to Canterbury.

So we cannot tell now whether Henry the Fourth lies in consecrated ground or not.

You will like to know that this proud and ambitious Henry of Hereford was the first person who gave its pretty name to the field mouse-ear, or *myosotis*. When he said good-by to his dear friend the Duke of Orleans, to come to England, he gathered one of these little blue flowers, and fastened it to the gold collar which was then worn by noblemen, and called the collar of SS,[16] and said in old French, "*Souveigne-vous de moi*—Remember me." And from these words that little flower has ever since been called the 'Forget-me-not.'

---

[16] The Collar of SS., so often found in monumental brasses and old engravings and manuscrips, was only allowed to be worn by nobles of the highest rank.

CHAPTER XXX.

The Greatest Glory of England

From 1413 to 1422

MADCAP Harry was now king of England. But King Henry the Fifth was a very different person from Madcap Harry. He sent away all his bad companions, and would have nothing more to do with them. He went to his confessor, and expressed the deepest contrition for his past life, and his conduct afterwards showed that it was a sincere contrition. He was always very devout at his prayers, and was very careful to defend the Church and the clergy, and to punish heretics. He put the whole kingdom in order, as far as he could, and then he set out for France, to try and get it for his own.

Poor Charles the Sixth, the French king, was mad; his queen Isabeau was one of the most wicked women that ever lived; the little dauphin was only ten years old; and all the nobles were quarrelling and fighting together; so it really seemed as if it would be a blessing for France itself to be conquered by England.

Henry had not a large army, but he was very brave. The French army was very large, and was commanded by the Duke of Alençon, who was a great general. The two armies met together at a castle, which was very near the village of Crecy. The night before the battle one of the nobles said, that he wished some of the brave knights who were sitting idle in England could be transported to the field of battle. The king heard him, and he said, "I would not have a man more than is here. If God gives us the victory, it will be plain that we owe it to His goodness; and if we lose it, the loss will be less to our country." These pious and courageous words ought never to be forgotten by our English kings.

Henry V praying before the Battle of Agincourt

When the morning came, Henry put on his brightest armor, and over it a gay coat, with the royal arms of England and France embroidered upon it, that every one might mark him as the king. The Duke of Alençon led all his men against him, and at last, after wonderful deeds of bravery, cut his way to Henry, and clove the crown on his helmet with his battle-axe. Every one thought the king was killed; but the duke saw that his own life was lost, and he cried out, "I surrender—I am Alençon." It was too late; the next moment he lay dead at Henry's feet.

After the battle Henry called the French herald to him, and asked what castle that was in the distance. "It is called the castle of Agincourt," replied the herald. "Then," said Henry, "let this battle be ever known by the name of the battle of Agincourt."

When the news of this victory was brought to England, the people seemed mad with joy. They jumped into the sea at Dover, and carried Henry in their arms to the shore. All London was hung with tapestry and flowers, and sweet wine was made to gush out of all the fountains instead of water. You may be sure that the clergy were not behindhand in welcoming their dear and pious king. There were processions of the Bishops and Abbots; and the *Te Deum* was publicly sung in thanksgiving.

The next year the king of the Romans, Sigismund, came to England to pay Henry a visit, and promised to help him to conquer France; and several other foreign princes came with him. Every one who knew Henry loved him. He was as frank and affectionate as a child; yet he was so full of truth and dignity that no one could help respecting him. The French said his magnificence was so great that one would have thought he was king of all the world.

Not long after the battle of Agincourt, Henry besieged Rouen. The poor soldiers and people held out so long that they were obliged to eat up their horses, and even rats and mice, and the weeds which they found. At last, after 50,000 persons had died, the garrison surrendered, and submitted to wear the Red Cross of St. George, which they hated so much, as being the badge of England.

Henry went to Paris; and at Troyes he married the daughter of the poor mad King Charles and wicked Queen Isabeau, whose name was Katherine. She is always called Katherine the Fair, for she was more beautiful than anybody in the world at that time. Henry brought her to England; and the people made the greatest rejoicings all over the country.

You would be amused to read of all the dishes that were set out at the coronation banquet. As it was Lent, there was no meat—nothing but fish, and what were then called *subtleties;* that is, confectionary and sweet things made into all kinds of shapes, and with mottoes painted and gilt upon them. Every kind of fish that can be named was there, even that hideous monster the porpoise, or dolphin, roasted. It was at this banquet that Katherine asked Henry to set James the First of Scotland free. He had been nineteen years a prisoner in Windsor Castle; and he was set free only under condition of serving under Henry's banner against his own countrymen in the French wars.

The next year Henry and Katherine went to Paris; and there they actually sat on the royal throne in the Louvre, as king and queen of France. The whole English court stood round them, and all the French people came in to pay them homage. The English were delighted to think how easily this great kingdom had become theirs.

In the midst of all his grandeur, and at the very height of

human glory, Henry fell sick; and his sickness increased so much that he knew he must die. The two sceptres were in his very hand, the two crowns were upon his very head, when God required of him his soul. But Henry seems never to have forgotten that he could not carry his glory with him. He does not seem to have even expressed a single regret at leaving all this splendour; and the only care he had was about his little baby son, who, he knew, would find it difficult to rule England in the turbulent state it was in at that time.

As he lay sick at Meaux, he called the Duke of Bedford and Lord Warwick to his bedside, and spoke to them very earnestly about his son and his kingdom. He made the Duke of Bedford regent while Henry should be too little to govern himself. When he had said all he wished to say, he called his physician to his bedside, and asked him how long he had to live. The physician said he should now attend to his soul, for he could not live more than two hours.

The king was not at all moved at hearing this, but he sent for his confessor, and turned all his thoughts to God. He asked his chaplains to chant the penitential psalms; and when they came to the verse, "Thou shalt build the walls of Jerusalem," he said faintly that he had always hoped to go to Jerusalem to free the Holy Sepulchre from the infidels. Then he said no more; and soon after he calmly gave up his soul to God.

This was the end of the last of the really great English kings. We shall read of many famous men, and of many noble deeds that were done afterwards, but Henry the Fifth was the last great king of Catholic England. He was so wise a statesman, that he kept England in perfect order when it was distracted with rebellion and heresy, and administered justice as rigorously as King Alfred himself, at a time when it was difficult to restrain even dreadful excesses.

He was so great a warrior, that no foreign power had ever overcome him when he fought in person, and he was adored by his soldiers as the bravest and kindest general in the world. He was so true, that even his enemies believed his simple word as if it had been an oath; so gentle and affectionate, that the poor loved him and spoke to him as to a father; and yet so terrible, that the bravest men feared him when they knew that they deserved his punishment.

The king's body was put upon a car, and under a rich canopy a figure of him, exactly like him, was dressed in royal robes, and with the sceptre in his hand. Five hundred knights in black armor, with black barbed horses, and trailing their lances, went before and behind the car, around which were several hundred torchbearers, and the priests of every district through which they passed in France. Behind came the nobles and princes of the blood, with the King of Scotland as chief mourner. The poor Queen Katherine was last of all.

When they got near London, fifteen Bishops in pontificals, and many mitred Abbots, with a long train of clergy, met the procession, chanting the Office for the Dead as they moved along. Every householder in London stood at his door with a torch in his hand. Solemn Mass was sung for him, first at St. Paul's, and afterwards at Westminster Abbey, where he was buried near St. Edward's shrine. Crowds of people visited his tomb, with nearly as much love and reverence as if he had been a canonised saint.

They had reason to mourn for their great and wise king, for sad days were at hand for England.

Chapter XXXI.

The Maid of Orleans
From 1422 to 1461

THE baby king, Henry the Sixth, was only nine months old when his father died. Katherine brought him to England; and he was sometimes shown to the people sitting or lying in her lap. The earl of Warwick was his governor; and on great occasions used to carry the little king on his arm in a long crimson velvet robe. The Duke of Gloucester got himself made President of the Council; and the Regent, the great and good Duke of Bedford, who was very like his brother Henry the Fifth, went to France to continue the war. Henry the Sixth had another uncle, the son of John of Gaunt and Catherine Swynford, who was Bishop of Winchester.

All these wise statesmen governed England so well, that at first every thing went on rightly, and there were no misfortunes. The Earl of Bedford won place after place from the French, and at last laid siege to Orleans. He built a line of forts all round the city, and blocked it up.

The poor mad king Charles was dead; and his son was

king, who was named Charles the Seventh. When he heard that Orleans was almost taken, he was nearly in despair, and thought of flying away from France, and giving it up entirely to the English. Just as France was on the very brink of destruction, it was saved by one of the most extraordinary circumstances that ever happened.

There was a young girl at a little village of Champagne called Domremy, who was remarked for being more modest, more pious, and more diligent than any of her companions. Every Saturday she used to go to a little chapel called the Hermitage of the Blessed Virgin, and offer to Our Lady a garland of flowers or a wax taper; and she never failed in these acts of love to the Mother of God.

Jeanne loved the poor so much, that she often gave away her own dinner to feed them; and slept upon the hard brick floor, that the harborless traveller might be lodged by her father. While her companions were dancing and making merry, she used to steal away to the church, or to her favorite hermitage, to speak with our Lord and His Blessed Mother alone. When the hour came for Complin, which was then sung every evening, if the beadle did not ring the bell in time, Jeanne used to give him some money to be more exact.

At night she spun diligently, and spent the evening often spinning with her young companions, who loved her very dearly.

One day, as Jeanne was watching her flock, she heard a voice telling her that she must go and deliver France; and sometime after, she saw St. Michael, with St. Catherine and St. Margaret, bidding her go to the governor, and ask him to send her to the court.

Charles heard of Jeanne after a while, and of the voices which spoke to her; and he sent for her. To try her, he dressed in plain armor, and stood amongst a great many other knights in a large hall lighted with torches. Jeanne did not once look at the lights or the company, but walked straight up to the king, and said, "God give you life, gentle king. I am Jeanne, the maid sent by God to help you and the kingdom."

"I am not the king," replied Charles, "but that one," pointing to another knight. "You are the king, and no other," answered the Maid. The king then spoke to her aside for a long time; and when he came back, he said that she had told him secrets which she could not have known, unless God had made them known to her. The next day Jeanne appeared before all the people on a beautiful horse, in bright armor, with her long black hair curling round her shoulders; and when she ran a course with her lance, like an accomplished knight, there was a general burst of enthusiasm in her favor.

She was examined by some learned priests, who were quite satisfied of the piety and truth of Jeanne; and very soon after, she was led out to the people as the deliverer whom God had sent to France.

And when they saw her, so young, and with her modest and holy face, in bright armor, with her dark hair floating in the wind, and riding on a beautiful grey war-horse, they shouted and wept for joy, and said that she was not a woman, but an Angel.

She spoke to them wisely and cheeringly. She first of all promised the king that he should be crowned at Rheims, where the French kings were always crowned. She exhorted the nobles to join together now to drive away the English altogether, and to restore their dear young king to his throne. She told the soldiers and people that our Lady and St. Michael would certainly help them to recover France, and to plant their corn and vines again, and to serve God in peace. She spoke so beautifully and simply, that every one was roused to do his utmost, and to put his trust in God.

Jeanne sent away all the wicked women from the camp, and forbade swearing and drinking among the soldiers; so that the army began to have a holy look, as if they were really fighting under the protection of Our Lady.

Joan of Arc at the Battle of Orleans

The English, on the other side, were dispirited by what they heard and saw; and when Jeanne appeared at the head

The Maid of Orleans

of her troops, fighting in the very thick of the battle, they lost courage at so extraordinary a sight, and were driven from their lines. All the forts that had cost so much labor were set on fire, and Orleans was saved. After this Jeanne was always called the Maid of Orleans.

A great many other battles were won by the French; and at last Jeanne fulfillled her promise that the king should be crowned at Rheims.

The French army entered the city in triumph, and went to the cathedral. Jeanne stood by the young king with the white Oriflamme[17] in her hand; and when the ceremony was over, she threw herself at his feet, and begged with many tears that he would let her go back to her father, and keep his sheep at Domremy; for now, she said, her mission was finished.

The king would not hear of her going back, and she was obliged to stay; but Jeanne was right—her mission was finished. Very soon afterwards she was taken prisoner by the English, and carried to the Duke of Bedford, who gave her up to the Bishop of Winchester, who was now Cardinal Beaufort. He and several other ecclesiastics decided that she was a witch, and she was sentenced to be burnt. The French, for whom she had done so much, basely deserted her, and the English treated her with a revengeful cruelty, which will leave a perpetual disgrace upon their name. Jeanne was forced in her weakened state to declare that what she had said of Our Lady and St. Michael appearing to her was an imagination, and that she would never put on armor again.

As soon as she was carried back into her prison, she felt the deepest sorrow for what she had declared; and taking down the suit of bright armor that had been hung there, she

---

[17] The ancient royal banner of France, covered with fleurs-de-lys, was called the Oriflamme.

put it on, as if to prepare for a crown of almost martyrdom.

Her enemies burst in triumph upon her, to take advantage of what they called her perjury. The Maid of Orleans was led to the market-place at Rouen, and amidst the crackling of the flames, with the fervent aspiration, "Jesus, good Jesus!" the soul of this pure and noble champion departed.

Coronation of Henry VI

Soon after this tragedy, little Henry was crowned king of France at Paris by Cardinal Beaufort; but it was only an empty show, for the French were daily gaining ground. Every one was tired of this endless war, which had made Henry a beggar, and the Pope called a congress at Arras to make peace. The Duke of Burgundy, Cardinal Beaufort, and very many princes were there; but it was of very little use. One of the nobles there declared, that it was the sixth peace he had sworn to, and all the other five were broken.

The great Duke of Bedford died next year, as much respected by his enemies as by his friends. He was buried by the high altar at Rouen; and when Louis the Eleventh was asked to remove his bones to a less noble place, he said angrily, "I will not war with the remains of a prince who was a match for your fathers and for mine. Let his ashes rest in peace; and may God have mercy on his soul!" These long French wars, and Henry's being so young, raised up sad quarrels in England, about which I am now going to tell you.

Chapter XXXII.

The White and Red Rose

BESIDES his two good uncles, the Duke of Bedford and Cardinal Beaufort, Henry had another, who was a very bad man. This was the Duke of Gloucester, who tried every means to get himself made Protector, and to usurp all the power in the kingdom into his own hands. In spite of all that his brothers could say, he would marry the Duchess Jacqueline of Holland, who had been living for a long time in England. This lady, whom Henry the Fifth always called *Dame Jake,* was very rich, and it was to gain her money more than any thing else that the Duke of Gloucester married her. This marriage offended the great Duke of Burgundy, Jacqueline's feudal lord, and made him help the French king instead of helping Henry, as he always had done hitherto.

After Gloucester had done this, Jacqueline was taken prisoner and sent to her own country, and instead of going to help her, and trying to get her back again, this wicked man married another wife, who was as bad as himself. This woman was said to be a witch, and she was accused of making a wax image of the king, and melting it before a slow fire. It was believed that when the image was melted, the king would die. She was condemned to walk through London with a lighted taper in her hand, as a public penitent; and the Duke of Gloucester, who was very proud, felt this disgrace very much.

It is not certain whether his anger led him to make any plots against the king, but very soon afterwards he was arrested, and died quite suddenly, some said of apoplexy, and some by poison. It is most likely that his angry passions caused him to die a natural death.

Soon after, the great Cardinal Beaufort died too; but not before he had married Henry to his beautiful and brave wife, Margaret of Anjou. She was the daughter of King Réné of Provence and Isabella of Lorraine, who was descended directly from Charlemagne, and she inherited from her mother all the valour and beauty of the great Carlovingian race. When she was quite a little girl, her father was taken prisoner by the Burgundians, and her mother went with her and her little brother Louis to live at a beautiful castle on the banks of the Rhone. The children were both so wonderfully beautiful, that whenever they went out, the people strewed flowers at their feet and sang songs about them.

Margaret was only fourteen when Henry the Sixth sent the Earl of Suffolk to ask her to marry him; and some time after, he brought her to England. The whole of King Réné's court wept bitterly when she came away, for they loved her dearly. When she came to England, and the people saw how good and beautiful and kind she was, they followed her about in crowds, made processions and shows to welcome and amuse her, and wore her badge, the daisy, in their caps and jackets. All the books that were made had daisies painted in them and nothing was talked of but the beautiful young Queen Margaret.

Margaret was very different indeed now to what she was afterwards driven to become by the cruelties and horrors of the last years of Henry's reign. She was very meek and gentle, and did all she could to make peace with France, and to set poor distracted England in order, and to establish new manufactures of silk and woollen, in which she took great interest.

But all that she could do was in vain. The holy and gentle Henry was too weak to control the fierce passions of the time, or to tame the powerful nobles, who had in fact changed the government of England from a monarchy into an oligarchy, that is, the government of a few nobles.

Peace was made with France; but Louis the Eleventh, who was the French king, was too cunning to make it without getting a great deal of land from the English. He knew that Henry was nearly ruined by the long war, and that he had great difficulty in getting money from the nobles and people. So he asked to have Maine and Normandy given up, before he would make peace. And when the English found that nearly all that Edward the Third, and their dear Black Prince, and Henry the Fifth had won was given up again to the French, they were very angry, and they said that the prime minister, Lord Suffolk, ought to be beheaded.

Lord Suffolk was a good and brave man, who had only done his duty as far as he could; but his defence was of no use, and he was obliged to fly to his own estates in Suffolk. As he was trying to escape to France, he was taken prisoner by some of his enemies, and cruelly murdered on the sands.

This savage murder roused all the bad passions of the people. A man named Cade collected an immense mob, and gave battle to the king's troops, whom he defeated; and then he marched to Blackheath, insisting upon seeing the king himself, who fled to Kenilworth with the queen.

Henry VI sits while Edmund Beaufort, 2nd Duke of Somerset, and Richard Plantagenet, Duke of York have a dispute in *A Chronicle of England*.

It was just about this time that there was a famous dispute between Lord Somerset and Lord Warwick in the Temple Gardens, in London, about which had the most right to be king, Henry, or Mortimer Duke of York, who was descended from Lord March, Richard the Second's presumptive heir. Somerset was Cardinal Beaufort's nephew, and Henry and Margaret loved him very much. He was very hot-tempered; and when he found that Warwick would not agree with him, he hastily gathered a red rose from a rose-tree that stood near, and cried out, "Whoever is for Henry of Lancaster, let him wear a red rose!" and he stuck it in his cap as the badge of the House of Lancaster. Warwick directly gathered a white rose, as the badge of the House of York, and all the gentlemen who followed him did the same; and rosettes of red and white ribbon, or red and white paper, were very soon made, and worn by every body all over England. This was the beginning of the Wars of the Roses, in which more blood was shed than can easily be reckoned.

The Duke of York gathered an army to fight against Henry; but soon after, leaving his men, he came to defend himself before the king, and to accuse Lord Somerset. This nobleman, whom he thought was in the Tower, was hidden by Queen Margaret behind the arras, or tapestry; and when he heard the duke accusing him, he rushed out, and began abusing him violently. The puzzled king, who did not know he was there, sat quite amazed, without speaking a word, till the queen sent in some soldiers and arrested the Duke of York.

Besides Somerset, there was another great noble who took the king's part in these unhappy wars. This was old Talbot, the brave Earl of Shrewsbury, whose name was used, in the wars with France, to stop the French babies from crying, just as the Saracen mothers had used Richard Coeur de Lion's name, some centuries before, in the Holy Land.

This brave old nobleman, whom the queen called "our good dogge,"[18] was killed about this time in Guienne; and as he was very clever and accomplished, besides being such a brave and faithful friend, Margaret was very unhappy at his death.

This poor queen had very few friends left, just when she wanted them most. The holy king was seized with a sad illness, which deprived him of his senses, so that sometimes he was like a baby, and could not speak or move. When he came to himself, he always went to church to return thanks,

---

[18] A Talbot, or tyke, was a large kind of deer-hound, and was the badge of the Earls of Shrewsbury.

and then made his offerings at the altar, and said his office again. But he could not attend to business, and he knew very little of the real state of England. He was more fit to be a holy monk than to be king of the rude and savage country England was then. The most touching account is given of him, when he recovered from one of these sicknesses, after his son's birth. He asked the Prince's name, and thanked God to hear it was Edward, having a great devotion to St. Edward. He then said *he was at charity with all the world, and he much wished all the lords were.*

Soon after his recovery he was taken prisoner by the Duke of York, and carried by him to London. He made Henry call a parliament and appoint him Protector of the kingdom; after which he sent the king, with Margaret and little Edward, to the palace at Greenwich, where he kept them in a kind of honorable imprisonment. While they were there, the brave and energetic queen called about her all the leaders of the Lancastrian House, and spoke to them about the state of the country, as if she had been king herself. After some time, by their advice, she took the king to London; and one day, when Parliament was sitting, Henry went into the House of Lords, and said, that as he was now quite recovered, he would rule again for himself; and he begged of them to declare that the Duke of York was no longer protector of the kingdom.

The nobles were so astonished to see their holy king again, and to hear him speak with such firmness and dignity, that they did directly what he asked, and Henry found himself again King of England. Several of the nobles got leave from him then to make pilgrimages to foreign shrines for his recovery; and the Duke of Norfolk went to the Holy Sepulchre for this purpose.

About this time the King of France threatened to invade

England, and Margaret entreated the angry Yorkist nobles to make peace, that they might all fight against their common enemy. Henry wrote a beautiful letter to them himself, to urge them to peace; and they came to meet him in London, with all their followers.

After a great many angry debates, peace was arranged; and on the Feast of the Annunciation all the nobles walked in procession with the king to St. Paul's, to offer a solemn thanksgiving. The queen walked with the Duke of York; and all the others walked hand in hand with those nobles who had been their most bitter enemies.

But unhappily this was only a show-reconciliation. The queen and Lord Warwick never could forgive each other; and this sad hatred of Margaret and the singular and most powerful baron soon caused fresh bloodshed. Directly the conference was over, the great Yorkist leaders, York, Salisbury, and Warwick, went to collect an army; and Margaret took the king and the prince through the midland counties, to show them to the people, and to excite a fresh interest in their saintly king and noble young prince. Every one loved Prince Edward, who was a most beautiful and valiant boy; and he distributed little silver swans[19] to all who came to look at him. While they were in Staffordshire, there was a great battle won by the Yorkists at Blore Heath, and Margaret was forced to fly to Eccleshall Castle. But a little while after, the queen, who had now learned not only to fight, but to fight well, won a battle in her turn, and drove the Duke of York to Ireland.

But the Red Rose was not destined to win many battles. Warwick and the young Lord March, the Duke of York's son, got together another army, and fought the queen at

---

[19] The swan was the crest of Edward the Third, his great-great-grandfather.

Northampton, where, as a chronicler says, "ten thousand tall Englishmen were slain, and King Henry, left all lonely and disconsolate, was taken prisoner." The Duke of Buckingham and the son of the "good dogge" Talbot were killed.

Margaret and the prince escaped to Harlech Castle, in Wales, where the Welsh people took every possible care of them; and when she went away to Scotland, they sung a wild song called "Farwel iti Peggy bau," in remembrance of her going. If you ever go into Wales, you can ask any Welsh harper to play you this song in remembrance of the brave and unhappy queen, Margaret of Anjou.

The Duke of York carried Henry a prisoner to London. Going in state to the House of Lords, he walked up to the throne, and laid his hand on it, expecting the lords to ask him to take possession of it as king—but they said nothing. After a time, the dead silence was broken by some of them asking him to visit the king at his palace. York, who was disappointed by their cold silence, said angrily that no one had so good a right to be visited as himself. He made Henry send for the queen and prince to London; and Margaret obeyed more quickly than the duke expected. She came like a lioness, with a gallant and devoted army, and appeared before the gates of York, defying the duke to meet her in the field, and taunting him with being beaten by a woman. The duke was so angry at her taunts, that, in spite of all his friends could say, he would go out with an army much less than the queen's; and at Wakefield he lost a bloody battle, in which he himself and a great many of his followers were killed.

Every body had by this time become fierce and savage; and at the battle of Wakefield such shocking things were done by Margaret's friends as make one shudder to read of. After the battle, Lord Clifford met an old priest flying across the fields,

The death of the Duke of York at the Battle of Wakefield

with a very handsome boy, who was beautifully dressed. Clifford asked the boy who he was; and the priest answered that he was Lord Rutland, the Duke of York's second son. "Then," said the fierce Clifford, "as thy father slew mine, so will I slay thee and all thy kin!" and he stabbed him to the heart with his dagger, and bade the old priest go and tell his mother what had happened to her son. The next thing Clifford did was to cut off the Duke of York's head, and to stick it on a lance, with a paper crown upon it. When he had done this, he took it to Margaret with these words: "Madam, your war is done; here is your king's ransom."

Margaret shuddered when she saw the bleeding and

ghastly head of her enemy, and turned away her head. But war and bloodshed make the gentlest and kindest natures cruel; and when the Lancastrian nobles begged of her to look at the head of him who had so dishonored her husband and her son, she looked and laughed at it, as they did, and then ordered them to stick it over the gates of York upon a spear.

Margaret went to London after the bloody battle of Wakefield, and won another battle at Barnet Heath; after which, to her great joy, she rejoined the poor king, who embraced her and the prince with transports of delight, for he never expected to see them again. If Margaret had controlled her passions then, and gone directly with calmness to London, these sad wars might have been ended, and Henry might have died king of England. But she was angry and indignant with the citizens of London, and she allowed her fierce northern soldiers to plunder and ravage all the country round Barnet in revenge.

They were so angry at this, in their turn, that they would not let her enter London, and she was obliged to retire to the north again. As soon as she was gone, Edward, the young Duke of York, with Warwick, took possession of London; and from that moment Edward was proclaimed king as Edward the Fourth, and Henry the Sixth's reign was ended, though his life of long and cruel martyrdom continued.

Chapter XXXIII.

End of the Red and White Rose

From 1461 to 1483

QUEEN MARGARET only seemed to grow braver and more resolute as her misfortunes increased. She fled to the north, and raised another large army. Edward the Fourth hastened after her, and a great battle was fought at Towton, which was the bloodiest of all the bloody battles that were fought in the wars of the Roses. Half of the Lancastrians remained dead on the field, and Edward was fixed more firmly on the throne.

Margaret then sailed to France, and asked King Louis to lend her some money; and when she came back she raised another army. The good king had been hiding himself all the winter in the caves and woods of the north of England, and was often nearly starved with hunger and cold.

The Yorkists met Margaret again at Hexham, and again the holy King Henry was forced to fly, and to hide in Lancashire. Margaret and the prince escaped; but as they were riding through the forests, they met a party of robbers, who robbed them of their rings and collars, and every thing valuable that they had. When they had taken their prize, they began to quarrel about dividing it; and while they were quarrelling, Margaret seized the prince by the hand, and ran away into the forest as fast as she could, and they could not catch her. But as they were running, they met another robber, who looked fiercer and stronger than those they had left; and Margaret knelt down at his feet, and asked him to save the Prince of Wales.

The robber was a kind-hearted man; and he took Margaret and the prince to his cave, and gave them food, and money to get to the Lancastrian camp.

The queen then determined to fly to Flanders; and after a great many dangers and adventures, she and the prince, with Dr. Morton, who was afterwards the Cardinal Archbishop of York, arrived at St. Pol, where her oldest enemy, Philip the Good, Duke of Burgundy, treated her with the greatest kindness and generosity. She then went on to her father's court.

In the meantime the saintly king was betrayed into the hands of his enemies, who were base enough to lead him into London as if he had been a thief or a murderer. He bore all their insults and taunts with the patience of a martyr; and they seemed only to fix his holy soul more firmly upon God.

Just when all hope seemed to be quite lost for the Red Rose, Warwick was accused of favoring Margaret; and as he would not obey the king and defend himself, he fled to France. All the Lancastrians then thought it was a good opportunity to make peace between him and Margaret; and this great baron, who played so extraordinary a part in the Rose wars, was invited to King Réné's court.

The end of the discussions and disputes was, that Warwick agreed to bring an army to help young Edward, and that the prince was betrothed to Warwick's daughter, the Lady Anne Neville.

It was a strange sight at Amboise on the day of that betrothing. For twenty years Warwick had been striving with his whole strength to rob Henry of his crown; and from the time of the Duke of Suffolk's murder, he had always shown the most bitter hatred to the queen. But now they stood together, side by side, before the altar, with Louis the Eleventh, and good King Réné and his queen, and all the banished Lancastrian lords; and the princely Edward and Lady Anne plighted their troth together in the presence of this strange assembly.

Warwick kept his word with Prince Edward. This time the "king-maker" did not change. While Edward the Fourth was, as usual, feasting and dancing, he heard that Warwick had returned, with the queen and prince, to England, and was marching with a large army against him.

The two forces met on Barnet-heath; but now even the king-maker's presence failed to bring triumph to the Red Rose. Poor King Henry was taken again; and the great Earl of Warwick himself was killed.

The unhappy queen fainted when she heard the sad news, and fled to Beaulieu Abbey. But the fiery young Somerset, and some other lords, went to her, and said they had another army to do battle in her cause.

This, which was Queen Margaret's only army, met King Edward at Tewksbury; and there, after her last most bloody battle, the unhappy queen and her brave son were taken prisoners, and carried to the king's camp. When they were brought before him, he asked the prince how he dared come

King Edward IV and his Yorkist troops are beseeched by a priest to stop the pursuit of their Lancastrian foes who have requested sanctuary from the abbey after the Battle of Tewkesbury.

to England against him, and the fearless young Plantagenet replied, "To recover my father's crown and my own inheritance."

At this answer the cowardly king brutally struck him on the face with his steel glove or gauntlet; and the lords who stood round him stabbed the brave boy with their daggers.

The unhappy Margaret burst out into the most frantic expressions of rage and sorrow; and Edward cruelly revenged himself by making her go in procession, with the poor young Princess of Wales, into London, where he lodged them both in the Tower.

That very same night he did a blacker deed still. The holy and gentle King Henry was put to death in the Tower by the Duke of Gloucester (Richard the Crook-backed), the king's brother. Henry had been a solitary prisoner there for five years; and his only companions were a few learned books and a bird, his oratory, and now and then a visit from his confessor. In this captivity he composed some touching lines, some of which I will write down here, that you may never forget the holy King Henry.

> "Kingdoms are but cares;
>   State is devoid of stay;
> Riches are ready snares,
>   And hasten to decay.
>
> Who meaneth to remove the rocke
>   Out of his slimy mud,
> Shall mire himself, and hardly 'scape
>   The swelling of the flood."
>
> "Patience is the armor and conquest of the godly;
> this meriteth mercy, when causeless is suffered sorrow."
>
> "Nought else is war but fury and madness,
> wherein is not advice, but rashness; not right,
> but rage ruleth and reigneth."

The body of the saintly king was carried to St. Paul's, through Cheapside, upon an open bier; and "there the silent witness of his blood, that welled from his fresh wounds upon the pavement," cried out against his foul murderers. When they came to Blackfriars the blood again flowed out, and this awful witness a second time bespoke the manner of his martyrdom.

That same evening the bloody hearse was put into a barge, and carried up the Thames to Chertsey Abbey, where he was silently buried. But the witness of God was with the holy martyr; and so many miracles were said to be performed at his tomb, that it was believed among the people that holy King Henry would be canonised.

It is said, indeed, that the process of his canonisation has been long begun.

King Henry VI

I am sure you will like to know what became of the brave and unhappy Queen Margaret. She went back to her good father's court, where sorrow worked such a change in her, that from being one of the most beautiful princesses in the world, she became quite dreadful to look at. She died when she was fifty-one years old, and was buried in the cathedral at Angers, where, until the French Revolution, the canons chanted in procession every year round her tomb.

The long sad story of the wars of the Roses is ended at last. But besides the interest which you will take, and which every one must take, in the great personages who make those wars quite like a romance, there is another thing you must understand. Besides liking to hear about holy King Henry and his brave and beautiful queen, the fiery Lord Somerset, the great and wise Cardinal Beaufort, and the wonderful "king-maker" Warwick, whose noble but capricious character seems to have been the hinge upon which all these miseries turned, it is right for you to understand the real reason of these cruel wars.

It was because the constitution of England had become changed from its original state, that the barons had gained such strength and power as to shake the throne. The monarchy, as you have been told, had become what is called an oligarchy, or the government of a few nobles; or rather there were two oligarchies, which broke out into war against one another. As long as the more warlike Plantagenet kings reigned, they had power to control these fierce barons, and to keep them at least within bounds. But when the gentle hand of Henry the Sixth took the reins, they broke loose; and it was because Margaret really endeavoured to restrain them in his stead that they hated her so much.

It needed all the seas of blood, which were poured out like water upon the English soil, to put down this destructive power. When the wars of the Roses were ended, the English barons found that their strength, as it had been, was for ever departed. Most of the great families had lost their heads; many had become altogether extinct; many were exiled or their estates confiscated; and thus, like Samson, in devoting all their strength to the last struggle, they perished in the effort. They destroyed themselves in overthrowing the Plantagenet line.

There is very little more to say about Edward the Fourth.

He was very handsome and merry, and was fond of fighting, and fine shows, and eating and drinking. He was clever, and had a warm and affectionate heart; but he gave himself up so entirely to pleasure, that he never did his duty as a king.

Edward married an English lady called Elizabeth Woodville, who had a very brave and good brother named Lord Rivers. He was one of the first gentlemen who improved printing in England; and one of the most celebrated printers then living, named Caxton, was his printer, and used to consult Lord Rivers about all the improvements he was making.

Edward had two brothers, George Duke of Clarence and Richard Duke of Gloucester. Clarence was foolish and vain, and Gloucester crafty, deceitful, and wicked. While Edward was enjoying himself, he let this bad duke do as he pleased; and he persuaded the king to do very cruel actions. One of them was to send the Duke of Clarence to the Tower, where it is said he was drowned in a butt of Malmsey wine. It is not quite certain whether he was drowned in it or not; but Clarence was very fond of drinking; and the Duke of Gloucester had a butt of Malmsey taken into his room, where it is most probable that Clarence drank till he killed himself.

At last Edward the Fourth died; for he had eaten and drunk and amused himself so much, that he had no more strength left.

Chapter XXXIV.

The Hunchback, and the End of the Plantagenets
A.D. 1483

EDWARD IV. had two little sons, Edward the Prince of Wales, who now became Edward the Fifth, and the little Duke of York, who was only eleven years old. Edward the Fifth was a very handsome and spirited boy, who was brought up by his uncle, the good Lord Rivers, in Wales; but as soon as his father died, his other uncle, the Duke of Gloucester, said that he must be brought to London. Lord Rivers was very sorry to let him go, for he distrusted the duke; but he was obliged to send him. The duke, who, as he was humpbacked, was always called Crookbacked Richard, next pretended that the little king wanted a playfellow; and he sent the Archbishop of Canterbury to Westminster Abbey to ask the queen to send the Duke of York to be with him; for Elizabeth had fled to the sanctuary there, for fear of

Crookbacked Richard.

When the Archbishop came, the poor queen said that she thought some other boy might be found to play with Edward; and that she much feared to send the Duke of York to his cruel uncle. When the Archbishop urged her to trust the lord protector, she said she would trust *him* (the Archbishop), and that she would give up her son. But she cried very much, and kissed him a great many times; and they led the poor little duke away, crying too so bitterly, that every one had tears in their eyes, who looked on at this sad sight.

Children of Edward IV by Jozef Simmier

When Crookbacked Richard had lodged both his nephews safely in the Tower, he next accused the good Lord Rivers of rebellion; and, before he could defend himself, he had him put to death at Pontefract Castle. Then he called a council at the Tower, and said that Edward the Fifth should be crowned. But he only pretended this, to find out if he could safely declare himself king. One day, while the council was sitting, Richard came in very angrily, and said he had found out that a great many traitors were trying to take away his life, and asked what they deserved. "If they have done so," replied Lord Hastings, "they deserve death."

"*If!* Dost thou answer me with *ifs?*" shouted out Gloucester; "by St. Paul, I will not dine till thy head is off!"

And he sent for his soldiers directly, and they took Lord Hastings down to the court-yard, and chopped off his head upon a block which they found there.

Crookbacked Richard had long been wishing to get rid of this good Lord Hastings, who was one of Edward's chief friends; and now he was dead, he set about another murder blacker still.

He went away to his castle in Yorkshire, and ordered Sir James Tyrrell to go to London, and murder the young princes in the Tower. Sir James went to the governor of the Tower, Sir Robert Brakenbury, and asked him to help him. Sir Robert said he would have nothing to do with such a shocking deed; but he gave up to Sir James his keys. Sir James then sent his own groom, Dighton, and another ruffian named Forest, to the king's room, where the two innocent boys lay asleep in bed. One of the ruffians was softened at the sight, and said he could not bear to kill such pretty creatures; but the other called him a coward; so, as the princes lay, they covered them with the bed-clothes and pillows till they were stifled and quite dead. They then went and fetched Sir James to look at them, who ordered them to be buried at the foot of the stairs, under a great heap of stones.

Their wicked uncle was very glad when he heard of their murder; but he ordered that they should be buried in consecrated ground. When some workmen were repairing part of the Record Office many years after, they found some bones under the stairs; and as the Record Office had been the chapel of the Tower before the Reformation, every one knew at once that these were the bones of poor little Edward the Fifth and his brother the Duke of York.

1483 to 1485. The wicked Hunchback was now King Richard the Third. He married the poor Princess of Wales, Lady Ann Neville (formerly wife of Edward, son of Henry VI and Margaret of Anjou), who hated him, but who was forced to marry him. Besides his wickedness, Richard must

King Richard III

have been a monster of ugliness. He was born with teeth, and with a long bushy head of hair. One of his shoulders was much higher than the other, and both of them were up to his ears. He was always restless and impatient too, so that his rolling eyes were never still; and he was always on the watch, thinking that some one was plotting mischief against him.

But though he was unkind to his wife, Richard was very fond of his son, whom he had had carefully educated, and upon whom he heaped all kinds of honors. This boy, for whom he had committed such dreadful crimes, died suddenly; and Richard was distracted with grief. "*There is no peace to the wicked.*" And, Richard's reign was full of trouble. His greatest friend was the Duke of Buckingham, who was as proud and ambitious as himself; and who had helped him in all his wicked actions. When Richard was crowned, Buckingham envied him; and from envying him, he began to plot against him; and at last Richard had him arrested and put to death.

The plots, however, still continued. They were all made in favor of Henry Richmond, whose mother was the great-granddaughter of John of Gaunt. His father was a son of Katherine the Fair, the widow of Henry the Fifth, who, after the king's death, had married a Welsh gentleman named Owen Tudor; and who was thus the founder of one of the most remarkable of the English line of kings.

Although Buckingham was dead, Bishop Morton was still alive. He had fled to Flanders after Margaret of Anjou left England; and there he wrote to Henry Richmond, and to Buckingham, and to the other English nobles who hated the crook-backed usurper Richard.

At last their plans were ready, and Richmond landed in Wales, when a number of gentlemen met him, and joined his army. When Richard heard of his coming, he was very much agitated. His eyes rolled more fiercely, and he never left off the secret armor which he had for a long time worn. But as he was very brave, he put the crown upon his head over his helmet, and went with a great army to meet Henry, whom he found near Bosworth in Leicestershire.

The night before the battle of Bosworth, as Richard lay in his tent, his guilty conscience brought before him all the black crimes of his life. He went back in thought to the bloody battle of Tewksbury, where he had been the first to stab the brave young Edward of Lancaster with his dagger; he thought of the gentle holy Henry, whom he had murdered in the Tower; and perhaps the last patient words of the royal martyr came back to his mind; probably a few short words of holy prayer, and a warning to himself. He thought then of the two innocent princes, whom he had so often promised to take care of; of the Duke of Clarence, of Lord Hastings, of Lord Rivers, and of Buckingham. All these he had murdered, to gain that worthless golden circlet upon his helmet.

He thought then of the punishment of these crimes; and his remorse became so unbearable, that he started up, sobbing and crying out; and when his guards came in, they found him standing in the middle of his tent, pale and trembling, with his drawn sword in his hand.

The next day his own nobles surrounded Richard in the battle, and overpowered him with wounds. But he died, as he had said he would, *with the crown upon his head, and King of England.*

Sir William Stanley took the crown, and putting it upon Richmond's head upon the field of battle, cried out, "Long live Henry the Seventh!" and all the soldiers saluted Henry Tudor Richmond as their king.

Chapter XXXV.

The First Tudor
From 1485 to 1509

HENRY VII was a very wise and cautious king. He was quiet and calm in his manners; and his fair hair and grave blue eyes were very unlike the dark restless face of Crookbacked Richard.

The first thing he did was wise. He knew that the nobles who had put him on the throne might put him off again if he allowed them to get too much power and to do as they pleased. He knew that although Richard was such a monster as a man, still he had been a very prudent and a very wise king, and had ruled the country extremely well. A great part of England, especially the north, was attached to him because he was of the House of York, and a Plantagenet, and the people were sorry that that great and splendid race of kings was come to an end.

Henry knew all this very well. He sent therefore to Elizabeth, Edward the Fourth's daughter, and asked her to marry him. Since, as she was the chief head of the White

Rose party, and as he was the chief head of the Red Rose party, he knew that by marrying her the two parties would be joined, and that no one would think any more about the wars of the Roses.

The wedding of Henry VII and Elizabeth of York
World History Archive/Alamy Stock Photo

So he married Elizabeth, and there were great rejoicings and feasts all over the country; and when Henry had a little son born, the joy was greater still. The little prince was named Arthur, and he became a very clever boy.

Henry did one thing that was very cruel. The Duke of Clarence, whose death had been caused or contrived by Crookbacked Richard, had a son, who was made Earl of Warwick. He was a simple, half-witted boy, who usually behaved more like a baby than any thing else. But some of the English lords, who were still restless and dissatisfied, said that this poor boy should be king; and they were always making plots and disturbances about him.

First they thought he had been murdered, and they wanted to find out the truth; so they brought a poor boy from Ireland, who was very like him, and they said he was Lord Warwick, and that he was the rightful heir to the crown. Some foolish people joined the friends of this boy, who was named Lambert Simnel, and gave Henry a good deal of trouble.

But he was soon taken prisoner; and when Henry found that he was a harmless, simple boy, he made him a turnspit in his kitchen, and afterwards a falconer, or man who takes care of falcons for hawking.

But there was another pretender after Simnel, who gave Henry a great deal more trouble. This was a young man named Perkin Warbeck, a Fleming, who pretended to be the brother of Edward the Fifth, that little Duke of York who was murdered in the Tower.

Perkin went to the Duchess of Burgundy, who was aunt to the real Duke of York, and said that he was her nephew. He was a very handsome, pleasing young man, and spoke very well. The Duchess thought, or said she thought, that he really was her nephew. She called him the White Rose of England and gave him some money and soldiers. He landed in England and managed to get an army together to fight against Henry; and he went to the Scottish court, where the king married him to his own cousin, Lady Catherine Gordon.

King Henry was sadly vexed by these disturbances, which lasted for seven years. But at last Perkin Warbeck was taken, and hanged at Tyburn.

It was then that Henry did the cruel action spoken of before. He thought there would be no peace as long as the Earl of Warwick lived; so he brought the poor innocent child out of the Tower, where he had been a long time a melancholy prisoner, and had him put to death.

Perkin Warbeck's widow, poor Lady Catherine Gordon, was the only person who was sorry for his death. King Henry treated her very kindly. He sent for her to the court, where she lived a long time as one of Queen Elizabeth's ladies, and afterwards married an English gentleman.

Henry seems never to have been so happy after Lord Warwick's death. His dear son Arthur, who was one of the most pious and learned princes that have ever lived, died suddenly; and the good queen died too, soon afterwards. Henry was very unhappy at her death, and it had a very bad effect upon his character: he became more reserved and crafty than ever, and grew very fond of money.

But although he had these great faults, Henry the Seventh's reign was a very important one for England. He was always watching the nobles, and restraining their wars and disputes with one another; and for this purpose, he forbade them to keep more than a certain quantity of retainers or soldiers. He encouraged them to spend their money in fine pageants and shows instead of on soldiers and armor; and by these means, by degrees, he changed the great feudal barons into temperate and useful nobles, who supported the monarchy without being able to overpower it and put it in danger.

This change, and the steady improvement in the customs and constitution of the House of Commons, were the solid fruit of Henry the Seventh's reign.

This led to another very good thing, which might have been the greatest blessing to England if it had not been seized upon by Satan, and turned into evil. As there was now peace, and time was no longer taken up in quarrelling and fighting, the English nobles and gentlemen began to think about learning. Magdalen College was just finished at Oxford; and Henry sent his nephews to the University to learn Latin and Greek. Now that there was time to think about these things, it was found that the English gentlemen were much more ignorant than the scholars of other Universities, and every one was ashamed to discover how little Greek was known in England.

There was one very learned man, whom we shall know more about by and by. His name was Sir Thomas More, and he was one of the wisest and cleverest, as well as the holiest, men of his time. He understood Greek very well, and he wrote a great many books, and often asked some learned friends from other countries to come and see him. Among these was Erasmus, a Dutch gentleman, who was a very famous scholar.

There were two other great scholars besides: Dean Colet, who was Dean of St. Paul's, and Thomas Linacre, a physician, who went to Italy to study. When he came back, he went to teach Greek at Oxford, and he soon had a great many good scholars of his own.

He was tutor to Prince Arthur as long as the prince lived, and built the College of Physicians in London. All these learned men did a great deal of good.

The art of printing was a great help to these learned men. You remember that the good Lord Rivers, whom Crookbacked Richard put to death, had a printer named Caxton. After Caxton there were a good many other ingenious printers;

and they helped to print the learned books which had been kept with such care in the monasteries, but which the nobles had been, for the most part, too ignorant to care for, and too busy to think about.

Besides learning Latin and Greek, there were a great many things for the English gentlemen to think about. Larger ships were built, and some daring and brave men began to make longer voyages. Christopher Columbus came to Henry, and asked him to give him some ships to discover a new westward route to the Far East.

Henry was too avaricious to give him any money, so he lost the great kingdom which he might have gained, for Columbus sailed soon afterwards from Spain and discovered America. Henry was very sorry then that he had not listened to Columbus, and he sent another brave sailor, named Sebastian Cabot, an Italian, to Newfoundland and Florida. A number of strange plants and birds were then brought to England, among which were potatoes and turkeys.

Henry sent for some good sculptors and painters from Italy to teach the English painting and sculpture by showing them good models. His own monument, and Queen Elizabeth's, was made by one of these, named Torregiano. It is in the beautiful chapel which Henry built in Westminster Abbey, and which I hope you will go and see some day. It is still called Henry the Seventh's Chapel, and is a most beautiful example of that kind of Gothic architecture which was called Tudor, from being adopted when the Tudors became kings of England.

At last Henry the Seventh fell very sick. He was twenty-seven hours in his death-agony, and suffered very much. He had taken a great deal of money unjustly from his subjects, and they did not love him. He was very reserved and crafty, so that no one ever knew what he really thought. For this reason, very few of the nobles loved him—they never knew what he was going to do.

His greatest and firmest friend was Cardinal Archbishop Morton, his chancellor. He was that Dr. Morton who had fled out of England with Margaret of Anjou, and who had turned his troubles and trials to good account in many ways. He was one of the wisest and most sagacious ministers that ever advised the king of England.

Sir Thomas More, who was brought up in his household, says of him, that "he was of a middle stature, not broken with age; his looks begot reverence rather than fear; his conversation was easy, but serious and grave; he spoke both gracefully and weightily; he was eminently skilled in the law; had a vast understanding and a prodigious memory. From his youth he had been all along practiced in affairs; and having passed through many traverses of fortune, he had with great cost acquired a vast stock of wisdom, which is not soon lost when it is purchased so dear."

Henry the Seventh was buried in Westminster Abbey, in his own beautiful chapel, and the magnificent monument of Torregiano was raised over the first Tudor king of England. You must try to distinguish the different races of our kings, because, besides the interest you have in themselves, they have each had a very different influence on our country, and their own peculiar character gave a different character to their people.

Henry the Seventh had *finished* the work which the Wars of the Roses had begun, of lowering the power of the nobles. He had *begun* another work, which afterwards, under another line, brought about another dreadful civil war—I mean, the increasing and strengthening the power of the monarchy; which afterwards became unjust and oppressive in its turn, just as the power of the nobles or aristocracy had been unjust and oppressive under the Norman kings.

The Plantagenets were often cruel and tyrannical themselves, and upon impulse, but they had always great and splendid qualities, which we cannot help admiring. They were a noble and a princely race of kings.

The Tudors were cruel and unjust from policy, and by calculation. They planned and designed whatever cruel actions they did, and hid their designs from every one. They were wise and clever, but had no greatness or generosity of character. They were a useful race of kings in many things, but we could never admire or love them.

Engraved portrait of King Henry VII (1457-1509) King of England and the first Tudor monarch. Dated 15th Century. World History Archive/Alamy Stock Photo

Chapter XXXVI.

The Splendid Chancellor

From 1509 to 1530

HENRY VII. had another son, a little younger than Arthur, whose name was Henry. He had two daughters as well: Mary, who married Louis the Twelfth, the king of France, and Margaret, who married the king of Scotland. Young Henry became king after his father's death.

Henry the Eighth began his reign with every prospect of doing a great deal of good to England. He was very much beloved by the people for his frank, noble-looking face and kind manners. He was very pious, and heard several Masses every day, and was charitable to the poor. He married his brother Arthur's wife, Katherine of Aragon, about whom I must tell you something. Katherine was the daughter of the greatest and best of all the sovereigns of Spain, Ferdinand of Castile and Isabel of Aragon, and was born and brought up in that holy and lovely country, in the enchanting Moorish palace of the Alhambra. It must have seemed very sad to her to come to England, where the people were so rude and barbarous, and thought of nothing but fighting, and childish

Catherine of Aragon, attributed to Johannes Corvus

pageants, which often ended in good rough blows.

Katherine had several sons, but they all died, and only one daughter remained alive. Henry was very much disappointed at this; and he became less kind to Katherine, and he did not lead so good a life as he had done before. The queen, who was very pious and sensible, behaved with the greatest sweetness and kindness to him, and continued to attend to all her religious duties and to her studies, in which she took great delight.

But after some time, Henry grew more and more passionate and capricious; and he at last determined to get rid of Katherine altogether, that he might marry a beautiful young lady named Anne Boleyn. He asked all his ministers and the clergy of England, and wrote to consult the Pope about this divorce, for he pretended that his conscience was always in trouble about marrying his brother's wife.

This was a sadly hypocritical pretence to indulge his passions, but as he was a very powerful king, he found many men who listened to him and who did not tell him the truth.

Henry's favorite minister at that time was Cardinal Wolsey. He was the son of a butcher at Ipswich; but his talents were so great that he had been sent to Oxford, where he made a wonderful advance in his studies. He was then ordained, and sent into the household of Bishop Fox, of Winchester, where the king saw him, and made him his almoner. Wolsey was very clever and agreeable, and the king became so fond of him that he could do nothing without asking his advice. He made him first a Bishop, then Archbishop of York, and the Pope made him a Cardinal. He had a great many houses and lands, and never went out without a grand train of servants and followers all dressed in scarlet, with crosses, and banners, and great silver pillars.

Every thing that Cardinal Wolsey did was magnificent. He built the college of Christ Church at Oxford, which is one of the most beautiful buildings of its kind in the world. He built Hampton Court, a splendid palace, for himself. But when the king said to him one day, "Why this is indeed a royal palace!" he replied, "It is then worthy of its royal owner," and he made a present of it to the king.

Wolsey was chancellor as well as a Cardinal and an

Archbishop. Notwithstanding all the load of business he had upon his hands, he constantly sat in the Lord Chancellor's court, heard and decided the law-suits that were brought before him, and, as a modern and Protestant Lord Chancellor[20] gives witness, justice was never better or more completely administered than under Cardinal Wolsey. Besides all this, he encouraged learning and the arts, and established a number of the higher and finer kinds of trades.

While Cardinal Wolsey was Henry the Seventh's chaplain, he had sent him once on a very important message to the Emperor Maximilian of Germany, who was near Calais. Wolsey set off as fast as he could, and gave his message so quickly, that when he came back and was going to say Mass for the king, he was displeased at seeing him, for he thought he had not yet set out.

When he heard that he had seen the emperor, and had besides settled something which was very important that he had not been told to do, and which it required great cleverness to settle so well, the king was very much astonished at his learning and quickness at knowing how to do so well what he had never been taught.

And now that you know this much about Cardinal Wolsey, you will understand why Henry the Eighth asked him above every one else to help him to marry Anne Boleyn.

The Cardinal loved the king very much, and he loved his state and dignity too; and I am sorry to say that he forgot for a time that his duty towards God was the first thing. He tried to help the king to send away the good holy Queen Katherine. All the courtiers in England were against her, because they were afraid of the king; but the people, who loved Katherine dearly, were very angry, and they said they

---

[20] Lord Campbell, *Lives of the Chancellors of England*.

would stone Henry if he sent her away.

The Pope was looking on all this time, and he sent a legate named Cardinal Campeggio to England, to see that justice was done to the queen. When Cardinal Campeggio came, the wicked king prepared in great state a court in London, and he sat on one throne with his lawyers before him, and Queen Katherine sat on another throne with her lawyers by her; and the two Cardinals, Wolsey and Campeggio, sat before them. Then the crier cried out, "Henry, King of England, come into court," and Henry spoke first, very hypocritically, about his conscience, and the trouble it gave him for marrying his brother's wife.

When he had done, the crier cried out, "Katherine, Queen of England, come into court," and then the noble and holy queen got up, and threw herself at the king's feet. She spoke very beautifully, and said that as she was a foreigner and a stranger, she hoped the king would take pity on her. She blamed Cardinal Wolsey very much, and spoke so indignantly to him that he was quite ashamed. She said that he had treated her badly, because her nephew (the Emperor Charles the Fifth) would not make him Pope. When she had done speaking, she went away out of the court, and though the king called her back, she would not come.

But the wicked king sent away good Queen Katherine, and she went to live at Ampthill, near London. He would not let her see her little girl, nor go to see her himself. He wanted her to say that she was not his lawful wife, and she would not— and this made him like a raging wild beast.

Cardinal Wolsey was so sorry for what he had done against the queen, that he would not help the king any longer, and then the king sent him away too, and banished him to Yorkshire, where he lived in his own diocese, and did a great deal of good. But the king was not satisfied with disgracing him; he wanted to kill him as well. So he sent for him to London, and the Cardinal set out directly to obey his master, whom he still loved.

But as he went along, he felt that his health was gone. Grief and trouble had broken down that great and powerful spirit, which once seemed as if nothing was too great for it to master. When he got to Leicester, he went to the monastery; and at the gate, he said to the Abbot, "Father Abbot, I am come to lay my bones among you." He was laid in bed; and after receiving the last Sacraments, he died in great contrition.

Nearly the last words he said were to commend himself to the king, his royal master; and then he uttered those most true words, which will always be remembered: "Oh! if I had served my God as faithfully as I have served my king, He would not now have left me in these straits."

The arrival of Wolsey at Leicester from the painting by Sir John Gilbert.

Chapter XXXVII.

The Holy Chancellor
From 1529 to 1546

We must now stop a little while in our history; because you must hear about some very sad and important things that were going on in some other parts of Europe. You know very well that in the early ages of the Church, when people had committed great crimes, they had heavy penances given to them, that were called *canonical* penances, or penances according to the canon. Afterwards, these penances were remitted for certain prayers and devotions, which, if said in the right dispositions remitted the temporal punishment due for the sin, just as the canonical penances had remitted it. And as this was done by the mercy and *indulgence* of the Church, these remissions were called *Indulgences*.

When the Popes Julius II. and Leo X. were building St. Peter's at Rome, they wanted money very much to finish it with; and amongst other ways, they granted *Indulgences* to all who would help in this pious work. They sent a Dominican friar to dispense these indulgences, and to receive the money in return for St. Peter's. There had long been a kind of jealousy or rivalry between the Augustinian monks and the Dominican friars, which always leads to mischief, and at this time was turned by Satan to very sad evils. The vicar of the Augustinians in Germany employed one of his young monks to write against the manner in which the Dominicans were dispensing the indulgences; and as this young monk was clever, ambitious, and very bold, he went a great deal farther than his vicar told him, and wrote, not only against the friars, but against indulgences too. The monk's name was Martin Luther.

He wrote a number of short propositions called *theses*, which he fastened to the door of the church at Wittenburg, and which were all intended to show that there were a great many abuses in the Church, and that the See of Rome was altogether wrong. There were certainly at that time a great many sad abuses in the Church, which several Popes had been laboring to amend by calling a General Council. They died without obtaining this end; but you know that abuses in the Church can never make the Church itself wrong.

And Leo X was now engaged in building St. Peter's, and encouraging the new desire for learning, which had sprung up with greater ardour in beautiful and learned Italy than any where else. You will understand this better when you read of the learned men in Italy who were doing all they could to devote their talents and their energies to the service of God, in restoring the fervour of piety and the practice of every virtue. You must learn to know the names of some of them. Among these were, Luigi Priuli, Sadolet, Cardinal Bembo, Cardinal Contarini, and the Colonnas. Priuli was a great friend of Henry the Eighth's cousin, Cardinal Pole, the grandson of the poor Duke of Clarence who was murdered in the Tower. All these great and good men often met together in the gardens of a villa at Venice, to talk about the state of the Church, the sad heresies which were springing up, and their hopes of a General Council. They not only talked, for they did a very great deal towards obtaining that Council, about which we shall hear by and by.

It was a time of great and wonderful events every where. In the very same year that Martin Luther went away from the Diet at Worms to write against the Church, St. Ignatius Loyola went to the cave of Manresa, where he wrote his Spiritual Exercises and prepared himself for that perpetual crusade against heresy, which will never end as long as one Jesuit remains in the world.

The Elector Frederic of Germany and Charles the Fifth helped to keep Luther from being punished as he ought to have been at first, and this made him more bold and bad than ever. He promised over and over again to submit to the Pope; but when the Pope wrote, he would not submit; so he became only more and more obstinate.

It was a very unfortunate thing that the Bishops in Germany were at that time nearly all secular princes as well as Bishops, and they neglected their duties, and lived like noblemen. This made the clergy neglect their duty too, so that they had become very bad. When the people saw this, and heard Luther say continually that he only wished to restore the Church to her purity, they thought he must be right, and that the Bishops wanted to punish him, so that they might go on living as they did.

Instead of being obedient and docile, as they ought to be, the people thus began to judge of matters with which they had no concern, and to give their opinions. The mischief was helped by the art of printing, which was now brought to great perfection. You remember that we said before that Satan afterwards turned this beautiful art to evil, and it was now that he did so. Books were written by all kinds of bad and ignorant men and were read by the common people with the greatest eagerness; and so they learned to wish to judge of all these high and difficult matters.

They were like children who had stolen the keys of the store-room, and who were making themselves sick with all kinds of improper food.

Henry the Eighth at first said he would defend the Church against Luther, and he wrote a very clever book against his theses, for which the Pope gave him the title of *Defender of the Faith*. But when, soon after, the Pope wrote to him, and told him to send away Anne Boleyn, and to live with Katherine again, he was so furious, that he roared like a wild beast and vowed that he would be revenged. It was then that Cardinal Wolsey's former secretary, Thomas Cromwell, gave him the wicked advice which threw England into schism. He asked the king why he obeyed the Pope, and said that there might be a separate Church made in England, and that the king ought to be the head of it.

Henry was wicked enough to listen only to his furious passions. He sent to Cranmer to propose to all the Bishops that *he* should be supreme head of the Church in England, and ordered them to accept this on pain of his displeasure.

It will make you very sorry to hear that many of them did as the king bade them. The very saddest of all the sad things that happened then in England was the apostacy of so many of her Bishops. They thought more of the king's anger, which could only kill their bodies, than of the wrath of Almighty God. One of them, however, refused to sign the proposal with indignation. This was the saintly Bishop Fisher, who had been Henry's tutor. Sir Thomas More would not sign the proposal either, and as he was so wise, and learned, and good, that every one, not only in England, but in all Europe, looked up to him, Henry was very angry indeed. He ordered that Bishop Fisher and Sir Thomas More should be taken to prison.

Sir Thomas More was the son of one of the judges in the King's Bench; and when he was quite a child he was taken into the household of Cardinal Morton, who, you know, was Henry the Seventh's best minister and friend.

The wise and sagacious Cardinal was very fond of the little More, who was a *very* graceful, accomplished, and witty child, besides being very pious and prudent. While he was there, he used to be very fond of acting in dramas and plays; and his quickness and readiness of reply, and his true and original genius, showed what he would be. Often while he was waiting on his master and the nobles who were with him, as a page, the Cardinal used to say, "Whoever lives to see it, will find this child a marvellous man."

It was a great advantage to a boy to be brought up in this way in a Cardinal's household, as was then the custom. There were very few books and no newspapers but in the conversation of the prelate, his foreign connections, and the learned and distinguished men of the time, a great deal more could be learned than by the pert shallow writings of a later time.

More listened in modest silence to what he heard, behaving himself with the reverence and docility which the rank and dignity of the prelate inspired, and he treasured up all that he had learned. When he was eighteen, the Cardinal sent him to Oxford, where he studied with the greatest ardour. He wished very much to become a Franciscan monk, but his father told him that he must be a lawyer instead.

More was very sorry for this, but he obeyed his father. He left his dear Oxford, his Latin and Greek, and his learned tutor, Grocyn, and went to be entered at Lincoln's Inn. All the time he was reading law, which is very hard work of itself, he fasted very rigorously, wore a hair-shirt, and regularly took the discipline, besides sleeping always upon a bench. He used to go very often to hear his confessor preach (Dean Colet), and to see the Carthusians, whom he loved very dearly. When you go to London, you must ask to see the Charter-House, which was then a Carthusian abbey, and it was near there that More went to lodge.

Sir Thomas More by Han Holbein the Younger

When he had read for some time, he began to give lectures, and was very much pleased to see his old tutor Grocyn among the crowds who came to hear his lectures. As soon as More was known, every one wanted to engage him as their counsel. But, ready as he was to help them, he never would undertake what he thought was an unjust cause. If he thought it was unjust, he gave it up at once. He was most ready to help the poor, and those who had no other friends, and he spent his time rather upon them than upon men who could have flattered and praised him.

When he found that his father absolutely forbade him to enter Religion, he determined to settle in his profession as a lawyer, and to marry, and if he could not lead the best life, he might become a good and useful member of society. He married and had a house at Chelsea, where he brought up his large family. He had several daughters, who were really learned, as he had a tutor for his little girls, who taught them Latin and Greek, so that they could read and write and speak both these languages. You may see by this how much the English were improved in learning since Thomas Linacre's time. Sir Thomas used to study with his children and to talk with them about their books. Even at dinner, he had some pious or useful book read aloud, that no time might be wasted or given to the appetite merely.

A great many learned friends used to come to the happy villa at Chelsea, and amongst them was Erasmus, the Dutch gentleman whom we spoke of before. Poor Erasmus was very unhappy. He tried to think that every body was right—the Pope, and Luther, and Sir Thomas More himself. Sir Thomas tried many times to show him that truth was *one*, and that the Church could not be wrong, even when some of the fathers of the Church *seemed* to contradict one another. Erasmus was too weak to act with the courage which it required to have to fight against heresy. Sometimes he wrote for the Pope, and sometimes for Luther, and so with all his learning, he was despised by both sides, and was never happy. Though as long as he lived, he used to write to Sir Thomas More and come to Chelsea to see him.

Whenever Sir Thomas went away from home, even for a few days, he used to make his children write to him and tell him about their lessons. And as they loved him so dearly, you may suppose what pains they took to get on, that they might please him. You will like to hear a letter that he wrote to them all, once when he was away from home, which will show you how this great and learned Chancellor fulfilled his duties as a father in the very least particulars.

"*Thomas More to his whole School.*

You see what a device I have found to save paper, and avoid the labor of writing all your names. But although you are all so dear to me, that if I had named one, I must have named all the rest, yet there is no appellation under which you appear dearer to me than that of scholar. The tie of learning seems almost to bind you to me more powerfully than even the tie of nature. I am glad, therefore, that Mr. Drue[21] is again safely returned to you, as you know I had some reason to be anxious about him. If I did not love you so much, I should envy you the happiness of having so many and such excellent masters. I understand Mr. Nicholas is also with you, and that you are, with his assistance, making such prodigious progress in astronomy, as not only to know the Pole-star and the Dog, and such other common constellations, but even, with a skill which

---

[21] The tutor

bespeaks truly accomplished astronomers, to be able to distinguish the Sun from the Moon. Go on, then, with this new and wonderful science, by which you ascend to the stars; and while you diligently consider them with your eyes, let this holy season of Lent remind you of the sacred hymn of Boethius, which teaches you to raise your minds also to heaven; lest while your eyes are lifted up to the skies, your souls should grovel among brutes. Adieu, my dearest children."

This holy and happy household could not remain undisturbed by the miseries of those sad times. When the king was trying every means he could think of to send away his good queen Katherine, he wished very much to get Sir Thomas More to take his part; but Sir Thomas said that he had nothing to do with such matters, and he could not think of giving any opinion. This made the tyrannical king very angry.

Cardinal Wolsey was angry too, because this question disturbed his ambitious plans, by which he hoped to be made Pope. His anger led to several circumstances which show us what a clever, witty man Sir Thomas was. One day, in the Privy Council, the Cardinal proposed to have a high-constable in England, and because he proposed it, every body else agreed to it except Sir Thomas, who spoke last. When his turn came, he gave such good reasons against making this office, that the other noblemen agreed with him. The Cardinal was very angry, and he asked Sir Thomas rudely how he could be such a fool as to set himself against all the wise men of the king's council? Sir Thomas More quietly replied, "Thanks be to God, that the king's Majesty hath but one fool in his right honorable Council!"

Another time the Cardinal came into the House of

Commons in great state, with his silver pillars and Cardinal's hat, and asked the Commons for a large grant of money for the king. The Commons were very much surprised, and were angry too, and they did not answer a single word. The Cardinal then grew angry as well, and asked Sir Thomas More, who was speaker, what they meant. Sir Thomas got up very politely, and said that he was sorry they were so rude, but he thought they must be quite amazed at the appearance of such an extraordinary personage. This quiet and sagacious answer made the Cardinal so angry that he said hastily, "Would to God you had been at Home, Mr. More, when I made you speaker!"

"Your Grace not offended, so would I too," was the witty answer, "for then I should have seen an ancient and famous city, which I have long desired to see."

But neither the Cardinal's anger, nor the king's, which was even much more terrible, made the slightest difference in Sir Thomas More. He knew the full value of honors and riches and pleasure, and he despised them all. When the king tried to flatter him into approving of his wicked conduct towards the Pope and towards his queen, Sir Thomas stayed away from court. And when the king, in a fury, ordered him to be sent to prison, he went with a light heart, because he had a good and pure conscience.

In prison Sir Thomas More was so badly treated that he had no clothes to wear nor food to eat; and if his favorite daughter, Margaret Roper, had not brought him some food, he would have been starved. Margaret, who was very like her father, came every day to see him, and it was his greatest comfort to talk to her.

At last the king ordered Bishop Fisher to be put to death. The Pope had sent him a Cardinal's hat, and when the savage king heard of it, he said, "Paul may send him a hat; but he shall have no head to wear it on." Then he had this saintly Bishop brought out and beheaded.

Sir Thomas More was to die next. When he was on the scaffold, he said he felt obliged now to declare, that the oath which the king wished the Bishops and nobles to take to him, as head of the Church, was unlawful and wrong. He told the lords who had condemned him, that he hoped they would be like St. Paul, who first helped to stone St. Stephen, and then became converted.

The lords told him that the king had been so good as to allow him to be beheaded instead of being hanged, and he said, "May God preserve my friends from all such favors!" The executioner shed tears, and asked him to forgive him. Sir Thomas smiled and said, "You will do me this day the greatest service; but I am afraid, as my neck is so short, you will gain little credit by me." He then knelt down, and said that he died a good Catholic, and a faithful subject to the king, and the executioner cut off his head, and stuck it upon a spike on London Bridge.

Every body in England was full of sorrow when they heard that Sir Thomas More was dead. When his friends in Italy and Germany heard of it, they burst out into the most indignant words against the king. Emperor Charles the Fifth said to the English ambassador, "Your master has put Sir Thomas More to death. If he had been my subject, I would rather have lost the best part of my empire than such a servant!"

One of the best things that have to be said about this great and good man is, that he wrote some books against Luther's heresy, which did a great deal of good, and showed a great many people how wicked that heresy was. Very many people, who had been led into reading Luther's books, gave them up, and became good and obedient Catholics again, and among them was Mr. Roper, Sir Thomas's own son-in-law, who had been corrupted by reading the forbidden books.

Archbishop Tonstal, who was so often at Chelsea, proposed to the other bishops to give Sir Thomas More a great deal of money for his books, because they had been of such use to the Church. But Sir Thomas said that he would never take one penny for what he had done; he would wait to be rewarded by Almighty God.

Margaret Roper rescuing the head of her Father by Lucy Madox Brown. She kept his head pickled in a jar until her death.

Chapter XXXVIII.

The Wicked King's End

THE next thing the wicked king did was to send away all the poor monks and nuns from their monasteries and convents. We cannot stop to tell of all the shocking things that happened from his doing this. The monks and nuns had nothing of their own; and he sent them out into the world, after they had given themselves to Almighty God, without any thing to live upon.

Henry had sent away Katherine, and had married Anne Boleyn; but he soon began to be tired of her, so he accused her of doing some bad actions, which perhaps she had never done, and sent her to prison, where her head was cut off. Her cousin, Lord Rochford, who was a brave and noble gentleman, had his head cut off too. The very day poor Anne's head was cut off, the cruel king married a lady named Jane Seymour.

She was not good, nor beautiful, nor clever; but she always did just as the king wished her, so he liked her better than any of his wives. But soon after her little son was born she died. Henry sent about every where to get a wife; and at last he sent to Germany, and married Anne of Cleves, because he liked her picture. But when she came to England, she was not at all like her picture, and the king was so angry because she was ugly, that he sent her away, as he had sent Queen Katherine. Then he married a young lady named Lady Katherine Howard, the Duke of Norfolk's niece.

You know that Henry had made Cranmer Archbishop of Canterbury. This bad man had broken his vow, and had married a wife abroad, but he married so privately that no one in England knew of his wickedness. When Henry made him Archbishop of Canterbury, instead of the good Archbishop Tonstal, Cranmer did all he could to get the king to allow the English priests to marry, that they might be all as bad as himself. He was always in a great fright lest the king should become reconciled to the Church, and that he should be punished. He hated the Catholics, and did all he could to prevent them from being with the king. The Howards were all true Catholics, and the leaders of the Catholic side, and he hated them the most of all. So he got some bad men in the council to accuse the queen of some wicked actions and to have her put in prison. She was not allowed to be properly tried, nor even to speak, and her head was cut off, like Anne Boleyn's. Lady Rochford and some gentlemen had their heads cut off at the same time, because Henry wanted to take their money and jewels.

After he had done this, the Bluebeard king sent all over Europe to get another wife. He asked an Italian lady to marry him, named Christina, the Duchess of Milan. She was a very witty lady, and she sent him word, "that if she had had two heads, she would perhaps marry him; but as she had only one, she was afraid." He married at last a widow lady named Katherine Parr, who was very learned and prudent, and

The Wicked King's End

Katharine Parr, attributed to Master John, circa 1545

who knew how to manage him. Katherine Parr was a Protestant; and she helped to bring up Jane Seymour's little son Edward, and Anne Boleyn's daughter Elizabeth, and their cousin Lady Jane Grey, to be Protestants too.

The Pope tried all he could to recover England to the faith. He sent Cardinal Pole to Spain and to France, to try to persuade Charles the Fifth and Francis the First to invade England, and to frighten Henry. But they were too selfish to do this. The great times of generous faith were gone by, and the kings of Europe thought more about their lands and merchandise than of the Catholic Church. Henry was so enraged at his dear Reginald Pole for undertaking this holy service, that he seized upon all his relations, and put them in prison, especially Courtenay Lord Devon and his little son, and the noble Cardinal's venerable mother, Margaret, the Countess of Salisbury.

Would you believe that the savage monster had this noble old lady put to death, because she would not try to make her son come back to England? She was very old, and her hair was quite white, but she was full of energy and courage, like a true Plantagenet. When the executioner told her to lay her head on the block, she said that her head had never been a traitor, and that if they wanted it, they might take it as they could. The cruel executioner followed her about, striking at her with his axe till she died.

The last evil deeds of this atrocious tyrant were to put the old Duke of Norfolk and his brave son Lord Surrey in prison. The old duke was one of the wisest and best ministers in the kingdom; and Lord Surrey was the handsomest, and politest, and bravest young nobleman of the time. He was very learned, and wrote beautiful poetry, which you must read when you grow up.

Thomas Cromwell by Hans Holbein

All this mattered very little. Cranmer and Cromwell, and some other low men whom Henry had put into his council, were never satisfied till they had destroyed all the brave and generous noblemen in England. Lord Surrey was at the head of the Catholic gentry, and they were determined upon his ruin. So his head was cut off, like Sir Thomas More's, and holy Bishop Fisher's, and Lord Rochford's, and Margaret Plantagenet's; and the stains of their blood are still to he seen in the Tower-yard.

Every one was wearied out with Henry's bloodshed and crimes. He was not cruel and brave, or cruel and generous, like the Plantagenet kings, who had generally been cruel only when they were angry, or when they were at war, or when they were defending their crown. Henry *thought* over his cruelty; he pondered it sullenly in his mind, and did the cruel acts in cold blood, while he deceived his victims by caressing them to the very last. He did not go to war; he sat at home, all full of sores and ulcers, enormously fat and swollen, and thought over which victim was the richest, and out of which he could get the most money and jewels. He never failed to rob the children of those whom he murdered. It did not matter to him if those who offended him were women or children; he killed all, without mercy.

The old Duke of Norfolk was saved by the savage king's own death. Henry died, as might be expected, in great misery, sometimes raving out in wild despair, and sometimes sullen and stupified. In his last agony he looked towards the door, and cried out with loud shrieks, "Monks! monks!" But whether his guilty conscience represented to him the images of all those whom he had forced from the holy service of God, or whether he was crying out in agony for a confessor, we cannot know till the Last Day.

One awful sign of the judgment of God upon this blood-stained apostate was seen. Henry's body was carried to

Windsor to be buried; and on the way it rested for one night in the ruined abbey-church of Sion, which he had caused to be desecrated, and where he had imprisoned poor Katherine Howard. The leaden coffin burst with the weight of the enormous corpse, and the blood gushed out upon the pavement. While the plumber was soldering up the coffin, there appeared a dog suddenly under his feet, licking up the blood; and thus was fulfillled Friar Peyto's prophecy, who, when Henry had hunted away the Franciscan friars, had compared him to Achab, and had declared that the dogs should lick up his blood also. And the people who stood round said that the dog appeared so suddenly, that they believed it was Satan, who had come to claim even the least particle of his lawful prey.

CHAPTER XXXIX.

The Misery of England

From 1546 to 1553

As soon as Henry the Eighth was dead, Jane Seymour's little boy became king, and he was called Edward the Sixth. He was only nine years old, and was very weak and sickly. He was, like his mother, very fair, with bright eyes, and a mild and pleasant face. He was made to learn a great many lessons, and to study so much, that it was bad for his health. You remember how ignorant the English gentlemen were in the time of Henry the Seventh. Now it was just the contrary; and, as is common when people become ashamed of a thing, the English ran into the other extreme; and every body was now having their little boys and girls taught Latin and Greek. Edward was a clever boy, and had a very learned tutor named Roger Ascham, who taught him and his cousins, Lady Jane and Lady Katherine Gray. The Princess Mary was even more learned than them all; and they all used to write Latin letters to the last of Henry's wives,

Katherine Parr, who was very kind to them.

Poor little Edward was made to read a great many Protestant books. Cranmer trained him so well, that the little prince hated the Catholic Faith, and was prejudiced against all his Catholic subjects, even his own kind, good sister Mary. Besides Cranmer, there was some one else who helped to drive all the Catholics away from the poor little king, and to deceive him into doing very cruel actions. This was his uncle, Lord Somerset, a daring, bad man, who got himself made Lord Protector and took all the power into his own hands. When he had done this, he built himself a fine house in London, and he pulled down five beautiful Churches to get marble and beautiful stone to build it with, and took all the Chalices and consecrated plate for himself. This house is standing in the Strand now, and is still always called Somerset House. In a little while, Lord Somerset got the king to order his own brother, Lord Sudeley, who was High Admiral of

Somerset House on the Thames River

England, and who had married Katherine Parr, to be put to death.

Somerset went to Scotland, to try to get the little queen of Scotland to marry Edward the Sixth. But her mother and uncles, who were very wise and pious, said that she should not marry a Protestant king; and they took her away to France, and betrothed her to the Dauphin, whom she afterwards married. When Somerset came back, every body blamed him for having managed the king's affairs very badly. Lord Warwick, who had got a great deal of power while Somerset was away, persuaded the weak little king to have Somerset's head cut off, as his brother's had been.

The people liked the Lord Protector for some things; because he had been kind to the poor, and had tried to get them work, and to make better laws about the commons and waste lands. When he was brought out to have his head cut off, there was a great bustle in the crowd, and the people thought he was going to be pardoned, so they cried out with loud shouts, "A pardon! a pardon!" Very soon, however, Somerset heard that it was a mistake, and that he was not pardoned. This disappointment made him turn pale for a little while, but he soon recovered, and he laid his head down on the block and was killed.

But the country was not much better off now; for Lord Warwick, who was made Duke of Northumberland, governed the king just as Somerset had done. The poor king began to be very ill too, and every body knew that he would soon die. Northumberland was very much afraid of Mary, who he knew would punish his injustice; and he asked Edward to make a will, and to leave his crown to his cousin, Lady Jane Gray. He went so often to ask this, that at last the poor little boy, whose mind was weakened by sickness, and was perhaps never very strong, did as the duke asked him, and made a will to say that Lady Jane should be queen when he was dead.

This was very wrong. Northumberland was wrong to ask it, for he did it from a bad motive of ambition—his son, Lord Guilford Dudley, had married Lady Jane. But he pretended to Edward that it was his zeal for religion which made him wish to have a Protestant queen. It was very wrong of Edward to give way to Northumberland, because he knew that in England the king's crown does not belong to the king; it belongs to the Constitution. And our Constitution has settled that the crown shall always go to the lawful successor, and to no other. No single man has a right to alter the Constitution. But Edward had been taught some very bad lessons by his bad ministers. In the first place, as soon as Cromwell and Henry the Eighth conceived the wicked design of making the king the head of the Church, the Bishops were obliged to teach a new doctrine, which the Church had never taught.

They said that the *king's majesty was sacred;* that is, that as head of the Church, he had become something more holy than he was before. They said of him exactly what the Pagan Romans said of their kings and emperors, who were half kings and half priests.

They were obliged to invent new laws to punish people for saying any thing against the king; and they were sent to prison, and fined, and even put to death, for the most ridiculous reasons. They were obliged, too, to invent new ways of naming the king, so as to show greater reverence and respect. These were so absurd, that some of Mary's and of Elizabeth's letters to Henry the Eighth are more like the letters of Turkish slaves to their Sultan, than of English princesses to their father.

Edward the Sixth had learned to like this. Whenever

his sister Elizabeth went to see him, she was obliged to kneel down upon the floor all the time. The noblemen and gentlemen who brought in his dinner knelt down always before they put each dish on the table; so that when the French ambassador came to England at this time, he was quite shocked to see free Englishmen behaving like slaves. So you see that because wicked men had destroyed what they called *the tyranny of the Church,* by which they meant her blessed and holy restraints upon sin, they had brought poor England under a real tyranny—the slavery of their own bad passions. And it is always so when men touch the Church.

Cranmer had made a great many alterations in his new religion. As soon as Henry the Eighth was dead, he had sent for his wife and children from Germany, and lived with them openly. The other clergy did the same; so that there were no more real priests in England. Those who kept their vows faithfully were punished. Some were put to death, and some were fined and banished out of England. Laymen were allowed to receive Communion under both kinds, and to drink from the Chalice, which was a very dangerous breaking of the Church's discipline. But besides this, instead of Mass, they made a new form of prayer called Common-prayer, in English, in which they put pieces of the Missal, and pieces out of their own heads—all mixed up together, with a new translation of the Psalms. They made, too, a new translation of the Bible, so that the holy Scriptures were fingered by every one in the parish, and each one interpreted them according to his fancy, and with what irreverence he pleased. By degrees the beautiful vestments were put away, the consecrated plate was sold, and the ugly German black gown was worn instead by the married and desecrated clergy.

And how do you think the English poor felt when they saw

all these changes? Certainly you have been longing to ask if no one had faith enough left to cry out against them. Yes, there was some one. The Bishops and the nobles had been most of them faithless to the Church, and, to their eternal shame, this is written down in history. But the Poor were faithful still. The poor cottagers and the village-people saw their Mass turned into a confused heap of prayers without any meaning, their dear Altars desecrated, their Tabernacles, robbed, their Lord taken away, their beloved pastors forced to fly, and to give place to a married hireling, whose greatest cares were for his own wife and children instead of theirs. There were no friendly Abbeys and convents for the houseless and starving, no sweet and kindly Religious to exercise the works of mercy for them. When the Poor saw all this, they did indeed cry out. They petitioned the king, and the protector, and the parliament. They begged to have their Altars and their priests restored; but it was of no use. The powerful men had plundered the Church of the riches of God, and they did not wish to give back their prey.

Soon after the little king had made his unjust will, he died; and Northumberland had Lady Jane Gray proclaimed queen.

Chapter XL.

Mary The Good
From 1553 to 1558

THE Duke of Northumberland thought that as Mary was only a woman, alone, and without any friends or soldiers with her, she would give up all hopes of the crown which rightly belonged to her. He was very much mistaken. Lady Mary knew that she had one thing to do, and she was determined to do it with all the energy which so great a work deserved. This was to restore the Catholic Faith in England.

As soon as she knew that the king was dead, Mary ordered her horse, and with her ladies and gentlemen, rode from Kenning Hall, which was the name of her house, to Framlingham Castle in Suffolk. It was forty miles from Kenning Hall, and they never once rested on the road; for Mary wanted to be within reach of the coast, that she might get to her cousin, Charles the Fifth, if her life was in danger. As they rode along, the ladies and gentlemen talked together about the king's death, which happened on the very date on which Sir Thomas More was murdered. Sir Thomas's granddaughter and her husband were among those who went with Mary to Framlingham, and very surely they must have thought a great deal about Henry the Eighth, and all his useless wickedness. He had committed so many crimes, and put so many people to death, that he might have a son. And now his son was dead without any children, and his Catholic daughter, whom he had treated so badly, was on her way to raise an army, and to take possession of her crown.

A great many faithful Catholics came to help Mary at Framlingham. Sir Henry Bedingfeld, Lord Edward Howard, the Jerninghams, and Pastons, all came round her, and she had soon an army of 30,000 men. With this army she marched to London, and sent for Elizabeth, who had always lived with her, and to whom she had been a true mother.

Elizabeth pretended to be sick, that she might wait and see who was likely to win the battle; but at last she thought it wisest to go to her sister, and they rode into London together. Mary was very slender and small, fair, but with beautiful bright dark eyes, which spoke all her thoughts. Elizabeth was tall and large, with blue eyes, and beautiful hands, of which she was very vain. Great was the joy of London that day; Aldgate was hung with gay flags, and all the Minories and Leadenhall were swept, and strewed with clean gravel, and all the crafts in London stood on either side, dressed in their guild-dress, with banners in their hands. The lord-mayor and all his men, with the city-mace, were there; and Lord Arundel, with the sword of state, and a thousand gentlemen in velvet coats, walked before Mary, as she rode on a small white palfrey. As soon as the queen got inside the gate, she sent away all her guards, and with the greatest courage showed that she trusted herself altogether to the care of the good citizens of London.

When the queen got to the Tower, she saw something

that made her very sorry. On the green before St. Peter's ad Vincula were all the prisoners which Henry the Eighth and Lord Somerset had sent to the Tower. There was Cardinal Pole's nephew, Edward Courtenay, who had been there ever since he was ten years old; the poor old Duchess of Norfolk; the holy Bishop Tonstal, Sir Thomas More's great friend; and the famous Bishop Gardiner, who had done so much to hinder Cranmer in his wicked apostasy.

Mary burst into tears when she saw them. She kissed them all, and said, "You are my prisoners!" In a day or two they were all restored to their property and offices.

The guilty Duke of Northumberland was taken prisoner. When he found that Mary was really queen, he pretended to be very glad, and to be a good Catholic. He and several others were condemned to death, which they fully deserved; but Mary was so merciful, that she could scarcely be persuaded to sign his death-warrant, and she pardoned Lord Suffolk, Lady Jane Gray's father, directly.

Bishop Gardiner and the Spanish ambassador, who came to England from Charles the Fifth, persuaded her to let Lady Jane Gray be executed too. Every one was sorry for poor Lady Jane. She was only a girl of sixteen, very good and clever, who spent all her time in her studies, and who did not wish to be queen at all. But when she was asked, she was not strong enough to refuse to do what was wrong, and she agreed to be crowned. A great deal has been said for her and about her which is not true; and most of the speeches which are called hers were written for her by Protestant historians, who are always trying to make Lady Jane Gray a kind of Protestant martyr. Her head and Lord Guilford Dudley's head were cut off in the Tower, which was very sad.

Mary wrote directly to Cardinal Pole, who with Friar

Peyto, had lived in Rome ever since they had left England. Cardinal Pole gave Mary a great deal of good advice, and was very glad indeed to hear the good news about England. The queen hindered all the heretical preachers from preaching, and had the beautiful offices of the Church restored. The new great bell of Christ Church, Cardinal Wolsey's college at Oxford, was baptized by the name of Mary; and there was nothing but joy and bellringing through England.

Mary Tudor, Queen Mary I by Antonis Mor, 1554

Well indeed might Cardinal Pole be glad, when he thought that his own dear England, with all her faithful poor, was become merry Catholic England again!

As soon as some certain news could be gained, the Pope made Cardinal Pole his legate to England, and he set out on his journey home. But it was a long time before he got to his own country, for a great many things had to be settled first.

In the first place, Charles the Fifth had proposed to Mary to marry his son, Philip the Second, the king of Spain, who was one of the wisest and best kings of the time. The English were pleased at this; but they were afraid that Philip would try to govern England himself, and bring in some of his Spanish notions of an absolute monarchy, which would alter their constitution. So they debated a long time; and the parliament made Philip promise a great many things before they would agree to his marrying the queen.

Next, the religion had to be firmly settled. So many lords and gentlemen had taken lands and houses and money belonging to the Church, that they were afraid the Pope would make them give them up again; and as some of these lands and houses had already been inherited by the sons and grandsons of the gentlemen who took them, they had come to look upon them as real property of their own. They need not have been so frightened about their houses and lands. The Pope and Cardinal Pole thought only of restoring England to the Faith, and of seeing her again united to the See of St. Peter. They sent word to the queen that nothing should ever be said about the Church property.

Then the parliament passed a bill, doing away with all the ugly wicked changes which Henry the Eighth had made and acknowledging the Pope's authority again. Then King Philip came to England, and Bishop Gardiner married him and Queen Mary. King Philip was dressed always in black velvet, with the most beautiful jewels. He was very grave and polite; and he drank beer to please the English, always calling it "the wine of the country."

Soon after the queen's marriage, Cardinal Pole came back to England. Some English gentlemen had gone to Brussels to meet him, and when he came on shore, so many lords and bishops went to welcome him, that he had a train of 1800 people. He came by water to Westminster Bridge, with the legate's cross stuck at the prow of his barge. How little he had thought when he was talking with his friends Luigi Priuli and Contarini about the sad heresies of the time, or when he had fled away in danger of his life to Rome, that he should see the happy day when he should be publicly received as the Pope's legate at Westminster!

A few days after, on St. Andrew's day, the queen and King Philip went in state to the House of Lords. King Philip sat on the queen's left hand, and Cardinal Pole on her right. The chancellor, Bishop Gardiner, read a petition from the two Houses, saying that they were grieved to think how they had departed from the ancient Faith, and begged the queen to restore it. Then, after speaking a little while, Cardinal Pole got up, and absolved the whole nation from schism and heresy, and restored it to the Communion of the Church, in the name of the Father, and of the Son, and of the Holy Ghost. And when he had finished, a loud "Amen, amen!" sounded from all sides of the House.

The members of parliament then got up from their knees, and went with the king and queen to the chapel, where the *Te Deum* was sung, and Bishop Gardiner preached at St. Paul's Cross, upon the blessings of unity and peace with the Church.

It was a very sad thing that, notwithstanding all that the queen and the parliament and King Philip had done, the country was still disturbed by continual riots and troubles. Cranmer wrote the most violent and disgusting papers, saying that the Mass was the invention of Satan, and that the Catholic Church was full of lies. At last the queen and her council had Cranmer and a great many Protestant bishops put in prison, and they were burnt for heresy. It is very difficult to say now what should or should not have been done. The whole country was unsettled and diseased with heresy, and it was clearly impossible to stop it by gentle means. In this case, you know, when men are determined to destroy not only their own souls, but the souls of many others, they have to be treated as malefactors, and are given over by the Church to the law, to be punished. It was very shocking that people should be burned; but it was much more shocking that they should be leading so many more people to be burned in the flames of hell for ever; and this was what Bishop Gardiner thought.

It is very difficult now to find out what Bishop Gardiner's real character was. He had certainly conformed to some points of heresy in Henry the Eighth's reign, for he was always bitterly lamenting his fall afterwards. He was very clever, and a most trusty and faithful servant to the queen, and he administered justice to all with the strictest integrity. He was too violent and anxious about the state of the country, and often differed from Cardinal Pole, who was very mild, and a great lover of peace. But it is clear that in the state England was then, religious peace was very difficult. Bishop Gardiner knew this very well, for he had seen the whole coming on and the growth of heresy, and the awful corruption of the nobles and gentlemen by avarice. It seemed as if, now that they had once tasted the wealth of the Church, they could not keep their hands from it, unless they were hindered by fear; and as long as Gardiner lived, he kept them in this fear. But at last this famous Bishop died. While he lay *on* his death-bed, he edified every one by his piety and his contrition. He often said, "I have sinned with Peter; but I cannot obtain Peter's tears and penance."

After the death of Gardiner, all went on badly. The French king went to war with Mary, and the Duke of Guise took Calais from the English. When the English governor was marching out of the gates, a Frenchman asked him, when the English would come to France again? He answered, what was really a prophecy, "When the crimes of your country shall be greater than ours." The next time the English soldiers landed in France was when the Duke of Wellington went to restore Louis the Eighteenth, after the dreadful Revolution.

Mary was so unhappy at losing Calais, that she said they would find the name 'Calais' written on her heart after she was dead. She had been very ill a long, long time, and had borne more pain than can be told. She spent all her time in her religious duties, in walking out to the cottages round Croydon, and giving the poor people clothes and money and physic. She was very kind to all her ladies, and especially to her sister Elizabeth.

King Philip had gone away and left her. He did not behave altogether very kindly to Mary; but it is no wonder that he did not like to stay in England, for notwithstanding all his kindness and politeness, the English behaved very badly and rudely to him. At last Queen Mary lay on her death-bed. She made a beautiful will, in which she left all her money to convents and hospitals, and to build schools. She had never spent any of her revenue foolishly, and had bestowed magnificent sums upon the wisest and most useful charities. One morning her chaplain came to say Mass for her as usual, and just after the Elevation, she died quite calmly.

The night after Queen Mary's death, the holy and generous Cardinal Pole died too. It is a good thing he died then, for he would have been very unhappy if he had lived to see all the sad things that happened afterwards. He was the last Cardinal legate who lived in England; and what is very strange is, that since he died, no Archbishop has ever been buried in Canterbury Cathedral. It seems as if the bones of schismatics could not lie in the church of St. Thomas and St. Anselm. For the night that Cardinal Pole died was the last night of Catholic England.

CHAPTER XLI.

The Court of Elizabeth

From 1558 to 1561

As soon as Queen Mary was dead, it was found out what a long train of falsehoods and deceits her sister Elizabeth had been acting. She had sworn with a solemn oath that she was a Catholic; and before her sister died, she had sent for a Chalice and candlesticks from Flanders, and had always heard Mass as regularly as the queen herself. You will soon see whether she had spoken the truth or not.

Among the statesmen who had proclaimed Lady Jane Gray queen, with Northumberland, was a gentleman named Sir William Cecil, a tailor's son, who was very clever and crafty, but very dishonest. As soon as Mary became queen, he went to her in great haste, and begged pardon for his mistake, the blame of which he threw upon another gentleman; and he told a great many falsehoods about his joining Northumberland, which he always laughed at afterwards himself. Mary, who was always more ready to pardon than not, forgave him; but she never would make this smooth-tongued gentleman one of her state ministers, for which he was always very unhappy.

As soon as Mary was dead, Sir William Cecil set off to Hatfield, where Elizabeth was, and offered her his services; and as Elizabeth knew how cunning and ready he was, she was glad to see him, and they talked together a great deal. Elizabeth was very cunning herself, and, with Sir William Cecil's advice, she planned a great many changes in religion, which she managed so cleverly, as to deceive every body. She went to Mass herself, and ordered that no one should preach but those who had license from her. This gave her time to think what she could do next. Very soon after, Bishop Oglethorpe, who was acting as her chaplain, was told that when the queen was present, he was not to elevate the Sacred Host at Mass. The Bishop, of course, answered that he could only say Mass in the right way, so the queen went out of church directly after the gospel.

The Archbishop of York, Dr. Heath, was told to send the queen the Great Seal and his title of Lord-keeper; and then the queen sent for all the Bishops, one after another, and told them to acknowledge her as head of the Church. They would not do this, and they were all sent to prison. We are glad to know that this time there was only one apostate Bishop. His name was Dr. Kitchin, the Bishop of Llandaff. All the heretical Bishops were then sent for from Germany and Switzerland, and put into the real Bishops' sees.

The next thing to be done was to make a new Archbishop of Canterbury. This was not so easy, because it is necessary that *four* Bishops should consecrate an Archbishop, and there was only *one* in the kingdom, that same cowardly Dr. Kitchin. Besides, the parliament had abolished the Church service-books, and nobody knew how to consecrate the Archbishop. However, the bishop-making queen imagined a very ingenious plan, which was this: she made four of the deprived Bishops commissioners, who consecrated Dr. Matthew Parker Archbishop of Canterbury, who then confirmed two of these very commissioners as Bishops, and with their help, he consecrated other Bishops.

These poor queen-made Bishops found that as they were Elizabeth's creatures, and she intended to use them as such; for she would not give them their sees till she had taken all the best lands out of them for herself. It must be owned that they could not have met with a fitter punishment for their wicked and cowardly conduct.

So all that Mary and Cardinal Pole had done was soon swept away. Mass was forbidden, and the Common Prayer-book was ordered to be used in every parish. The Altars were pulled down again and sold; and it was a curious thing that the Altars of Westminster Abbey, as they were stripped and broken up, were laid piece by piece on Mary's grave, as if that was the only place where they could be safe from desecration.

After Elizabeth had settled the Bishops to her satisfaction, she sent to a conjuror to tell her what would be a lucky day for her coronation; and when he had told her, she made a great progress through London to be seen by the people.

I have told you before that the queen was tall, and fair, and graceful. She was very clever and ready in speaking, especially in giving sharp and witty answers; and she pleased the people by listening to them all, whether they were poor or rich, with the same attention. She *acted* very well too, sometimes smiling, and sometimes sighing, and sometimes turning up her eyes to heaven, and clasping her hands. Indeed it is difficult to hear of any one who was so clever at pleasing people, when she chose, as Queen Elizabeth. She was very vain of her beauty, though she was not really beautiful; and liked to be told by every body that she was the most beautiful woman in the world. All the courtiers and ladies used to flatter her about this. They used to powder their hair with red powder, that it might be like the queen's red frizzled curls, which they pretended to like, and to call her '*golden* hair,' though they always laughed at it behind her back.

Elizabeth was crowned by Bishop Oglethorpe only, and there was no other Bishop present at this sad coronation. All the Bishops who would not say that she was head of the Church were called *Non-jurors,* and were treated very cruelly afterwards by Elizabeth. The people wanted her very much to marry; and one prince after another asked her to marry him. First came Philip, king of Spain, who thought he could make England Catholic again; but Elizabeth would not have him. Then came Eric of Sweden, and the Archduke Charles of Austria, and the Count of Anjou, and his brother the Duke of Alençon. Besides these, a great many English noblemen tried to marry Elizabeth—some because they wanted to get power, and some because they really loved her. The chief of these were the Duke of Norfolk, the Duke of Sussex, Robert Dudley the Earl of Leicester, and the Earl of Essex. Elizabeth would not marry any of them. She said she was determined never to marry at all, and she kept her word, though she behaved to each of these gentlemen just as if she really intended to be his wife. In the end, indeed, she behaved so badly that it would have been much better if she had married any one of them. But she was too proud and ambitious to obey any body. She delighted in being looked at, and waited upon, and flattered so much, that she never could bear to submit to a husband. This pride led to some very sad and wicked things, as you will hear by and by; but first of all, you must hear about some of Elizabeth's ministers, and some other people, whom you ought to know.

Sir William Cecil was made Lord Burleigh, and he stayed with the queen as her prime minister till he was quite old, and died. As he grew older, he grew more and more clever, and cunning, and careful, till he became one of the craftiest statesmen in the world. He was always making plans and schemes, either against the poor Queen of Scotland, whom he hated, or against the Kings of France and Spain, or against the Catholic lords at home. He promised all kinds of things, and always broke his promises, and deceived every body whoever had any dealings with him, except Elizabeth herself. She prized him very much. When he had the gout, she never let him stand up; and when he was very old and dying, she went to see him, and gave him his broth and medicine with her own hands.

The grey-headed old statesman wrote to his son after this, "to serve the queen, for that every other service was the service of Satan."

We cannot help fearing that this poor Lord Burleigh, with all his wisdom, knew nothing about the service of God; for he never seems to have thought of Him, except to make false oaths by His name. Another of Elizabeth's clever ministers was named Walsingham, and he was almost as famous as Lord Burleigh for deceiving people. Besides these, there was the great Lord Bacon, the chancellor, who has written some very wise books, which you must read by and by. He seems to have known almost every thing that men do and think and feel. He was, besides, very learned in mathematics and natural philosophy.

The two greatest of all the English poets lived in Elizabeth's reign, Shakspeare and Spenser. You have often heard of Shakspeare. He wrote beautiful plays, which Elizabeth, who was very clever, delighted to hear; and she kept Shakspeare at court, and gave him money and jewels for writing his beautiful plays. Spenser wrote a long poem called the *Faery Queen*, in which he calls Elizabeth Gloriana, and praises her very much.

Elizabeth's godson, Sir John Harrington, wrote too. He was a very merry, witty gentleman, whom she loved very much. But one day he offended her, and she gave him a sound box on the ear, as she often did to her ladies when she was angry.

Lord Leicester was Elizabeth's great favorite among all her nobles. He was tall and handsome, and very clever; but he knew how to deceive and to tell falsehoods nearly as well as Elizabeth herself. He asked the queen once to go and see him at Kenilworth Castle, where he lived; and there he entertained her and all her court, for twelve days, with the most splendid shows and games. This bad man had a poor wife, whom he sent to live in a lonely house in Berkshire, that nobody might think he was married. She died there by a frightful accident; and many people say that Leicester had her killed.

Lord Essex was a brave, high-spirited nobleman, but he was rash and obstinate. He offended Elizabeth so much by marrying, that she never forgave him; and she had his head cut off.

Another very brave gentleman at Elizabeth's court was named Sir Walter Raleigh. He was walking out one day, with a number of her courtiers, behind Elizabeth, and they came to a very muddy place in the road. Elizabeth did not like wetting her feet, and was going to turn back, much against her will; for she did not like any thing to interrupt her. Sir Walter saw that she was not pleased, and he very quickly unfastened his new purple plush cloak, and spread it over the mud, so that the queen stepped on the cloak, and crossed over to a clean path. She was so much pleased at this chivalrous attention, that she always liked Sir Walter afterwards, and made him one of her admirals. Sir Walter made such good use of his favor that he was always asking for money and offices; and one day the queen said to him pettishly, "I wonder, Sir Walter, when you will leave off being a beggar." He answered, very cleverly, "When your Majesty leaves off being my benefactor."

This ready, sharp way of answering was become so fashionable, that no one could get on without it. In Elizabeth's time it did not matter whether a gentleman was religious and just and good, or whether he were very irreligious and bad; for if he was witty and merry, and wore fine clothes, he was sure to be liked at court.

There was one gentleman at Elizabeth's court who was merry and pleasant and handsome, and brave and good and religious as well. His name was Sir Philip Sidney. He wrote beautiful books in poetry and prose too, and was one of the most accomplished men and bravest soldiers that ever lived. He might have been king of Poland;[22] but Elizabeth said she could not spare him, for he was the brightest jewel in her crown. When Sir Philip heard this, he said that he would rather be Elizabeth's subject than the king of any kingdom in the world.

Sir Philip Sidney was killed at the battle of Zutphen, in Holland. Just before he died, he was in an agony of thirst from his wounds, and he begged for a cup of water. The cup was brought to him; and just as he was going to drink eagerly, he saw a poor dying soldier look at the water with longing eyes, but he dared not ask for it. "Poor fellow!" the generous Sir Philip said,

---

[22] He was elected by the Diet of that country.

"he wants it more than I do." He took the cup from his own lips and gave it to the soldier, and in a few minutes died of the pain of his wounds. It is a pity that there were not more gentlemen at Elizabeth's court like Sir Philip Sidney.

Sir Walter Raleigh was a sailor as well as a courtier. He went to America, and found out all kinds of new plants and vegetables and brought them home. Among the rest, he brought potatoes and tobacco. No one in England had then ever heard of such a thing as smoking a pipe; and one evening, as Sir Walter was smoking in his study, his servant took in a great jug of ale. When he saw the clouds of smoke coming out of his master's mouth, he thought he was on fire, and was so frightened that he threw all the jug of ale in his face. This was afterwards a great joke against Sir Walter Raleigh.

There were some other great admirals, too, besides Sir Walter. One was named Admiral Drake; and he sailed round the world, and found out all kinds of curious things, and took a number of Spanish ships, with all their gold and silver cargoes. When he came home the queen went to dine with him on board his ship. She looked at all the strange birds and things he had brought home, and liked them very much. But what she liked best was the gold and silver plate which Admiral Drake gave her. Elizabeth knighted the admiral, and he became Sir Francis Drake.

Another clever admiral was named Sir John Hawkins. Elizabeth was fond of him; but no one else can like him at all, for he was the first Englishman who ever bought slaves and sold them to other countries. Elizabeth herself encouraged him in this wicked trade, for she liked every thing that gained money.

Another great admiral was Sir Martin Frobisher, who sailed to North America, and discovered Hudson's Bay, and all the country round it.

The last gentleman we can speak of was Sir Christopher Hatton. He danced so well at a ball at Lincoln's Inn, that Elizabeth took a great fancy to him, for she liked to see tall and well-made people. She sent for Sir Christopher to court, and at last made him Lord Chancellor, which offended all the lawyers very much. However, Sir Christopher turned out to be a wise man; and he did a great deal of good in the queen's council, so the lawyers forgave Elizabeth for choosing a dancing chancellor.

Elizabeth liked to have all these gentlemen round her, that she might hear very often how beautiful and clever she was, and what a splendid court she kept. She was very kind to them, and spoke to them about their concerns, and visited them at their houses, so that she made friends with them all. But if they offended her, and especially if they married, she was in a violent passion. She swore at them dreadfully, sent them away from court, and never employed them again. Some of them were ashamed of the soft life they led there, and got away; and then she had them sent for, and scolded them soundly for going away.

It was very bad for the country that all these gentlemen should be taken away from their own properties, and forced to lead such an expensive, useless life. The noblemen were taken away from seeing how their tenants and people went on, and the tenants began to lose their respect for the nobles. The noblemen, indeed, were led into such an idle, bad life at court, that no one could respect some of them; so that, though Elizabeth's fine court is so pleasant to read about, it did a great deal of mischief to England in many ways.

Elizabeth became so accustomed to spend money upon dress and jewels, that her court might be very splendid, that there was soon no money left in the royal treasury. She had a new gown every day, and all her gowns were covered with pearls and rubies and diamonds. She wore pearls and diamonds in her red frizzly hair, and pearls and diamonds round her waist, round her cloak, on her gloves, and even on her shoes. When she rode out she had riding-dresses of purple velvet and silks, and strings of jewels round her waist and in her hat. Every time she went out, some of this wonderful finery was lost, and she had to buy more. She made all her noblemen and gentlemen and soldiers, and even her milliners and cooks and washerwomen, give her presents. Because of this, besides all the fine furniture and plate and jewels in her palace, she had three thousand gowns in her wardrobe, and one thousand wigs of red curly hair!

This makes you laugh. But soon we shall hear of some things that this "glorious Queen Bess" did, which will not make you laugh at all.

Queen Elizabeth, the Darnley Portrait, named for a previous owner, circa 1575

Chapter XLII.

Mary Stuart
From 1561 to 1587

YOU recollect that, a few chapters since, you were told that the Protector Somerset went to Scotland to ask the little Queen of Scotland to marry Edward the Sixth; and that she was taken away to France, and married to the Dauphin. The Dauphin became King of France, and was named Francis the Second, and his queen grew up to be one of the most beautiful and charming ladies in the world.

She was brought up by Catherine de Medici, who taught her all kinds of accomplishments; but, above all, she had her taught to be a good and pious Catholic, and devoted to her religion. Francis the Second soon died, and then Queen Mary thought she had better go back and govern her own country, so that she is always called Mary Queen of Scots.

When Mary was sailing away from France, she looked back at the shore, and burst into tears; and she stayed looking at the blue land, till she could see it no longer. It seemed as if she felt beforehand how much sorrow and trouble she should have in her own country.

When she got to Scotland, she found all the nobles at Leith ready to meet her; and when they saw how good and kind and beautiful she looked, they burst out into loud shouts, and carried her in triumph to Edinburgh. But very soon they began to be displeased with her, because she had brought some priests with her, and because they said Mass. Scotland was in a worse state of religion even than England. A rude, violent fanatic named John Knox had preached so much

Mary Queen of the Scots, after a portrait by Nicholas Hilliard

against Popery, and altars, and stained glass, and images, and every thing which the beautiful Church raises up to do honor to our Lord's Presence, that the people had pulled down most of the fine old churches, and broken the stained glass and carvings.

When they found that Mary was determined not to send away her priests, and to hear Mass, and to restore, if she could, the true Faith, the people were quite enraged. They abused their young and beautiful queen in the vilest terms, and made riots against her. This made Mary very sad. After awhile she married Lord Darnley, who was her cousin. At first they were very happy, and they had a little son named James. The people were pleased at having a prince of Scotland.

But Darnley was vain and foolish. He behaved very badly to Mary, and she was sadder than ever. Some of the nobles began to make bolder plots, and to say that James should be king, and that they would not have a woman to rule them. At last some very shocking things happened. Lord Darnley was ill, and was taken away from the palace to be nursed at a house called the Kirk of Field, where the queen used to go and see him. One night, as the queen and her ladies were dancing merrily at a ball given by the queen upon one of her servants' marriage, some wicked men got some gunpowder, and blew up the Kirk of Field, where Lord Darnley was. His dead body was found in a field near the house; but none of the murderers could be found.

The queen's enemies said that she had done this to get rid of her husband, and many people believed it. Among these, Elizabeth and Lord Burleigh pretended especially to believe it. Elizabeth treated Mary, whom she was jealous of, like a criminal. The real murderer was most likely a wicked man named Bothwell, who took Mary prisoner, and he then forced her to marry him. When he did this, her enemies cried out more than ever, and poor Mary's son was taken away from her, and she was put in prison in a castle on an island in Loehleven.

I cannot tell you of all the brave deeds of Mary Queen of Scots, nor of all that her wicked enemies did to her because she was a Catholic, nor of all her charity and generous behaviour to them. It would fill a large book to tell you all about Mary. But I am sure if you had lived in those days, you would have loved her very much; and, if you could, you would have helped her.

Her bad husband, Lord Bothwell, ran away when he found that he could not have any more power. There were but few people left in Scotland to help Mary, but these few were faithful and brave. They managed to let her know that if she could steal the keys of Lochleven Castle, they would be ready with horses on the other side of the lake: and Mary really got out, and rode away as fast as she could with her friends. But her little army was beaten, and, in an evil hour, Mary resolved to trust herself to the craftiest and most deceitful of all her enemies, Queen Elizabeth.

Her friends knelt round her, weeping and begging her not to go to England, but Mary was generous herself, and she thought Elizabeth would be generous too. She came to England, and wrote to tell Elizabeth, who treacherously took her prisoner, and sent her to Tutbury Castle, where Lord Shrewsbury was her keeper.

They allowed her to ride and walk about, and to see her friends; but, in spite of all that Mary could beg and entreat, Elizabeth would never see her, nor allow her to go to France, where she might have lived very happily. Nothing went well in England after this sad injustice. For eighteen long years there was nothing but plots, and conspiracies, and murders, and burnings. Everybody was so angry with Elizabeth for keeping Mary in prison, that they tried to help her to get out.

The King of Spain and the King of France made war with Elizabeth. She was always promising to let Mary go, and always broke her promises. She became more cruel every day, and more like her wicked father, Henry the Eighth. She persecuted and burnt all her rich Catholic subjects, and seized their estates, and made the most cruel laws against them. She was determined, she said, not to have a single Catholic priest ordained in England again.

But all would not do. The priests fled; but they only went to Rome to beg to be allowed to come in disguise to England. Cardinal Allen founded a college for them at Douay in Flanders, where hundreds of English priests were educated, and came thirsting for martyrdom to England. The faithful children of St. Ignatius, the Jesuits, were all asking to be sent to England, because here they were sure of torture and every kind of hardship.

Among those who came in disguise from Rome were two celebrated Jesuits, whom you must learn to love. One was named Father Persons, and the other Father Campian. Father Campian was young and brave, and very clever and eloquent. Whenever he spoke, everybody listened with the greatest attention. His intense zeal won many souls to gain the martyr's crown. Father Persons was older, and was very calm and wise.

Father Persons came first disguised as an officer, and said that he was expecting a French merchant in a few days. In a little while the merchant came, who was Father Campian. They both said Mass secretly in London, and gathered all the Catholics together. In a week 10,000 people had returned from their apostacy to the true Church, and Elizabeth was frightened. She promised all kinds of rewards to any one who should bring her the two Jesuits; and at last, after a great many escapes, Father Campian was taken in a hiding-place in the wall of a gentleman's house in Norfolk, and was carried to London. Elizabeth was so curious about this famous Father Campian, that she went secretly to see him, but the sight of his pale, beautiful face did not make her less cruel. She ordered him to be hanged, and before he was dead to be cut open, and his heart to be torn out. The brave martyr bore this

Painted glass window from Campion House College, Osterley; now in the Jesuit Community Chapel at Stonyhurst College. Image © 2012 Jesuit Institute

horrible torture without a groan; and his blood, as it sank into the ground, watered many souls, who were converted to the faith.

In many villages Elizabeth had several hundreds of people hanged at once; and when the high-sheriffs wrote to beg her to be satisfied, she was violently enraged, and swore at them.

At last, after pondering and thinking upon her hatred and revenge many long days in cold blood, Elizabeth resolved to murder the holy and beautiful Queen of Scots. She first tried to get Sir Amias Drury to poison her; and was very angry because he would not, and said he was *over-nice*. Then she determined to send some gentlemen to cut off her head.

It was not known for many years how cruel Elizabeth was, and how much she hated this poor innocent queen, only because she was more beautiful than herself, and because she was the next heir to the English crown. But now all her own letters and her ministers' letters have been found, and now at last every body knows what "glorious Queen Bess" really was like.

When the gentlemen came to Fotheringhay Castle, where Mary had been taken, and Lord Shrewsbury had bid her prepare for death, she said he was heartily welcome for the news he had brought, and that she died a true Catholic, and innocent of all the charges brought against her. She then begged to see her confessor; but these cruel men refused to let her have this last consolation. When the noblemen were gone, she told her servants to rejoice, for they would soon see the end of her sufferings. She prayed nearly all the night, and the next morning went into her oratory and prayed for some time. Then she got ready to be executed. The scaffold was made in the great hall, and Mary looked at it without being at all frightened or growing pale. She had put on her richest dress, to show that she was rejoiced to die, and she carried her Crucifix in her hand. She spoke beautifully to them all, and said she was innocent of ever trying to do any harm to Elizabeth, and had always been her friend. After her death, she said, many things would be known. A very rude man, named Dr. Fletcher, then began to preach to her, and to beg her to become a protestant. The queen gently begged him to stop; and as the rude man went on preaching, Mary repeated some psalms to herself in Latin. Then she looked at her Crucifix, and said, "As Thy arms, O God, were stretched out upon the Cross, so receive me into the arms of Thy mercy, and forgive my sins." The rude Earl of Kent, who was there, told her to leave her popish trumperies, and to carry Christ in her heart. Mary firmly replied, "I cannot hold the image of His sufferings in my hand, without having Him in my heart too." Then she knelt down and said, "Lord, into Thy hands I commend my spirit!" and laying her beautiful head on the block, it was cut off, and her soul went to the rest she had sighed for so long. Dr. Fletcher said, "So perish all the queen's enemies!" The puritanical Earl of Kent, in a louder voice, cried out, "So perish all the enemies of the Gospel!" But nobody said "Amen." Most likely they were all glad that the beautiful and unhappy Mary, after all her long life of sorrow, was gone where no cruelty could reach her any more.

Chapter XLIII.

The Cruelties of Elizabeth, and the End of the Tudors

From 1587 to 1603

THERE is no need to tell you how all the kings and princes in Europe cried out shame upon Elizabeth, when they heard what she had done. The great Philip the Second, the King of Spain, fitted out a grand fleet to invade England, and he wrote to the Pope to help him, that he might be King of England, and make it a Catholic country again. Perhaps there never was such a fleet seen as that which Philip sent out. It was called the *Invincible Armada,* and there were one hundred and thirty-five large ships, commanded by the Marquis of Santa Cruz, who was a very brave old soldier.

When this great Armada came sailing towards England, you can fancy how busy every one was in getting ready to fight. All the great lords gave as much money as they could, to build ships and to pay sailors; the gentlemen got out all their horses, and put on red coats, and went to fight; and all the shopkeepers and farmers and cottagers put on red coats, and got swords and muskets, and were drilling all day long. The shops had to mind themselves, and the ploughs stood still in the furrows; for every Englishman was thinking only of how he could best defend his country.

All down the Thames, from London to Blackwall, and from Blackwall to Greenwich, and Chatham, and Deptford, and Tilbury Fort, there was nothing but shipbuilding, and hammering, and sawing, and rolling in casks of flour and meal, and bags of shot and powder. Day and night, every body was busy, and every one worked as hard as he could, that the Spaniards might not take England.

There never has been such a time since, except when Buonaparte was coming to invade England. Our grandfathers and grandmothers can remember that time, and they give just such an account of it as we have been telling about the Spanish Armada.

Elizabeth was very busy too. She spoke to the lords and to the people, and told them what to do, and how to behave themselves. She reminded them of their duties, and encouraged them to fight for their friends and their homes and their queen. She put on armor and a riding-dress, and rode on a beautiful white horse in front of the army at Tilbury Fort; and there was not a man there who did not feel more encouraged by the sight of his queen. Altogether, the words that Elizabeth spoke, and her actions at Tilbury, are the best of her life; and it was no wonder that the people felt cheered by seeing her, for *they* knew nothing of her bad life, her deceit, and her crimes. Mary Queen of Scots and the Catholic priests were both now, alas, very little to *them*.

The Cruelties of Elizabeth, and the End of the Tudors

The Spanish Armada, artist unknown

It pleased Almighty God to save England from Philip, and as He did so in a very singular manner, we must hope that our dear country is intended to return willingly to the true Faith, and not because she is conquered by a Catholic king. A very great and strange storm broke and scattered all the Spanish fleet, and of all the one hundred and thirty-five ships of the Invincible Armada, scarce one returned to Spain.

Lord Howard of Effingham, and Sir Francis Drake, and Sir Walter Raleigh commanded the English fleet and took a great many of the Spanish ships. There were bonfires and feasts and great rejoicings all over England. But after the defeat of the Spanish Armada, Elizabeth became more wicked and cruel than ever. A great many Catholics were put to death only for being Catholics, and among these was one of the chief noblemen of the court, Lord Arundel. For a very long time the queen had been so cruel as to forbid him to see his wife or children, and at last he was put in the Tower, where he died suddenly, and was most likely poisoned. After his death, Elizabeth persecuted his poor wife and children very cruelly. Like her father, Elizabeth spared neither man, woman, nor child, when they offended her.

The queen behaved very cruelly to the English Catholics, but she behaved even worse to the poor Catholics in Ireland. She sent a very cruel man, named Lord Grey, to be lord-lieutenant of Ireland, and to force the people to be Protestants. Lord Grey killed, and fined, and tortured the poor Irish in the most shocking manner, but he never could make them give up their religion.

When Elizabeth found that Lord Grey was so wicked, she made him come home, and sent her brother, Sir John Perrot, to be lord-lieutenant instead. Sir John Perrot was kinder than Lord Grey, and much more just; and because he was kinder, Lord Burleigh's son and Walsingham said that he wanted to make himself king of Ireland. Elizabeth was so angry at this, that she sent for Sir John, and was going to have his head cut off. He had once offended her very much, because when she had made Sir Christopher Hatton Chancellor, he had brought in a dancing-master, and asked her to have him for her Chancellor instead. When Sir John Perrot heard that his head was to be cut off, he cried out, "What! will my sister sacrifice her brother to his frisking enemies?" for he thought Sir Christopher Hatton had done it. When they told Elizabeth what he said, she tore the death-warrant in two, and said they were all knaves that condemned him. She still kept him in the Tower; and Sir John Perrot, whose proud spirit could be broken but never bent, died in his prison, just as an eagle

The Cruelties of Elizabeth, and the End of the Tudors

would die in a cage.

After he died, there were nothing but cruelties in Ireland. Lord Mountjoy fought against a brave Irish earl named Lord Desmond, who was the head of the Fitzgeralds, or, as they were called, the Geraldines. They were some of the oldest and bravest of the Irish chiefs. Lord Desmond, who was very old, and his countess, escaped a great many times from the English soldiers. But at last they found him sitting in a poor cabin in the bogs, and when they found that it was Lord Desmond, they cut off his head.

Another great Irish chief was Hugh O'Neale, Lord Tyrone. It is impossible to tell you of all his adventures, for they would fill a large book. But at last Lord Mountjoy killed all the men, women, and children that he could find who were of old Irish blood, and Catholics. Then he burnt all the houses, with the cows and sheep and standing corn, so that there was nothing left to eat, and those miserable wretches who escaped being murdered were starved. The misery was so great and so shocking, that to this day that frightful war is called "The Hag's War" by the Irish, in remembrance of Elizabeth. One of the bravest of the Irish lords who were left alive, named Lord Baltinglas, fled to Spain, and died of a broken heart. Elizabeth pretended to be sorry for Ireland, but she took good care to take Lord Baltinglas's houses and lands for herself.

But it is time to finish telling you about this long reign and all its cruelties. You have heard about Lord Essex, the last of Elizabeth's favorites. He was young, and very high-spirited; and when the queen scolded him, he scolded her in return. She sent him to Ireland amongst the rest; but he disobeyed her orders there, and she sent for him to come back, and put him in prison. He had a great many enemies who were jealous of the queen's love for him; and the chief of these were the dark and crooked-minded Walsingham, and Sir Robert Cecil, the famous Lord Burleigh's pert little son. They contrived and planned it so that Elizabeth misunderstood Lord Essex, and Lord Essex misunderstood Elizabeth; and at last they persuaded her to say that this bold and brave young noblemen should be put to death.

Robert Devereux, 2nd Earl of Essex, by Marcus Gheeraerts the Younger.

He sent Elizabeth a ring which she had given him, and had told him to send her whenever he should be in danger. But the child by whom he sent the ring gave it by mistake to a lady who hated him, instead of to her sister, who was his friend. This lady gave the ring to her husband, who kept it. Elizabeth had expected to have this ring sent her, because she really loved Lord Essex very much; and when it did not come, she thought he was too proud to beg her to forgive him. So poor Lord Essex was taken out of the Tower, and his head was cut off, when he was not much more than thirty years old.

After his death, the lady who had kept the ring confessed it to the queen, and begged her to forgive her; but Elizabeth was so angry and unhappy, that she cried out, "God may forgive you, but I never will!" She never looked cheerful or laughed any more; and now, at last, we see of what real value were all the shows and merriment and splendour of the reign of "glorious Queen Bess."

She still went on wearing longer and longer strings of jewels, and finer and finer gowns, and every year she had a larger and stiffer ruff made than any she had worn before. She would not let any shading be put into her pictures; and was very angry indeed if any body called her old. But at last she became very ill, and would not take any of the medicine that the doctors ordered for her. She sat upon a heap of cushions on the ground, with her finger in her mouth, and would not speak or move. But when at last Sir Robert Cecil came and told her that she *must* go to bed, she said scornfully, "Little man, little man, thy father would not have dared to use such a word! But thou art grown presumptuous, because thou knowest I shall die." When he went away frightened, her cousin the lord-admiral begged of her to go to bed, but she said, "My lord, I am tied with an iron collar round the neck; I am tied, and things are altered with me now."

Of what use now to this poor old queen were her three

thousand fine gowns, her jewels, and her thousand wigs of hair? The gay, frolicking courtiers could not make her laugh any more, nor tell her again of her "divine" judgment and her "divine" beauty.

The last Words of the last of the Tudors were words of pride. All through her life, she never would say who was to succeed her; and on her death-bed, she would not say distinctly who was her successor. When they named to her Lord Beauchamp, a cousin of Lady Katherine Grey, whom Elizabeth hated, and had treated very cruelly, she cried out angrily, "I will have no rascal's son in my place!" and soon after she died.

When they knew that she was dead, Lady Scrope let a sapphire ring down from the window to her brother, Sir Robert Carey, who picked it up and rode away as fast as horses could carry him to Scotland, to tell James that he was now king of England. The last and the proudest of all the proud and revengeful Tudors was buried with great magnificence in Westminster Abbey. However, it seemed as if the haughty and restless spirit of Elizabeth could not rest even in death, for the night before she was buried, her coffin split with a loud noise, and with such force that the leaden covering was burst open. Which is there among you, dear children, that would not rather have been the most miserable of all the poor Catholics who were persecuted at that time, than Queen Elizabeth in all her glory?

Chapter XLIV.

Foolish King James
From 1603 to 1625

AS soon as Sir Robert Carey, all splashed with mud, from the great haste he had made, had got to Scotland, and told King James that he was now King of England, James set out, for he was very fond of money, and he was glad to go to a country so rich as England. He took a great many Scottish lords and gentlemen with him, and came to London as fast as he could. It is said that as soon as he heard the news of Elizabeth's death, he had cried out to his nobles, "Now, my lords, we have got to the Promised Land at last."

When King James was a very little boy, he had been taken away from his good dear mother, the beautiful Mary, whom Elizabeth had put to death, and had been given to some tutors to take care of, under the protection of his uncle, the Regent Murray. He was a clever boy, and was very fond of learning, and remembered what he learned; but his learning was never of any use to him when he grew up, because he was a foolish man. He was always a quiet, solemn, comical creature, except when he was angry; and then he used to scream and curse and shout in a dreadful manner. His uncle had him brought up a protestant, which was a great misfortune to him and to England; so that he did not learn to overcome his passions. When he was about four years old, James was taken to open the Parliament; and he read his speech with great *gravity*, as was his custom. But it chanced that a slate had been blown off the roof of the Parliament House, which had left a space open. James looked up at the end of his speech, and said very drolly, "There is *ane* (one) hole in this Parliament!" He used to call all his companions by nicknames, and one day, as he was playing at quoits with the little Lord Marr, he

James I/VI, K of England, Scotland, and Ireland, and Queen Anne of Denmark. Engraving by Renold Elstrack, c. 1610-15

cried out, "Johnny has *slaited* me!" (cheated me). And always afterwards he called Lord Marr Johnny *Slaites*. This foolish habit of nicknaming his friends continued all through his life.

James had married a Danish princess named Anne. She was very pretty and amusing, but she was not very wise. She was fond of spending money in dress and plays and shows, and always acted herself, which was not fit for a queen. She spent almost all her time either in these amusements or in hunting.

James had a great many children, but they died very soon. He had two sons and one daughter when he became king of England, named Henry, Charles, and Elizabeth. Anne of Denmark and Prince Henry came to England soon after James. The people went to meet her as she came along, and entertained her with the most beautiful shows or *pageants*, written by one of the greatest of our poets, next to Shakspeare, named Ben Jonson. These pageants were called *Masques*, and were full of pretty stories about fairies and elves. They were always acted in the open air, and generally in some gentleman's beautiful park.

Anne of Denmark was not very wise, as we said before, and she offended the stately old English ladies by refusing to let them keep their places at court. She would keep her own Scottish ladies; and although King James scolded and swore, she would have her own way. James gave great offence, too, by making a great many new nobles and knights. There were so many, that even the common people laughed at the mushroom-nobles; and they stuck up a witty piece of poetry in London, begging the king to give them some new way of remembering their titles. A good many of the old English lords were turned out of their places at court to make room for Scottish noblemen, and this raised up endless quarrels and jealousies.

Altogether, James was a very mischievous king. You know that Scotland was joined to England, and the two kingdoms together were called Great Britain, instead of England; and if James had been a wise and prudent man, instead of a very foolish one, he might have taught the two nations to love one another very much. As it was, there were a great many troubles and plots, and a great many people wanted to make Lady Arabella Stuart, a cousin of James's queen, instead of him.

All the time that England was so troubled, and there was so much business to settle, James would not attend to his affairs, but spent all the mornings in hunting, and all the evenings in drinking, and laughing at foolish rude games. The wise old ministers, who had been used to Queen Elizabeth's business-like habits, were quite amazed at James's folly. They begged of him to attend to the affairs of the country, at least in the mornings; but he said he did not become king to be nailed to the council-board. One day he lost his favorite dog Jowler; and the next day the dog came home with a piece of parchment tied round his neck, on which was written a droll petition to the dog, because, as the people said, the king very often listened to him, but never to his people. Whenever this foolish king did attend to business, it was to business which did not concern him. He was very learned, it is true, and he had read a great many books, especially upon theology; and he fancied himself a great theologian, and quite fit to settle all points of doctrine. Several times he left off hunting to write addresses to the Pope, and to all the Catholics of Europe, to try to make out that he was right in calling himself head of the Church in England. He only got laughed at for his pains; and the French king's prime minister, who was a very witty gentleman, named Sully, said that James was the wisest fool in Europe.

Foolish King James

We said that the king had a son named Henry. He was not at all like his father, for he was very wise and good. He spent most of his time either in studying, or going about the country to see the different manufactures, and to encourage them in building ships, and a number of useful things. Prince Henry was the peace-maker between his father and mother in their foolish quarrels; and as long as he lived, there was some kind of order at the court. But when he grew up he was very tall and thin, and at last he fell ill, and died of consumption, just when he was most needed in England.

The king's other son was named Charles. He was a very handsome and graceful boy, with grave, quiet manners, and as unlike his father as Prince Henry had been. King James was so fond of Prince Charles, that he could not bear him to be out of his sight. He used to call him Baby Charles, even when he grew up to be a man, and talked to him in such a ridiculous, childish way, that all the gentlemen at court laughed at him.

Soon after Prince Henry's death, Queen Anne of Denmark died too; and then James grew worse, and more foolish and mischievous. He never chose his ministers for their wisdom in managing the country, but for their good looks, and because they were tall. The chief of his favorites was a nobleman named the Duke of Buckingham. He chose him because he was very handsome, and could dance and fence well, and was witty and pleasant, and never thought about his being a bad man, and a bad friend for his son. James called him Steenie, though his name was George, because he was like a picture at Hampton Court of St. Stephen the Martyr.

Buckingham was very ambitious, and he wanted to be admired by all Europe. So he proposed to Prince Charles a wild plan of dressing up, and going to Spain to see if he should

George Villiers, 1st Duke of Buckingham, circa 1625 by Michiel van Mierevelt

like the king of Spain's daughter for a wife. Prince Charles was pleased with this mad frolic; and he and Buckingham borrowed all the king's jewels and fine things, dressed themselves up in disguise, and called themselves John and Thomas Smith. The king cried like a child, and begged of his dear Baby Charles and Steenie not to go; but they only laughed at him, and set out. They went through France, where they were treated very well; and Prince Charles danced at a ball with the French princess Henrietta Maria, who afterwards became his wife. When they got to Spain, they were received with great joy by the king, who was pleased that Charles wished so much to marry his daughter. He gave the prince and Buckingham two gold keys, with which they could let themselves into the palace whenever they pleased.

But instead of marrying the Infanta (as the princesses of Spain are called), Buckingham behaved so badly himself, and made the young prince do such foolish things, that they were obliged to come back to England. The king of Spain was angry at this, and the English people were angry too, because the prince had been so foolish. Perhaps it was partly this mad frolic that made them lose their respect for him. After a great many disputes and changes, it was settled that Prince Charles should marry the princess Henrietta Maria, and that she should be allowed to fulfill all the duties of her religion.

The Duke of Buckingham did a great deal more mischief before the king died. He quarrelled with all the other great men of the kingdom; and the brave Sir Walter Raleigh was put to death, although the king did not really believe him guilty of any crime. The king disgraced Lord Bacon too, who was so great and wise a minister, because he had not courage to oppose his bad and foolish favorite.

The only use King James ever made of his cleverness was to find out the plot commonly called the Gunpowder Plot. Some Catholic gentlemen who had been very badly treated, and who were very discontented, made a wicked plan to blow up the king and all the parliament with gunpowder; and they spoke of it in confession to two Jesuits, named Greenway and Oldcorne, who did all they could to prevent them. The chief planners of this plot were Richard Catesby and Guy Fawkes; Guy Fawkes was to fire the train of gunpowder, and then to escape with Catesby to Dunchurch in Warwickshire, when they were to proceed to the king's court to take possession of Prince Charles. They were to name a regent, and to form a government favorable to the Catholics.

One of the two Jesuits had told their Provincial, Father Garnet, of this dreadful plot, and he did all he could to stop them, but they were determined. Meantime, one of the conspirators wrote a letter to his brother-in-law Lord

Monteagle, to warn him of a *great blow* which would be struck at the parliament. Lord Monteagle took the letter to the king, and he said that the great blow must mean that it was to be *blown up*. He sent some gentlemen to search under the Parliament House, and they found Guy Fawkes there, and a great many barrels of gunpowder.

Soon after Guy Fawkes was taken prisoner, Catesby and the Jesuits were put in prison too. The judge, whose name was Sir Edward Coke, hated the Catholics. He behaved unjustly at the trial of the Provincial, Father Garnet, who was put to death, even though he had been doing all he could to hinder these wicked men from doing as they intended. The king was very proud of finding out this plot, and boasted of it ever afterwards. Following the failed Gunpowder Plot, new laws were instituted in England that eliminated the right of Catholics to vote, among other repressive restrictions.

One admirable thing King James did in the years 1604-1611 was to sponsor an English translation of the Bible that became known as the *Authorized King James Version*. It is still considered today to be a beautiful translation—with poetic cadences and vivid imagery—and the most famous one. It is one of the most printed books in the world. However, since the translators' knowledge of Hebrew was limited, some of their translation differs from the Catholic (original) bible. Also, later versions left out some books of the Bible that Protestants did not consider to be the inspired Word of God.

Soon after it was settled that Prince Charles was to marry Henrietta Maria, King James fell sick and died. He had written a good many clever books, and had said a great many witty sayings; but he had *done* nearly as much mischief as a man who is fond of peace can ever do.

Chapter XLV.

The Cavalier King and the Civil Wars

From 1625 to 1649

When James I died, "Baby Charles" became king. Notwithstanding his foolish name, Charles the First never seems to have been babyish, or even childish at all. He was always very steady and grave, and had, even when quite young, the noble manners of a high-bred gentleman. He was not exactly handsome, but he had a sweet and majestic face, with that particular kind of grave sadness in it which is always said to speak of coming troubles and sorrows. He wore his long brown hair in curls over his lace collar, as was the custom of the gentlemen of that time, and he wore lace cuffs with long points to them, like his collar.

You know that, after many disputes, it was settled that King Charles was to marry the Princess Henrietta Maria of France. Soon after he became king, he sent the Duke of Buckingham to Paris to fetch her. He brought her to England, and Charles met her at Dover. The princess was the daughter of the great

Henrietta Maria of France, Queen consort to King James I, miniature painted by John Hoskins

Henri Quatre, and was very high-spirited and beautiful. She was of course a Catholic, and brought a great many priests with her to England. Her mother was Mary de' Medici, an Italian lady, who gave her daughter some beautiful advice before she left home, part of which is here written down for you:

"You are the descendant of St. Louis. I would recall to you, in this my last adieu, the same instruction that he received from his mother, Queen Blanche, who said to him often, that she would rather see him die than live so as to offend God, in whom we move, and who is the end of our being. Be, after his example, firm and zealous for the religion which you have been taught, for the defence of which he exposed his life, and died faithful among the infidels. Never listen to, or suffer to be said in your presence, aught in contradiction to your belief in God, and in His holy Son your Lord and Redeemer."

Henrietta Maria was very young when she came to England, and she was not so prudent as she should have been in obeying her mother's beautiful and true advice. She offended the bigoted people by bringing with her so many priests, and by having Mass said so publicly and with such splendour. She and the king had a great many quarrels about this, and it is not easy to say what mischief would have happened if her mother had not sent a wise old French officer named Marshal Bassompierre to England, to make peace between Charles and his wife.

This old marshal was a fine brave old soldier, and he told the queen his whole mind without any dattery. He blamed her for quarrelling with her husband, and he blamed her ladies and gentlemen too, who helped to make her behave like a spoiled child.

At last, Charles said he would send away all these French ladies and gentlemen. So one day he took the queen by the hand, and led her away from her own part of the palace, while he sent a number of his guards to drive her household out of Whitehall. They would not go at first, but at last they were obliged to leave, and they sailed back to their own country in very great anger. Henrietta was very angry too at first; but Charles was so gentle and reasonable that she could not help seeing he was right, and she became one of the best and most faithful wives that ever was known.

Every thing might have gone well in the country then, but for the miserable state into which the Reformation had brought it. There was a large party in the House of Commons at this time who said that the Anglican was nearly as Popish as the Catholic Church, and that they would not have any Bishops, nor surplices, nor singing, nor painted windows in the churches.

They were called *Puritans*, because they said they were purer in doctrine than the Anglican Church. They wore loose greatcoats, without any lace collars or cuffs, which they called worldly finery, and they had their hair cropped quite close to their heads. They had a great many ministers, who preached very long and very violent sermons. They pretended to imitate the way in which the prophets in the old Scripture spoke, and they often called the king "the man of sin," and the queen "Jezebel."

From calling the king names, the puritanical party went on to oppose him openly in the House of Commons, and instead of behaving with prudence, and looking to see if there was any thing in which he was wrong, the king did some things which were very wrong. This was partly his own fault, and partly owing to the great schism. You know that ever since Henry the Eighth's time, the kings of England had been accustomed to consider themselves the heads of the Church, and something sacred. They said that they held their power by "Divine right," and that no one had any business to control them. This was quite contrary to the English constitution, as it was laid down by Alfred, and St. Edward, and all the Anglo-Saxon kings, who had with such great wisdom establishing the Witan on purpose to control the monarchy, and to prevent the king from getting too much power. It was contrary, too, to the principle which those great and good ministers, Lanfranc, and St. Anselm and Cardinal Langton, had upheld, which they always helped the barons and the gentlemen to maintain, and which were written down for perpetual remembrance in Magna Charta at Runnymeade.

The Cavalier King and the Civil Wars

The Tudors had done their best to violate these principles, and the Stuarts imitated them in their tyrannical conduct.

The bad friend whom James had chosen for his son, the Duke of Buckingham, stayed with Charles, and helped him by his advice to do more mischief. He was so proud and ambitious, that he was always quarrelling with the other noblemen, and getting into scrapes with the great men of foreign countries, which he persuaded Charles to make war against.

The Commons were not willing to give the king money to make war for the Duke of Buckingham's pleasure, and they told him so. They were right in this, for the country was very much in debt, and the people were all complaining of being taxed. But instead of listening to them, Charles was very angry with the House of Commons; and he sent away the parliament, and said he would rule by himself. This was altogether wrong. When he had sent away the parliament, Charles sent a number of men about the country to inquire how much money every one had; and whatever he had, he was obliged to lend some to the king. This was very unjust indeed.

The chief speakers on the parliament side were Denzil Hollis, Pym, Selden, John Hampden, and Lord Fairfax. John Hampden was the bravest and really the best of all those who opposed the king, and only did it because he thought it a duty to defend the English constitution.

The king was so indignant at Hampden for opposing him, that he ordered him and some other gentlemen to be put in prison, though they had done nothing to deserve it. This made the Commons very angry indeed. They began to do all they could to vex and oppose the king. First of all they found fault with his ministers, who they said gave him bad advice.

One of these ministers was Wentworth, Lord Strafford. He was a very brave and high-spirited nobleman, who upheld the king in all his injustice, because he thought that kings ought to have absolute power, and that no one should be allowed to control them at all. He had a great contempt for the House of Commons; and, next to the king, he thought that the nobles ought to be allowed a large share of power. The king sent him to Ireland to be lord-lieutenant; and he behaved so cruelly to the poor Catholics, that they rose up in arms all over the country.

The Commons took advantage of this—though they hated the Catholics much more than Lord Strafford did—to find fault with him, and they said that he should have his head cut off. The king said that Lord Strafford's head should never be cut off, and he was very unhappy, for he loved his faithful friend and servant very dearly. But in spite of all he could do, Lord Strafford was tried; and although he spoke so eloquently and beautifully that even his judges were drowned in tears, his enemies would have his blood. He was sentenced to die, and they asked the king to sign his death-warrant.

Poor King Charles then did one of the worst acts of his life. He was so afraid of offending the angry Commons, that he gave way, and condemned the most faithful of all his servants to death. When Lord Strafford heard it, he started, for he had always trusted the king, and he said, "Put not thy trust in princes, nor in any child of man."

This brave lord had his head cut off without even changing his countenance. Soon after Lord Strafford was beheaded, the puritans put Dr. Laud to death. He was the protestant Archbishop of Canterbury, and had done all he could to persecute the Puritans, and to make them conform to the Anglican Church. The Puritans, you know, had as much right to interpret the Bible for themselves as Dr. Laud and the Anglican Church had, and it was unjust of him not to allow them to do so. He tried to make every one think that the Anglican Church was infallible, like the true Church, as he wished to believe himself.

It was often said that Dr. Laud wished to be a Catholic, and to make England Catholic again; and it is very sad that he was not a Catholic, for he might then have been a glorious martyr. He was beheaded when he was seventy-two years old and behaved with great dignity and courage.

After this, the Parliament grew more insolent; and they raised an army against the king, and the king raised an army against the Parliament. So England was in a civil war again, like the wars of the Roses, but a more dreadful one even than that. The gentlemen who fought on the king's side were called "Cavaliers;" and the Parliament or puritanical party were called "Roundheads."

Charles sent to Germany for his nephew, Prince Rupert, to come and fight for him. He was a clever and learned man, but very proud and harsh.

The Parliament army chose Lord Essex for their general, but they had a great many others, among whom you must remember particularly Oliver Cromwell and Harrison.

Poor Charles was obliged to part with his dear queen. She went to Holland to get money and arms to carry on the war. She was nearly shipwrecked on her way home; but while all her ladies were shrieking and crying, she sat quite quiet, and laughing at their fears, she cried out, "Courage, dears! Courage! Queens of England are never drowned!" She had taken with her a number of the crown-jewels, which she left as pledges in Holland, and she obtained a good deal of money for the king. She left her eldest daughter, Mary, in Holland, to be married to the Prince of Orange.

There were soon some terrible battles, the names of which will never be forgotten. One was at Edgehill, another at Chalgrove, and another at Newbury. At Chalgrove, John Hampden was killed; and at Newbury, a greater man still, Lord Falkland, who was the best and bravest of all the parliamentary leaders. Like Hampden, Lord Falkland had only opposed the king, because he wished the English constitution to be kept as it was established by Magna Charta, for he knew that that charter was the great standard and rule by which the liberties of our dear country are preserved. He had very often spoken with the king, who loved him very much, and had tried to persuade Charles to keep the promises made in the charter. He was very unhappy when he found that the king would not follow good advice, nor learn while there still was time. And when the war began, he was more unhappy still. His own friends, especially Lord Fairfax, grew more and more violent and bloodthirsty, and began to do as tyrannical actions as the king, and at last much worse. Lord Falkland was always talking and wishing for peace; and before the battle of Newbury, he said he hoped he should soon be dead, for he had no happiness now. And very soon his words came true, and this brave and accomplished nobleman was left dead on the field at Newbury. If he had fought *for*, instead of against his king, most likely he would have died more happily; for though it was very difficult at the beginning to see who was the most right, it is always safest to submit, as the Apostle tells us, to our rulers, even when they make us suffer.

Just before the battle of Newbury, the king bid goodbye to his dear and faithful queen, whom he never called Henrietta Maria, but always Mary. She went to France to try to get help for her husband and his brave Cavaliers, and she never saw

Charles again.

After the battle of Newbury, Prince Rupert fought two other bloody battles with the Roundheads; one was at Marston Moor, the other at Naseby. Both were gained by the Roundheads, and a great many brave Englishmen lay dead on the field, killed by their own countrymen.

Lord Fairfax took two brave royalist generals prisoners. They were named Sir George Lisle and Sir Charles Lucas. He ordered them both to be shot; and Sir Charles Lucas opened his waistcoat first, and said, "Fire, rebels." They shot him dead, and then Sir George Lisle kissed his friend's dead body, and was shot too. It was one of the cruellest actions of this cruel war to put these two brave gentlemen to death. When the king heard of it, he could only say, "Lucas and Lisle!" and burst into tears.

No one can help loving and pitying this poor king in his misfortunes. He wandered about from one place to another, sometimes sleeping on the open downs, and sometimes hiding in cottages and sheds. He often said that he had no where to lay his head, and compared himself, as the Prophet-king says, to "a partridge hunted on the mountains." Yet whoever met with him in these adventures, during which he and his friends were often nearly starved, never forgot his gracious and half-sad face, and his noble and kingly manners. One of the bravest and dearest of his friends, who went every where with him, was named Sir Richard Fanshawe.

At last, the king escaped to Scotland, his native country; and there he might have been safe, if the mean and cowardly Scots had not sold him to his enemies, the parliamentary Roundheads. He was imprisoned for a little while at Carisbrooke Castle in the Isle of Wight, and then at Hurst Castle, which is just on the opposite shore. But very soon the

Parliament had him brought to London, and they said his head must be cut off.

They pretended to give him a trial, but it was only a mock one, for he was not allowed to be heard in his own defence. Besides, you know the English law says, that every man must be tried by his peers, which means by his equals.

The people, who loved the king very much, and who now saw clearly that the parliament Roundheads were much more tyrannical than he had ever been, were very angry that they should ever think of putting him to death. But the parliament army was so large that the people could do nothing. The roundhead generals put soldiers along all the streets and all round Whitehall when the king was to be tried, and then they brought him in. Lord Fairfax, who was very tired of his roundhead friends, would not have any thing to do with the king's trial, which disappointed them very much. His wife was a great friend of the king's, and she persuaded him too to stay away, though she went herself in a mask to see if any thing could be done to save Charles.

When the judge said that Lord Fairfax was one of the commissioners, she cried out, "No, he has more wit than to be here!" and when he afterwards said that the king was condemned by the whole English people, she said again, "No, not by one-tenth of them!" The people began to clap and shout for joy at these brave words, but the soldiers made them leave off; and then Lady Fairfax was seen to go out of the gallery, though no one dared to stop her.

This brave lady, however, could not save the king. The wretches who had so thirsted for the blood of Lord Strafford and old Dr. Laud were determined to have the king's too. He was condemned to die, and then the soldiers began to spit at him, and to puff their tobacco-smoke in his face. The people cried out, "God save the king! God bless your Majesty!" but they were punished and beaten by the soldiers. When he went back to his room, his children were brought to see him, and to say goodbye to him.

The king took the Princess Elizabeth and the Duke of Gloucester on his knees, and spoke to them both. The princess was older than her brother, and very sensible. The tears rolled down the king's face while he talked with them, and they all wept together. He gave them very good advice, and they promised to do all that their father bade them. He bade his daughter tell her mother that his thoughts had never strayed from her, and that his love for her was the same to the last.

He then took the little Duke of Gloucester on his knees, and said to him, "Now will they cut off thy father's head. Mark it, my child, they will cut off thy father's head, and perhaps make thee a king. But mark what I say, thou must not be a king as long as thy brothers Charles and James live; therefore I charge thee, do not be made a king by them." The brave child replied, "I will be torn in pieces first!"

The king then gave them his blessing, and sent them away, and the parting between the father and his children made the iron-hearted Oliver Cromwell really weep.

The next day Whitehall was hung with black, and a scaffold was raised next to the street, but the people were driven nearly out of sight on each side by soldiers. The king came out with a calm and majestic look, and kneeling down, he had his head cut off by a man in a hideous grey-bearded mask. When the axe fell down, a deep groan of horror rose from the people; but Cromwell had strong bodies of soldiers sent to ride up and down amongst them till they were all driven away.

A contemporaneous print showing the 1649 execution of Charles I outside the Banqueting House, Whitehall

Chapter XLVI.

The Parliament Out of Place

From 1649 to 1658

YOU may imagine, dear children, how angry the kings of Europe were when they heard that the English Parliament had dared to put their king to death. The young French king, Louis the Fourteenth, and his mother, Anne of Austria, were very kind indeed to Charles the Second, who was then about sixteen years old. They gave the Queen Henrietta Maria some money, and a house to live in.

Poor Queen Henrietta was very unhappy that her dear and faithful husband should be killed in such a shocking way. She was in great trouble herself; for there was a civil war in France too, called the war of the Fronde, about which you will like to read some day. Paris was besieged, so that every one forgot the poor English queen in their own troubles. One day a very famous minister named Cardinal de Retz found Henrietta by herself, nursing her youngest daughter, who was in bed. She had nothing to eat, and no fire, though it was very cold; and if Cardinal de Retz had not found her, she must have been starved to death. He took her home with him, and never allowed her to be forgotten again.

The Irish were very angry with the Parliament; and they knew very well that the savage and bigoted Puritans would treat them much more cruelly than even their worst enemy, Queen Elizabeth, had done. So they asked Charles the Second to come to Ireland, and said they would fight for him.

The Scots were angry too, because some of their countrymen had disgraced themselves so much as to sell their king. And those very men who had done this base action were now so ashamed of themselves, that they wrote to Charles the Second, and said they would help him against the Parliament.

The Parliament generals saw that something must be done to keep the power they had gained in their hands. They chose a council, which was called the Council of State; and in that council they chose three men, who chiefly ruled it, and told the other councillors what to do. These three men were named Cromwell, Ireton, and Marten.

Oliver Cromwell was the cleverest of the three, and indeed he was one of the cleverest men that has ever been seen. He pretended to be a saint, and was always singing psalms, and talking what they called "godly and profitable talk" with the other Roundheads. Sometimes even he preached to them, and expounded Scripture to them, in the drawling canting voice their own ministers always used. But when he was alone with the more sensible or ambitious generals, Cromwell left off talking through his nose, and spoke promptly and clearly. His great object was to make himself Protector of England, that is, to be king without being called king.

The Parliament Out of Place

The first thing he did was to get rid of the House of Lords. He called the Parliament, and said that they would have a republic in England, and that there should be neither king nor lords, but that the House of Commons should rule the country. All the Parliament agreed to this, and the government was called the Commonwealth.

Oliver Cromwell by Samuel Cooper

But after a while some of the members became jealous of Cromwell, and began to see through his ambition; so he determined to get rid of the House of Commons too. One day, as Parliament was sitting, he went in, and began to speak to the members as usual, praising them for what they had done, and so on. But at last he began to say that there was a great deal more to do for the country, and that the Lord had not chosen them for the work; and he pretended to be very sorry for this. So he called in the soldiers and told them to clear the house, that is, to turn all the members out. One gentleman, named Sir Harry Vane, said that it was dishonest of Cromwell to turn out his own friends, but Cromwell said angrily, "Oh, Sir Harry Vane, Sir Harry Vane! the Lord deliver me from Sir Harry Vane!" and he turned him out of the house with the others.

This was the end of what is called the Long Parliament, because it sat for twelve years. It began by defending the English constitution and ended by disturbing and altering it quite as much, if not more, than any of the Tudors or Stuarts had done.

And now you see that no one of the three parts of the English constitution ought to get more power than it is intended to have, and this is a very important and useful lesson for you and for every one to learn.

In the time of the last Plantagenet kings, the nobles, or Aristocracy, got too much power, and they did very unjust things, which ended in the cruel civil war of the Roses.

In the time of the Tudor kings, the king, or the Monarchy, got too much power; and the kings did unjust things. They put on unjust taxes, and broke the promises in Magna Charta to give every man a full right over his own "life, liberty, and property."

This ended in the civil war of the Great Rebellion, and cost Charles the First his head.

Then the commons, or Democratic part of the constitution, got too much power, and did worse injustices than either of the others. For much as the kings and nobles had done to oppress and injure each other, the people had not been in general the sufferers. It was the commons who invented the plan of taxing the food we eat, and the clothes we wear, and the soap which makes us clean; and these taxes are more hard upon the poor than upon the rich. The commons, too, quartered their soldiers upon all the farmers and shopkeepers and cottagers, so that they were often nearly starved.

You will see, too, that as long as England was Catholic, there was a refuge and protection for the people in the Church. They found help and comfort from their priests in the worst times of the wars of the Roses; and even when both parties were most savage, there were always the Churches, the Abbeys, and the Convents to fly to for shelter.

But when they were robbed of the true Church, then the English people began really to suffer, and in the Great Rebellion it was a cruel suffering indeed. The Puritans would not hear of any more merry singing or dancing, or playing at manly and innocent games. The dear old maypoles were cut down, and all the pretty mumming and may-games were forbidden. Whatever painted glass and images and carving remained in the beautiful old Churches was beaten down and broken to pieces. Whatever sweet-toned bells, baptized by holy Church, still hung in the old towers and steeples, were pulled down and sold. All the rich brass monuments and colored pavements were torn up and broken in pieces with great hammers. Whenever old books still remained, they were torn up too; so that a great many beautiful remains, which had escaped Edward the Sixth's and Elizabeth's bigotry, were utterly destroyed by these savage and ignorant fanatics. This was the carrying out and completing of the great schism in England. At last Cromwell had established himself firmly in power; and he was always called the Protector of England. He was always at war, but he was a very determined and brave man, and was generally victorious.

He sent a great many soldiers to Ireland first, and he went himself. He found that the Irish hated him, and were every where in rebellion. He went and besieged a good many large towns; and when the garrison surrendered, he always killed them all, or at least the officers. At Wexford and at Drogheda he ordered some thousands of the poor inhabitants to be put to death, and among these were several hundreds of ladies and women, who ran to the great cross in the middle of the town, crying out for mercy. But the cruel soldiers, who were called Cromwell's "Ironsides," had no more mercy than their general, and they killed all these poor defenceless women with their swords. Very soon Drogheda was full of dead bodies, and the streets ran with streams of blood for many days.

Cromwell went about the country killing every one his soldiers could catch, even the women and children, and then he ordered that a great many of the Catholic gentlemen and farmers should be banished, and sent out of Ireland. A good many were glad to go; and a good many others went because they were obliged. Some of them went to France, some to Spain, some to America, and some to Venice, and their descendants are still to be found in all parts of the world.

When the cruel Protector had got rid of all these Catholics, he sent some ships, and made their wives and children get into them, and sent them to the West Indies, and some other places, where he sold them for slaves. This was the liberty which the Great Rebellion gave to Great Britain. After all these massacres and horrible deeds, there were still seven times as many Catholics in Ireland as Protestants. Do what they will, men cannot root the true faith out of Ireland.

Next there was a war in Scotland. A very brave and noble gentleman named Lord Montrose got an army together and tried to win Scotland back for Charles the Second. He had a number of German and French soldiers with him, and he fought many battles, and behaved in the bravest manner. He could not bear that his dear country should be given up to the sour-faced, canting Puritans, who were as cruel as they were hypocritical; and he laughed at them, and wrote songs about them, which made them very angry.

After great deeds of bravery, and wonderful adventures, Lord Montrose was taken prisoner by the Puritans, and they were so delighted at having got him, that they sang and danced for joy. They invented a high kind of carriage to carry him to his trial, and had him bound and treated in the most disgraceful manner. They pretended to try him, but it was no more a real trial than poor Charles the First's was. His enemies read over to him all his evil deeds, as they called them, and then condemned him to be hung on a high gibbet.

All the time of the trial they watched him to see if he was frightened, but the brave lord was as calm and dignified as if he had been at home in his own castle. When they told him that his body should be divided and stuck up on some of the city gates, he said he wished he had limbs enough to hang up in all the cities of Christendom, to show how loyal Montrose had been. When the hangman hung a book with the history of his life, in mockery, round his neck, he smiled, and said he had given him a finer ornament than the Collar of the Garter itself.

They took him outside his prison at last, and hung him on the gibbet, and cut off his head, and stuck it over the prison-door: but they gained nothing by this base cruelty; for when the crowds of people saw this brave Lord Montrose behaving so nobly, they loved him more than ever. Many who had thought him wrong when he lived, praised and honored and imitated his loyalty, after they had seen him die.

Before Lord Montrose died, he wrote some beautiful verses about his country, which he called his "dear and only love." He meant to say that he loved his country as much as other men love their wives. Montrose's bold, rough song is written down for you, that you may see how much he wished Scotland to be loyal and faithful to her king.

> " My dear and only love, I pray
>   That little world of thee
> Be governed by no other sway
>   Than purest monarchy;
> For if confusion have a part
>   Which virtuous souls abhor,
> And call a synod in thy heart,
>   I'll never love thee more.
>
> Like Alexander, I will reign,
>   And I will reign alone;
> My soul did evermore disdain
>   A rival in my throne.
> He either fears his fate too much,
>   Or his deserts are small,
> Who dares not put it to the touch,
>   To win or lose it all.
>
> Then in the empire of thy heart,
>   Where I alone would be,
> If others should pretend a part,
>   Or dare to share with me,
> By love my peace shall ne'er be wrecked,
>   I'll spurn thee from my door,
> I'll smiling mock at thy neglect,
>   And never love thee more.

But if no faithless action stain
Thy truth and constant word,
I'll make thee famous by thy pen,
And glorious by thy sword;
I'll serve thee in such noble ways
As ne'er were known before;
I'll deck and crown thy head with bays,
And love thee more and more."

Soon after Montrose was killed, Charles the Second went to Scotland himself, to see if *he* could not get back his kingdom. But though a great many of the lords and gentlemen joined him, Charles found that they meant him to obey them, instead of their obeying him as a real king. They wanted him to be a Presbyterian, and found fault with every thing he did. Sometimes they made him listen to six long sermons in one day, so that he was quite tired of the Scotch Puritans, who were then generally called *Covenanters,* because they had made what they called a covenant to keep the presbyterian religion.

When Cromwell came back from Ireland, he went to fight with Charles, who had come down by degrees into England, and the two armies fought a great battle at Worcester, in which Charles and the Cavaliers were beaten, and were obliged to run away. Some of the bravest of Charles's friends in that sad battle were Catholics, and among them were Captains Hornyhold and Gifford. After the battle, the king dressed up in disguise, and fled from one place to another. He had the strangest adventures, and was only saved by the great faithfulness of his friends. Captain Gifford took him to Boscobel, an old house belonging to a puritan lady, who did not live there, but who had some faithful royalist servants named Pendrell (there were four brothers of the

Pendrells), who might have got a thousand pounds by selling Charles to the Parliament. But though they were only poor woodcutters, they never betrayed him. They carried him about very carefully from one wood and from one cottage to another, when the soldiers came after him; and when they did not, they spread their cloaks on the ground for him to lie upon under the trees.

Sometimes Charles was dressed in ragged green baize, like a beggar; and sometimes he rode on horseback, as servant to a lady; and once he was obliged to sit with Colonel Careless all day in a bushy oak-tree at Boscobel, while the soldiers were looking about in the meadows for him. One of the faithful Pendrells and his wife stayed close by the oak, cutting wood, and the soldiers never suspected that the king was so near. When you see all the children carrying boughs of oak on the 29th of May, you must think that it is in remembrance of Charles the Second's being saved in the oak of Boscobel.

After a great many such escapes as these, in one of which he was hidden at Mr. Whitgreave's house, at Moseley Court, the king got into a small boat at Brighton, and landed at Fecamp, in Normandy, where he was at last safe from the cruel Protector and his Roundheads; but for some years he was obliged to live as he could, in France or in Germany.

The next war Cromwell had was with the Dutch. They had a very famous admiral named Van Tromp, and another named De Ruyter, who were thought to be the best admirals in the whole world. The cause of the war was this: for a long time the Dutch merchant-ships had brought all the spice, and cotton, and drugs, and dye-woods, to the other countries of Europe; and they were very glad to be the carriers to these countries, because they paid them for bringing these goods. But Cromwell was offended with the Dutch for asking to have the life of Charles the First spared, and they were offended with him for making them no answer. Cromwell said that the English ships should bring home their own spice and cotton and sugar, and that he would not allow the Dutch ships to bring goods to England any more.

The Dutch were very angry at this; and they sent Van Tromp, with a large fleet, into the English Channel. But there was an English admiral as brave as Van Tromp, and he had better ships. His name was Admiral Blake, and he fought Van Tromp, and burnt some of his ships, and took some more, so that Van Tromp was forced to go back to Holland. Afterwards, De Ruyter, with De Witte, another Dutch admiral, fought Admiral Blake; but they could not conquer him; and the Dutch were glad to make peace, and to promise to punish their friends who had been behaving ill to the English in the East Indies, and to pay a good deal of money besides.

You see that the Protector knew very well how to fight, and how to choose good soldiers and sailors to fight for him. He chose good judges and magistrates too; and he sent away from his court every one who led a bad life. He was very much feared and respected by the kings of Europe on account of these qualities; and he was feared and respected in England too, because every one knew that Cromwell was certain to punish rioting and drunkenness, and other bad actions, though he allowed his friends to commit every kind of robbery and cruel injustice towards the Royalists.

But, notwithstanding all his power and greatness, Cromwell was very unhappy. He was a usurper, and he knew it, and he was always afraid of being murdered. He wore a thick leather jacket under his clothes, and always kept loaded pistols in his pocket. He had two or three bedrooms, and never slept in any of them for many nights together. And notwithstanding that he did all these things to make himself safe, he never slept in peace. How often in those restless nights he must have thought of his king, whom he had helped to murder, and of his poor fatherless children, who were driven away from their own country!

He grew more and more unhappy. He had a favorite daughter, whom he loved very much, named Elizabeth Clavpole; and before she died, when she was very ill, she cried out, that *there was blood to be answered for;* and it made Cromwell very miserable. He had never been afraid in the hottest battle with the Cavaliers; but now he was afraid, because his conscience accused him.

At last he was quite worn out; and after praying a great deal for his Roundheads and for the Commonwealth to continue, Oliver Cromwell died. He did not pray at all for himself; for he thought he was sure to go to Heaven, as a reward for what he had done.

It is very difficult to say whether or not Oliver Cromwell was sincere in his religious enthusiasm; but it is most likely that he was. The whole of England began then to be in that extraordinary state in which there were as many sects as there were counties in it. Some of them believed that they were God's elect, and could never do wrong; some of them called themselves Fifth-Monarchy men, because they believed that Our Lord Himself was coning again to reign upon earth: and others were like madmen, preaching and singing psalms all day, and afterwards committing every kind of sin and crime. No country could be so sad as England has been since she left the ancient Faith, for some kind of religion is necessary for our hearts. When our poor countrymen ceased to be Catholics, they ran into every kind of religious madness and delusion.

Chapter XLVII.

The King Again, and his Bad Ministers

From 1658 to 1685

WHEN Oliver Cromwell was dead, his son Richard was made protector instead. But Richard was a very quiet man, and not at all ambitious; he had no wish to be protector. He was certainly not fit to govern England. While every body was wondering what was going to happen, a very clever man, who had been nearly forgotten, settled the matter in a way which no one expected. His name was General Monk, and he had been left in Scotland by Cromwell when he came back to England to fight Charles the Second at the battle of Worcester. He was very quiet and silent, and no one could ever make out whether he was a Roundhead or a Royalist. Even Cromwell was not certain himself; and once he wrote a letter to the general, in which he said, "Every one declares that there is a sly rogue called George Monk lying quiet in Scotland, waiting for an opportunity of bringing back Charles Stuart; if you catch him, send him to me." General Monk, however, was too cunning ever to say whether this was true or not. But when Richard Cromwell plainly said that he did not wish to be protector, General Monk thought it was time to declare himself plainly, and he brought his army back from Scotland into England. He wrote to Charles the Second, who was at Breda, in Holland, and said that if Charles would write some letters to the Parliament, he would be there to support him, and to say that it would be better to have a king again. Charles the Second was very glad to do as the general advised him. He wrote some letters to the Parliament, and said that if he came back, he would pardon every one who had had any hand in putting his father to death, and that all the troubles of the Great Rebellion should be forgotten.

Every body was delighted to get these letters; they were quite tired of the crop-headed, sour-faced, and psalm-singing Roundheads, who, although they talked so much about liberty, were the worst and cruellest tyrants that England ever had.

So General Monk wrote to Charles the Second to come to England; and every body set to work to dress up the streets, and to hang out carpets and flowers, and every thing they could find, to welcome their king home again after his long exile. And, on the 29th of May, 1660, the bells were rung, fireworks were let off, cannon were fired, and every one shouted and sang for joy; so that the king said, "Why, it must have been my own fault that I did not come before; for I have not met with a single person who did not declare that he has done nothing but wish for my restoration."

When Charles came near London, General Monk met him with all his life-guard, and a great many officers in splendid uniforms. The lord mayor was there too, carrying a naked

The King Again, and His Bad Ministers

sword, and a great many thousand people, with all the train-bands of London. The king embraced General Monk, and made him walk with him; and afterwards the general rode with the king and his two brothers, the Dukes of York and Gloucester, into London.

The king called the two houses of parliament, and they all told him how glad they were that he was come back, and how much they hoped that he would govern them well. So you see the English constitution was now again established in its true and ancient manner.

But it is a great pity, when every body was so glad, and all the people who had been bitter enemies were making friends with one another again, that General Monk did not ask the king to promise to keep Magna Charta, as the Plantagenet kings had always done. If Charles the Second had promised to do this, perhaps James the Second would not have been driven away from his kingdom, and England might have been reconciled to the Church again. This will remind you of what we have told you several times, and what you must never forget, that *the Church* has always been the most faithful guardian of English liberty, and that when there was no longer the Church to defend it, our poor country fell into the hands of many tyrants. Lanfranc, and St. Anselm, and Cardinal Langton, and St. Thomas of Canterbury, would have been certain to remember what General Monk forgot.

The king was very much liked at first. He was very good-natured, and fond of laughing, and he made every body else as merry as himself. He liked dancing and games and amusements, but he hated trouble and business.

All his friends were gay too. The Puritans, with their cropped heads, and brown coats, and grave faces, were all driven away, and the gentlemen dressed in gay-colored silk and satin coats, with satin shoes, and long curled wigs reaching down to their waists. The Cavaliers had it all their own way now. There were, however, some very grave and good ministers, who looked after the king's affairs for him. The best of these was the Chancellor Hyde, Lord Clarendon, whose daughter Anne married the king's brother, the Duke of York. Then there were the Duke of York himself, and General Monk, and Lord Ormond, who were good men of business.

The Duke of York was one of the greatest admirals that we have ever had; and whenever any ships came against the English ships, he went out to fight them, and generally conquered. He beat Van Tromp's son, and Opdam, who was another great Dutch admiral, in several battles; and at last the Dutch were very glad to make peace with England.

The king married a Portuguese princess named Catherine of Braganza, who was a very good and zealous Catholic, and who loved him very much. But he behaved very badly to her, and went away from her very often to amuse himself with a number of wicked ladies and gentlemen, who were as irreligious and careless as himself. He spent nearly all his time in this manner, playing at cards, and dancing and jesting and laughing with these bad companions. No one could have believed that such a good and steady man as King Charles the First, and such a pious woman as Queen Henrietta, could have had such a riotous, disorderly son.

The names of some of the most famous of Charles the Second's bad friends are, the Duke of Buckingham, Lord Rochford, Lord Wilmot, the Duchess of Cleveland, and the Duchess of Portsmouth. They made jokes about the queen, whom they hated because she was a Catholic. The Duke of Buckingham was so wicked as to try to persuade Charles to send her away, and get another wife. But though Charles was

The King Again, and His Bad Ministers

so fond of bad and foolish company, he was not hardened. He would never send away his queen; and once, when she was very ill, he sat by her bedside all day and all night, and promised that he would never go away from her again, if she got well. But when she got well, he forgot his promises, and went on as before. He had not the courage to send away his wicked friends, nor to resist their temptations.

And at last he allowed them to govern the country as they pleased, and they did such wicked actions as made all good men sorrowful and ashamed. There was a very bad minister especially, named Lord Shaftesbury, who was very clever and witty and learned, but who was an infidel. He was foremost in governing the country badly, and in disgracing the very name of England. Amongst other shameful things, this minister took a great deal of money from the French king, Louis the Fourteenth, and promised that he would not fight against France. Several of the other ministers and friends of Charles were bribed by the French king, that they might speak in parliament against any one who proposed a war with France. This was very disgraceful and dishonest indeed.

These bad ministers caused a great many plots and conspiracies. Not a few of these were invented by people who hated the Catholics, and who wished to have them sent out of the kingdom altogether; for these conspiracies were always said to be carried on by Catholics, and especially by the Jesuits, who are always the first to suffer. The Duke of York, who was a very zealous Catholic himself, tried to show the Parliament that these plots were invented by the accusers of the Catholics, but they would not listen to him. Two of these plots are very famous, and are called the Meal-tub Plot and the Itye-house Plot. But there is not time to tell you anything about them now, except that they were invented by the malice of the enemies of the Church, and of the queen, and especially by a wicked man named Titus Oates, who wished the king to persecute the Catholics much more severely than he did, and to send away his good wife.

Charles, with all his faults, was a straightforward, good-hearted man. He laughed at the plots and at the fears of his subjects, and would not make any new laws against the Catholics. But it is sad to say that he allowed his wicked ministers to persuade him to put some of the chief Catholics to death, and amongst these was a grey-haired old nobleman named Lord Stafford. This brave and good old lord went through a long and painful trial with the greatest fortitude; and his daughter, who was as brave as himself, sat by him all the time, and wrote down the notes for his defence at the risk of her own life; for Titus Oates had written and spoken so many falsehoods against our holy religion, that the mob were ready to tear any Catholic in pieces.

After these persecutions, there were some more plots made against the king. One by his own son, the Duke of Monmouth; and others by some gentlemen who thought, like Hampden and Lord Falkland, that the king ought to keep the promises of Magna Charta.

You must not forget that you were told, when Charles the Second came back to England, that General Monk had forgotten to make him promise this. This was the chief cause of these last plots, which were very sad and wrong in themselves; and sad too because two very brave and noble gentlemen joined in them, and were put to death. They were named Lord Russell and Algernon Sidney. Lord Russell had a very good wife, who thought that her husband died a martyr for the good of his country. She stayed with him to the last, and sat by him at his trial, to write for him, and remind him of every thing that was likely to save his life. You see that if Charles had kept the promises made in Magna Charta, his bad ministers could not have done such wicked things, and these good men would not have been so sorry, and made such mistakes in trying to do good, and the people would not have been so angry.

Besides all these plots, there were two very great misfortunes in this reign. The first was a terrible disease called the Plague, which is very common in Turkey and Egypt, but which is quite unknown in England now. It broke out in Holland first, and then came to England. Many thousands of people died each week; and wherever any one had the plague, a red cross was marked on the door, and every one but the nurses were forbidden to go to the house. When the person died, he was not buried in the usual way, but was put into a cart which came round for the purpose, and was called the dead-cart, which took all the bodies, and they were buried in a large cemetery near London. At last so many people died, that all who remained alive were frightened; so frightened that they did not think any more about their friends, nor care whether they died or not. It struck people when they were walking in the streets, or were talking together merrily, or playing with their children. First they felt a little head-ache, and then a great sickness, and then a swelling came under their arms, and then they were dead, almost before they had time to commend themselves to God. If people wanted to buy any thing, they were obliged to go and write down what they wanted on a piece of paper, and then to put the money into a trough of running water; and often people went away without the money for what they had sold, because they were afraid of catching the plague.

When you grow older, you must read the *History of the*

Plague, written by a man named Defoe, and another very pretty book written by a man named Christopher North, who had had the plague himself when he was just a baby, and whose mother stayed to nurse him. He wrote the book when he became a man, to tell how his dear mother took care of him, and how he loved her for it.

After the plague came a great fire. It began in a baker's shop in Pudding Lane, and burnt for six days before it could be put out. The king and the Duke of York were the foremost in setting the people to work and in saving lives. By their prudence and energy, Westminster Abbey, the Tower, and the Temple, were saved, although the Temple caught fire twice. Three hundred and seventy-three acres within the walls were turned into heaps of smoking ruins and ashes; and hundreds of thousands of people were sent into the fields without a home, or clothes to cover them. King Charles exerted himself to the very utmost to help these poor people. He left off dancing and playing at cards, and went about himself to visit every part of the city, and to give money and food and clothing to them; and the kind and good Duke of York went every where with him. It was such behaviour as this, which Charles always showed when he was roused from his slothful love of pleasure, that made him so universally and ardently beloved.

There were great troubles in Scotland during this reign, Charles sent one of his bad ministers there to govern the country; and he was determined to make the Presbyterians use exactly the same prayers as the Anglicans used, and to have Bishops, whom they hated. The Scotch were very angry with the duke, and the duke behaved very cruelly. He invented a new kind of torture, which was an iron boot, into which iron wedges were hammered, one after another, till the agony made the person who was tortured faint away. The cruel Duke of Lauderdale used to stand by and look on at these tortures, and make jests upon the people who suffered.

At last the most obstinate and fanatical of the Scotch Covenanters went away with a man named Cameron to the mountains, where they prayed and sang psalms, and made all kinds of wild prophecies against King Charles and his cruel ministers. They were hunted about like wild beasts by a nobleman named Lord Dundee, who is better known by his name of James Graham of Claverhouse. He was one of the bravest and most accomplished gentlemen that can be heard of; but he was very cruel. He hunted the Cameronians, as they were called, day and night among the mountains, and never spared one alive whom he took. He always rode upon a famous black horse, which had not a single white hair all over his body; and he and this beautiful horse did such wonderful deeds of bravery, that the superstitious Cameronians said that Lord Dundee had a charm from Satan, which prevented both him and his horse from being killed by common lead bullets. So they melted down silver buttons and shillings, and shot at him with them, but never killed him. Cameron was shot himself at last; and his followers were all either sent to prison, or forced to go as soldiers to Spain.

Ireland suffered as well as Scotland in this reign. At first Charles sent the Duke of Ormond there, to help to govern that poor country better; and as he was an Irishman himself, and had suffered from the want of good laborers and good food in Ireland, he did all he could to show the people how to work better, that the land might be better cultivated, and that the farms should be improved, so that more corn could be grown. There had been so many riots and disturbances, that the land was badly managed, and a great deal of it was wasted. But the Duke of Ormond's enemies got round the king, and persuaded him to send for him to England; for they said the duke loved Ireland too much. Charles knew that they only envied him because the Irish loved him so much; but with bis usual weakness, he allowed his enemies to make him ill-treat his friends, and he sent for the Duke of Ormond to England. After this, Ireland was badly governed till the end of his reign.

There is only one thing more to tell you about Charles the Second; but that one you will be very glad to hear. There had been, as usual, a great many quarrels between the ministers; and the king, as usual, was putting off from day to day settling whether to send away one of them or not, when he was taken ill. The poor queen, who loved him very much, was very unhappy, and the good Duke of York came and sat by his bed, without ever leaving him again. He watched for an opportunity when no one who was there could hear him, and then he asked the king if he would see a priest. Charles seized his brother's hand, and said, "For God's sake, send for one!" but he added afterwards, "but it will be dangerous for you." The duke said he did not care for that, and he brought Father Hudleston, who had been at Moseley when Charles was hiding there after the battle of Worcester, into the king's room. The duke said to the king: "Sir, this worthy man once saved your life; now he is come to save your soul." The king then said to Father Hudleston, that he bitterly repented of all his sins, that he pardoned all his enemies, and was at peace with all men; and that if God spared his life now, he would try to amend it entirely. He then made his confession, and the priest anointed him, and gave him Holy Communion, and went away. After suffering great agonies of pain all through that long night, which he bore with perfect patience, Charles died the next day at noon.

You must nearly understand already the chief faults and mistakes of Charles himself; but our country suffered so much during his reign, that it is better to say a few words more about them, that you may remember them better. The first was, that when he came to England, General Monk and the Parliament forgot to settle that the promises of Magna Charta, and the good old laws of St. Edward, should be kept by the king and his ministers. Secondly, Charles allowed his ministers to govern the country as they thought fit; and when they were bad ones, which was often the case in his reign, he would not take the trouble to send them away and to choose better ones. He was so fond of dancing, and playing at cards, and laughing, that he did not like to be interrupted by business.

Thirdly, whenever it did happen that Charles had a good minister, who really tried to do his duty, his enemies could always persuade him to send him away; for as he hated trouble, he would not take the pains to defend his friends when they were accused. And so it generally happened that he treated his enemies and bad men well, and behaved very ill to his dear and trusty friends. The wicked Lord Shaftesbury and the infamous Titus Oates were allowed to do all the mischief they could without being punished for it. Whereas, Lord Stafford, and Archbishop Plunket, and other good men, like Lord Russell and Sidney, who were driven by bad ministers to do what was wrong, were beheaded. And this is one of the worst of the things a king can do, for it is a great injustice.

King Charles II by John Michael Wright or his studio

Chapter XLVIII.

Doly King James
From 1685 to 1689

THE Duke of York was now become King James the Second. Athough he had been very often badly treated by some of the ministers and by the House of Commons, who were afraid of him because he was a Catholic, he was proclaimed king without any opposition at all. The bells rang, cannon were fired, and all England seemed full of joy; though they loved Charles so much, as to be really sorry for his death. But King James was even more beloved still; for besides that he was a much better man than Charles, he was very handsome, and agreeable, and good-natured, and had the frank, bluff manners of an English sailor, which he was. No braver or better sailor indeed has ever been seen in England than James the Second; and whoever had seen him fight, either on land or at sea, was quite astonished to see such fearless courage.

James had first married Anne Hyde, the daughter of Lord Clarendon, Charles the First's wise minister. She was an ill-tempered woman, and no one liked her much. She had two daughters, Anne and Mary, about whom we shall know more hereafter. After Anne Hyde's death, James married the Princess of Modena, which, you know, is in Italy. This princess, whose name was Mary Beatrice, was the most beautiful and the most unfortunate of all the foreign wives of our English kings. She was only fifteen when she came to England; and she was very unhappy at being made to leave her own beautiful Italy, to come to a country she had never even heard of, to be married to a husband whom she had never seen. But James went down to the beach, as his brother Charles had done, to meet his wife; and when she found how kind and gentle and brave he was, she soon loved him very much; and as he was a Catholic, she had much less to suffer in that respect than her poor sister-in-law, Catherine of Braganza.

Every body was very kind to the new Duchess of York' and indeed no one could help loving her. She was quite a child, and as innocent and simple as a child; but she had very good sense and judgment. When the ministers and Parliament quarrelled with James, and persuaded Charles to banish him to Scotland, Mary Beatrice went with him, and by her good humour and sweet Christian virtues made every place pleasant to him; and made all the people who saw them love her and the duke too. Scotland, in the winter, must have seemed dreary and desolate enough to the beautiful Italian princess. She no doubt suffered a great deal from the cold, and the rough ways and speech of the Scots; but she bore every thing well, and was really grateful to these loyal and warm-hearted people, who loved the Stuarts with a faithful and constant love.

When Charles died, and James became king, he and his queen were crowned together at Westminster Abbey; and, as you know, there was very great joy all through the country. But the usual troubles of the unfortunate Stuart kings soon began again. Charles had left his brother a very troublesome legacy of bad ministers; the chief of whom were named Lord Sunderland, Lord Halifax, and Lord Godolphin. They were bad men, without any principle, who never spoke the truth, and were secretly plotting against the king the whole time of his reign. Besides these, there was also Lord Churchill, who afterwards became very famous.

James was so honest and truthful himself, and so affectionate, that he could not believe his ministers were deceitful. He trusted every one belonging to him in the same generous but imprudent manner—especially his two sons-in-law, who afterwards behaved very wickedly to him. One of these was Prince George of Denmark, who married Anne. He was a stupid, indolent prince, who was nicknamed at court *Est-il possible?*[23] because he was always asking this question. The other was the cold, selfish Dutch Stadtholder,[24] William of Orange, who married the Princess Mary.

James had no son for a long time; and this caused a great many quarrels and plots. The Princess Anne thought she should succeed to the crown; and as she was selfish and ill-tempered, she hated the beautiful young queen, and hoped she should never have any little brothers. The Princess Mary, on her side, wished her husband to become King of England; and though she spoke kindly, and wrote kind and affectionate letters to her mother-in-law, she was as deceitful and ambitious as her sister Anne.

King James did not know of all these plots and treacherous

---

[23] Is it possible?
[24] Holland was then ruled by a sovereign called by this name, instead of king.

wishes of his children; if he had, he would perhaps have acted differently in many ways, for he was very imprudent. In the first place, he built a large new chapel in Whitehall, where Mass was celebrated with great splendour. This offended and frightened the strong protestant party in England. Next, he quarrelled with the Anglican Bishops, and sent seven of them to the Tower because they would not read in the churches some papers which the king ordered to be read. This was very foolish; especially because two of these Bishops, Dr. Sancroft and Dr. Kenn, were very excellent men, and very zealous in upholding the king's authority against the puritanical or Dutch party. When they saw that he was bent upon forcing everything to give way to his wishes, they began to oppose him as they had never done before. James did another very imprudent thing, which ended by bringing about more mischief than he could ever have foreseen. He had a holy Jesuit for his confessor named Father Petre; and James was so fond of him, that he insisted on making him one of his Privy council. It was contrary to Father Petre's rule to do this, and he was very unhappy at being forced so entirely out of his place; but to try and save the king from the ruin which he foresaw, he consented. All the mischief that followed was, of course, laid at his door, and, what was worse, at the door of the Society to which he belonged, which suffered a great deal in consequence.

Soon after the king had sent the Bishops to the Tower, a little Prince of Wales was born; and it would have been a good opportunity to have pardoned them. But the king would not; he only set them free to be tried, which made the people very angry. And when they had been tried, and found not guilty, there were bonfires made all over the country because the king had been beaten. This ought to have shown

James how imprudent he was; but he would not be stopped in his rash endeavour to make England a Catholic country again. To bring about this more quickly, James asked the Parliament to repeal a law which ordered that no one but Anglicans should hold any places or offices in England. This law was made to prevent Catholics from getting any power in the country; and *Nonconformists,* or, as they are now called, *Dissenters,* were forbidden under the same law to hold any office or place under government, without taking an oath that they were of the established Protestant religion. This law was called the Test Act, because it was made to *test,* or try, who were Catholics and who were not.

King James wrote to the bishops, and did every thing he could to get the Test Act repealed; but he could not persuade them to agree to this, and his son-in-law, Wiiliam the Dutchman, said that he would bring an army against England to support the Protestant cause. He fitted out ships, and raised soldiers very quietly, thinking that at last the time was come for him to be king of England. That he might be more sure of the crown, he and Mary declared that the Prince of Wales was not really the queen's child, but a little baby which the nurse had brought with her. This wicked lie was told and believed by most of the king's enemies. All the time William was doing this, Mary was pretending the greatest love and affection for her father, and writing the most false letters to Mary Beatrice, who besought of her to speak the truth now, and to say what the prince really intended. Anne went away about the same time, pretending that she was sick; but in reality that her father might be more completely betrayed.

At last these false and unnatural children, and the base ministers who were helping them, obtained their end. William of Orange sailed towards England with a large fleet, which was, however, broken to pieces by a violent storm, and he was obliged to go back again to Holland. Louis the Fourteenth, who loved James and his queen very much, begged of him to accept a fleet and army from him, to fight against William. He did this because he knew that William would send away or persecute the English Catholics, if he became king. But nothing would induce James to use the French ships or soldiers. He said if he could not fight with his own English soldiers, he would not fight at all. It was a great pity he did not fight; for he had by far the strongest army, and the greatest number of friends. But this brave and fearless soldier was so unhappy at the treachery of his ministers, whom he had trusted, and above all, of his children, whom he had loved so dearly, that he could only sit still, saying over and over again, "God help me! my own children have deserted me!" In the mean time William landed at Torbay, in the south of England, where several English gentlemen were base enough to join him. The false ministers went into the country, and excited the people into open rebellion. Still the people loved their dear, brave sailor-king so much, that very few, comparatively, joined the Dutch. If James had collected his army then, he might easily have driven them back to Holland.

There was one of his friends who told him all this, and who felt so bitterly the miserable way in which England was given up to what may be truly called a small band of robbers, that he implored the king to let him go by himself and raise an army. This was our old friend, the gallant Lord Dundee, who never left the king while he remained in England. But James was too unhappy to listen even to hopeful words. His heart, like King Lear's in the old story, was quite broken by the cruelty of his daughters; and not only was his heart broken, but his head was so confused, that he did not know what he was doing. His great care was to send away the Queen and the Prince of Wales, who were taken care of by a kind French gentleman named De Lauzun, who came from Paris on purpose to fetch them. This gentleman put the queen and her baby into a little boat at Westminster Bridge, and then took them in disguise to the coast, when they sailed to France in a small vessel. The queen was dressed like a washerwoman, and the baby-prince was rolled up in a bundle of linen. In this way they passed through the whole Dutch fleet, and landed safely in France, where the great Louis the Fourteenth received them with the most generous kindness, and gave them the palace at St. Germains to live in.

Some time after, James resolved to go to France too; and though his friends told him that if he once went away, he would never be able to come back to England again, he would go. This was exactly what William wanted, and he allowed him to escape without trying to prevent him. He went away in a small fishing-vessel, as the queen had done, and suffered all manner of hardships and insults, which he bore with the greatest patience and cheerfulness. When the English people saw their dear king led down the river by the Dutch guards, they sobbed and wept aloud; and kneeling down in crowds on the river's edge, they asked for his blessing. It was indeed a sad and sorrowful sight; and if his unnatural children had been there to see it, I should think even their hard hearts would have melted. But William took care they should not be there. That very night he came to London, and the next morning Whitehall was full of Dutch soldiers, who forced the people to be quiet, and to give up speaking of good King James.

James lived for some years at St. Germains. He came once

to Ireland with an army to try to get back his kingdom; but he lost the battle of the Boyne, and he never came again. Great numbers of Irish, Scotch, and English followed him back to France, and lived at St. Germains with him. They were called *Jacobites,* that is, friends of Jacobus, or James. At one time he had a large body-guard of these brave and faithful friends, who were all gentlemen; and you must hear a beautiful story about them.

Louis the Fourteenth at last thought it was not prudent to have such a large body of foreign soldiers in France, and he told James he must send them to be soldiers in the French army. Before he bade them goodbye, James ordered them to be drawn up in front of the palace, that he might review them once more himself. When he had thanked each one of them for his faithful services, and shaken hands with them, he went back a little, and bowed to them all, with that graceful dignity for which the Stuarts were so celebrated. Then he went away, but he could not help coming back again, and bowing to them once more. When he thought that these dear and loyal friends were going to leave him, and of how much they had suffered for his sake, he burst into a passion of tears. All the gentlemen knelt down, for they could only weep too, and then they got up and saluted their dear King James for the last time, as soldiers do; but no one could speak a word.

Every one loved James, and his beautiful Queen, and the Prince of Wales, and pitied them in their great sufferings. They sold all their jewels to buy food for the poor Jacobites, and at last they had nothing left. The little prince and his sister never bought any sweetmeats or playthings, but always gave all their pocket-money to the poor emigrants, and they ate as little as they possibly could, that they might have more to give them. Every one who saw the prince said that he was

Holy King James

more like an Angel than a human child; and his mother brought him up in the most pious manner possible.

After living in this way for some years at St. Germains, and becoming every year more pious and devout, King James died a holy death, thanking God that He had taken his earthly crown from him, that he might know what the true happiness of an eternal crown in Heaven is. Before he died, he sent for the prince, and spoke to him these beautiful and touching words: "I am now leaving this world, which has been to me a sea of storms and tempests, it being Almighty God's wish to wean me from it by many great afflictions. Serve Him with all your power, and never put the crown of England in competition with your eternal salvation. There is no slavery like sin, nor any liberty like His service. If His holy Providence shall think fit to seat you on the throne of your royal ancestors, govern your people with justice and clemency. *Remember, kings are not made for themselves, but for the good of the people.* Set before their eyes, in your own actions, a pattern of all manner of virtues. Consider them as your children. You are the child of vows and prayers; behave yourself accordingly. Honor your mother, that your days may be long; and be always a kind brother to your dear sister, that you may reap the blessings of concord and unity."

King James was so passionately fond of his people, that even when the French were fighting for him against them, he delighted to hear that the English had won the battle; and once when they told him that the English fleet had been driven away by the French, he said, "Well, well, it is the first time, then!" In one great battle off Cape La Hogue, he stood by to see the English frigates, under Admiral Rooke, run into the very mouths of the French guns; and when he saw their desperate bravery, he cried out, "See, see my brave English!"

This made the French say that he loved his enemies and hated his friends, and this saying, though a little exaggerated, certainly is more or less true of all the Stuart kings.

King James II (1633-1701) portrayed in his role as head of the Army, wearing a General Officer's State coat, attributed to Benedetto Gennari II

Chapter XLIX.

The Dutch King and England's Shame

From 1689 to 1702

T is a pity there is not time to tell you some other interesting stories about the last of the Stuarts, and especially about his dear beautiful Queen and the Prince of Wales; stories which certainly would make you cry over their sufferings, and which would make you love them dearly. But you must be satisfied with looking forward to knowing more about them when you can read larger histories than this. We must go back to England, and to some things which are not so interesting, but which are very important; and you must attend while you read about them.

You know enough already to see that James was an imprudent king; and besides all his own misfortunes, and the sufferings of the poor Jacobites, his imprudence was the cause of other greater evils. Like all the Stuart kings, James had gone beyond the powers which properly belong to the king in the English constitution. He had made other courts besides the courts of Parliament by his own authority, without asking the Parliament's consent; be had imprisoned some of his subjects before they had been tried, and without any warrant of the law; he had forced some of his other subjects to choose superiors or heads for their colleges in Oxford whom they did not wish to choose, with which he had nothing to do; he had kept a standing army, and levied taxes without the consent of Parliament; and he had created a kind of military judges, who went about the country trying and condemning a great many people almost by force.

It is very true that the unsettled state of the country required strong measures, especially after Lord Monmouth's rebellion; but the king should never go beyond the powers which the constitution has given him. He has never done so, nor ever can do so, without either weakening some other part of the constitution, or his own power; and in either case the country must suffer from the injustice. This time, the evils that happened were very sad; for, in the first place, the enemies of the Church laid all the blame upon the king's religion, and upon his holy confessor, who had deserved no blame at all. Next, the moderate Anglicans, those Bishops and noblemen who were friendly to the king, were overpowered by the base and violent ministers, Lord Halifax, Lord Godolphin, and Lord Danby; so that James not only lost the crown himself, but these men persuaded the Parliament to say that the Prince of Wales should not succeed to it either. All hope of a Catholic king of England was thus gone for the present, and the country was overrun by Dutch Calvinists, who were even more bigoted than the English Puritans, if that is possible.

For some time after King James had left England, William of Orange was not proclaimed king. There were three parties who disputed together for a long time, first, whether the

Prince of Wales should be king; secondly, whether there should be a republic again, as it was under Oliver Cromwell, with William for Protector; and, thirdly, whether William and Mary should be proclaimed king and queen of England. After a great deal of disputing, the last party (the leaders of which were Danby, Halifax, and Churchill) gained their point, and William and Mary were proclaimed.

There were several things, however, to be settled first. The Parliament had learned something by experience; and this time the Lords and Commons determined to make William swear to keep the promises of Magna Charta, so many of which had been forgotten. They wrote them down on a long sheet of parchment, which was called the Declaration of Rights, because all the rights of English subjects were written in it, and William was forced to sign it, very much against his will, for he wanted to be a second Oliver Cromwell. However, as he did not wish to sail back to Holland again, he signed it at last, and he and the cold-hearted Mary were crowned.

You will be glad to think that "the laws and customs of good King Edward" were to be kept again; but you will see how sadly some parts of the constitution which St. Edward had done so much to frame had now been spoiled or destroyed. That constitution declares that the crown shall always go to the lawful successor, and this has no doubt been one of the greatest securities of the monarchical power in England. But now the English crown was literally *stolen* by William from the Prince of Wales, just as it had been stolen by Lady Jane Grey from Queen Mary; and as the thieves were the strongest this time, they kept it. The English laws no where say that the king is to be elected or chosen by the people, or that they may choose another when they happen to be tired of the one they have. That would be a republican government, with a man called a king at the head of it. The English constitution is a *real Monarchy*, and the English kings are real kings by the right of descent and of law, and till this time this truth had always been acted up to and preserved, in some way or other, through all the Rose wars and other bloody disturbances of our history. But now this great and useful truth was changed; because the Dutch prince had no right, either of descent or of law. In order to prove that he was a king at all, that is, that any one had a right to say he should be king, the ministers were obliged to say that the English people had a right to change their king when he used any power which the constitution had not given him. This was quite a new doctrine in England, and a dangerous one every where and at all times. The Anglican Bishops were as much puzzled as the Parliament; for, at the Reformation, they had declared that the king was at the head of all spiritual and temporal power; and that one whom God had anointed could never be harmed without committing a great crime. And yet now they had allowed their king to be driven away, and robbed of his crown and kingdom, without raising a voice against it. Some of the Bishops felt this difference between their actions and words so much, that several of them refused to sign the papers William wished, or to own him for their king. Among these was King James's friend, Dr. Sancroft, who was sent to prison. These Bishops are always called the *Nonjurors*, because they would not take the oath the king asked of them.

And now that it is to be hoped you understand these things, which are rather difficult for you, you must hear what happened in William and Mary's reign.

Every one thought that Mary the Second would have shown some sorrow or sadness at coming and taking possession of her father's palace, and at seeing all his things, which he had left behind him, and which were still lying about in the rooms. He had been the very kindest father to her, and had always loved her the best of his children, so that even if she could not help being glad that her husband was king of England, you would think that she would show a little sorrow for her dear father. But, on the contrary, Mary did nothing but run about the palace at Whitehall, looking at the furniture, and laughing, and talking loud, as if she was glad she had so many fine things, and could not think of any thing else. Even her own friends, and the flatterers at court, who were all trying to get what they could, were disgusted with this heartless and unnatural woman; and even the greatest flatterer of all, the man who has written a book full of falsehoods, which he calls a history of the times, Dr. Burnet, allows that Mary's behaviour shocked him.

When King James heard that his daughter was actually crowned with the crown of which she had robbed him, he wrote her a terrible letter, in which he told her that the curse of an injured and betrayed father would certainly come upon her for her crime. William of Orange was frightened at this letter; but Mary said angrily, that "he had only himself to thank, for letting her father go." These cruel words were carried to the king at St. Germains, and he exclaimed that his own children had now lost all compassion for him, and were ready to cry, "Away with him from the face of the earth!" After this, the Jacobite poets compared Mary the Second to the Roman Tullia, the daughter of Tullius Hostilius, who drove over her father's body after he was dethroned; and the Scotch called her always in scorn, " Mary, the *daughter.*"

William was liked still less than Mary. He was a little, peevish, ordinary-looking man, who spoke very little, and then only a few dry words. He smoked a great deal, and drank a great deal of Hollands gin, but never allowed any one to eat or drink with him but his own Dutch friends. If the English noblemen came in while he was at dinner, they were forced to stand behind his chair like so many footmen.

It must be confessed that they richly deserved such treatment, and even worse, for their base treachery to their kind and noble king—for it was only the traitors and flatterers who became William's courtiers. Most of them behaved so ill, and robbed the country of so much money, that poor Duke Schomberg, William's favorite Dutch general, said that he never saw a nation so willing to steal. Another of William's Dutchmen, named Bentinck, asked his master one day if he thought there was one honest man in all Great Britain. "Yes," the king answered with a sigh, "there are as many honorable men in England as in any country, but *they are not my friends.*" He spoke the truth: the bravest and most loyal British nobles were across the sea, at St. Germains, or serving foreign kings in other countries, or lying dead upon Irish or Scottish battle-fields.

You already know that King James came to Ireland to try and get back his crown. This was during William and Mary's reign. Lord Tyrconnel, and most of the brave old Catholic Irish, joined him; and after the battle of the Boyne, they were most cruelly punished for it by the savage Dutchmen. All the miseries of Elizabeth's and Oliver Cromwell's reigns were revived again, till the best of them would not bear such treatment any longer, and 20,000 brave Irishmen went abroad and served in the French wars as the Irish Brigade.

In Scotland William behaved as cruelly. Our old friend Bonnie Dundee went into the Highlands, and raised an army to fight for King James. He won a great battle at Killiecrankie; but just at the end of it, he was killed, and his soldiers were obliged to give up the struggle. It was a long time, however, before Scotland was quiet, or would submit to William of Orange; for although King James was a Catholic, the Scotch had never loved any of the Stuarts more than they loved him. They made beautiful songs about him and the Prince of Wales; and many of them wrote to him as long as he lived, and told him all that was going on.

William was always at war somewhere or other. He did not think or care about any thing else; and all the money that could be got out of his people, and all the gold and silver furniture in Whitehall, which he melted down, was spent in battles and sieges, which did no good to the country. So much money, indeed, was spent, that William was obliged to ask his Parliament to raise *loans;* that is, to borrow money from merchants and bankers, who were paid so much a-year for lending it. The money that was borrowed and shot away by William has never been paid back again; and every year the government, or rather the country, has to pay so much for his borrowing it. So we are none of us much obliged to William of Orange. These debts are called the National Debt, about which you cannot understand much till you grow up; but you must not forget that it was Oliver Cromwell and William the Dutchman who put this great burden upon the country, which they professed to be delivering from oppression. Whenever men sweep away what is just and right, to make way for something *they fancy* to be more just and right, they always bring this kind of punishment upon themselves. Most of William's wars were with Louis XIV. on the borders of France and Flanders, or what is now called Belgium. They were ended by the Peace of Ryswick, which was signed at Ryswick, in Holland. While he was away, he always left Mary to govern for him; and she governed very well. She was a clever and sensible woman, and very brave and determined. She amused herself between whiles with planting the gardens at Kensington, spoiling Hampton Court by turning it into a Dutch palace, stitching at every kind of fancy-work, and knitting fringe.

After six years' reign, Mary died of the smallpox. William, who had behaved very badly to her all her life, was extremely unhappy at her death. Her best friends were unhappy too; for she died at enmity with her sister, and without once confessing that she repented of her wicked conduct to her kind father. William lived seven years after Mary's death. He was killed by a fall from his horse at Hampton Court. No one loved him, so no one was sorry for his death.

We are very often told that the Revolution of 1688 was very "glorious," and that William and Mary's reign was of the greatest use and good to England; and because this has been said so often, it has been believed. But as the truth has been found out in the history of Elizabeth and Mary the first, so it has been found out too of Mary the second and the "glorious" revolution. You have already heard that one of the greatest burdens of our country was given us by William. Great taxes were another of his "benefits;" and the shameless custom of taking bribes for services became so common, that the House of Commons was afraid to ask which of its members was guilty, because nearly every one of them felt conscious that he was one who ought to be punished! This is one of the most disgraceful facts in our history.

Indeed, the state of morals in this country was altogether so bad, that there was scarcely a single book written in this "glorious" reign which can be read. All the books that were written were either bad plays and poems, or jesting stories and foolish tales, full of impurity and wickedness. Mary often went to see these wicked plays acted, and she made one of the worst of the play-writers her Poet-Laureate instead of Dryden; that is, the poet who is chosen by the court. It was very sad to think that the beautiful poets of Catholic England, or who had been nourished in the spirit of the Church, were all gone; and that instead of Chaucer, Spenser, Surrey, Shakspeare, and Jonson, there were only a race of vile and wicked scribblers. All that was in any way high or noble seemed to have departed out of England with its last Catholic king, or to have joined in hating the rule of William and Mary; for every writer in prose or verse of this time, who possessed a single merit, was a Jacobite. The most famous of these was John Dryden, who wrote some really magnificent poems, full of bitter satire upon the ministers and other characters of his time. Very few of these poems, however, are fit for you to read. Some of the Jacobites made droll songs and verses to ridicule William and Mary's life at Hampton, and the perpetual wars in Flanders. Their life at Hampton Court must have been a real Dutch one; for Mary's only occupation at home was gardening, knitting white fringe, and eating great dinners and suppers. William never spoke but smoked, drank, and slept a great deal. The whole court always went to bed at ten o'clock.

The Jacobites made some bitter, but admirably true verses on the established Church, its unbaptized king, and unbaptized Archbishop Dr. Tillotson, which are here put down for you:—

> "Here lies the widowed Anglican Church,
> Half-buried, half-dead, and left in the lurch!
> Oh, sick and sorrowful English Church,
> You weep and wail, and sadly search

> *To hide from the mocking enemy*
> *The utter shame of your misery!*
>
> *Let not Rome know*
> *The depths of your woe.*
>
> *By fanatics bit, from the land of fogs*[25]
> *Defiled and choked by a plague of frogs;*
> *Oh, sorrowing wretched Anglican Church,*
> *Speak not of your head*[26] *or archbishop;*
> *For that schismatic primate and Holland king*
> *Are still in want of christening!"*

It was certainly no chance accident that inflicted so awful a punishment on this wretched country for its sins, as a king and a primate who had neither of them been baptized. The more we look into the history of that time, the better we shall be able to judge the depth of moral misery and evil that had fallen upon it. The jails were full of abandoned wretches, huddled together without any order or discipline, and at night the very jailors themselves went out to steal. Every kind of cruelty, vice, and disorder was committed in these prisons, and every one who went in came out a great deal worse instead of better for his imprisonment. Mary tried a dreadful ways of lessening thefts, but she only succeeded in taking the lives of a number of innocent persons, and encouraging still greater wickedness. This way was, to offer a sum of money to any one who should inform against a thief, which was called *blood-money,* and to get this money, many wicked men went and accused innocent persons, who were put to death. The most famous of these blood-seekers was Jonathan Wild, who boasted at his execution that he had

---

[25] Holland
[26] William of Orange

taken the lives of *sixty-seven* persons. Another great cause of crime was the encouragement William gave to drinking gin, and other distilled liquors, instead of beer, which soon became a frightful habit among the English and Irish poor.

There were no improvements in architecture or painting in this reign. William's only idea was to build heavy, ugly Dutch palaces, and to plant stiff Dutch gardens, in which the poor trees were cut into wigs, ducks, drakes, dragons, and every kind of monster, and Mary followed his tastes in every way. The last good painter was Sir Godfrey Kneller, who was, like all the other men of talent of the time, a zealous Jacobite. The court-paintings afterwards became nothing but miserable daubs.

The English language was as much injured by the bad taste of the time as every thing else. The sentences became, like the court, heavy and Dutch, and were stuffed with unnecessary conceited phrases, which led to no conclusion. Dryden and Swift were almost the only exceptions to this great fault. Burnet, the court-bishop, court-flatterer, and court-liar, was among the very worst writers of this style.

The most useful thing done during this reign was issuing the new coinage. The money had become so light by being *clipped*—that is, by having pieces cut off the coins—that it was good for nothing. Mary recalled all the light money, and issued a new good coinage. She did this while William was away on some of his perpetual wars, so that she has all the merit of this act of justice to her subjects.

It was Mary also who gave Greenwich Palace for a hospital for wounded sailors. It has been ever since the noble Greenwich Hospital, which you have either seen or must see some day, where the brave sailors who are wounded, and lose their arms or legs in battle, live comfortably for the rest of their lives at their country's expense.

These are very nearly all the benefits our country received at William and Mary's hands, for in the Bill of Rights, you know, they had no share.

Prince William of Orange and Mary Stuart by Gerard Honthorst

Chapter L.

Kind Queen Anne and the Fierce Duchess

From 1702 to 1714

WHEN William and Mary were dead, Anne became the peaceable possessor of the crown. We have spoken of her before; and there is not much need to describe a face which you must have seen so often, in pictures and statues, in town-halls and other public buildings. She was very fat and broad, like her mother, and very fond of eating, like her sister Mary. Her face was kind and goodnatured, and she had a very sweet melodious voice, which made it pleasant to hear her speak. She had, too, been taught to speak well and distinctly, so as to be heard at a great distance without talking loud which is a very necessary accomplishment for queens, who have to speak in the House of Parliament and in large assemblies.

As has been said before, Anne was a very ignorant woman; and her understanding had never been cultivated nor improved; so that she spent most of her time in gossiping, cardplaying, and dressing. The chief history of her reign belongs to her ministers and generals, and not to her, for she was all her life only a cipher, or, as she most justly called herself, a "crowned slave."

She had a great favorite, whom she had raised from a low rank, and married to the base Lord Churchill, who had betrayed and deceived King James the Second. This favorite's name was Sarah Jennings, and her husband was made Duke of Marlborough by Anne. This Duchess of Marlborough, who was one of the proudest and fiercest women that were ever known, ruled Anne entirely. She managed all the state affairs, gave away all the places and offices at court, and spent the queen's money just as she chose. She was so proud, and passionate, and ungrateful, that she treated her kind and too indulgent mistress with open contempt. Although she had heaped favors upon her, she even calumniated and misrepresented her character in the blackest manner. Certainly Anne could expect little that was good from so bad and ungovernable a woman; but Lady Marlborough's conduct embittered and saddened her whole life.

The fierce Duchess had a friend named Lord Godolphin, who was one of her ministers, and a very mischievous one. Godolphin and the Duke, or rather the Duchess, of Marlborough were both Whigs, and, with one or two others, were the heads of the Whig party. Lord Bolingbroke, Lord Shaftesbury, and Harley, were the heads of the Tory party. The Whigs wished the Elector of Hanover to be Anne's successor; the Tories wished to restore the crown to James, the son of their Stuart king, James the Second. In this the Tories were just and right; but as men, it is difficult to say which side was the most profligate and corrupt. Lord Bolingbroke was a man of the most extraordinary genius and talents, and a beautiful writer, but he was too an open infidel. Lord Shaftesbury was the same; and both of them were bad and dishonest ministers.

Louis the Fourteenth, whose conquests had been spreading on every side of France, at last began a war with Austria, and tried to get possession of Vienna and Bavaria. The English were afraid that this great king would really conquer the whole of Europe; and they sent the Duke of Marlborough with an army to help the Austrians. The Austrian general was named Prince Eugene; and he was a very holy and excellent man, as well as being one of the greatest generals that have ever lived. He spent all his spare time in meditation and in reading the *Imitation of Christ;* so that, after a great battle, or just before the battle began, when all the preparations were made, he might be found in his tent, reading as calmly and peacefully as if he were sitting at home in his own library.

The Duke of Marlborough's success was most extraordinary. He very soon forced the French to leave Flanders; and although Louis's generals, Marshal Villeroy and Marshal Tallard, were both brave and celebrated soldiers, they were obliged to give up Bavaria very soon after; and at the battle of Blenheim the French were completely routed and beaten, and their fine army broken to pieces. There were three other great battles fought at Oudenarde, Ramillies, and Malplaquet, which Marlborough won; and he afterwards took Bouchain, which Marshal Villars thought could never be taken, and which opened the way directly into the heart of France.

It was these continued and overwhelming losses which at length broke down the venerable old age of Louis the Fourteenth, who, whatever the errors of his life had been, was always the devoted and most faithful champion and guardian of the interests of religion, not only in France, but throughout Europe. As long as he lived, his great name and authority kept in check the growing heresies and infidelity which had crept in and sprung up in France, always the hotbed of every kind of novelty and excitement. Under his sheltering protection Catholic education had been steadily preserved from dangerous innovations; and pious and learned missionaries had added many thousands of souls to the Church, particularly in South America and in China; while in every branch of science and literature enlightened and religious men were encouraged by him to make greater efforts for the benefit and instruction of his people. At his death the glory of France may be said indeed to depart; for notwithstanding the efforts of many good and capable men, under his weak and unfortunate successors that unhappy country became a prey to infidelity, and finally to the most terrible convulsions of wickedness and impiety.

Marlborough's splendid victories saved Austria; but they did very little good to England. The French composed a song called *Malbruk,* which immortalised the fame of the great soldier; and the English nation gave him a magnificent palace, and a park near Woodstock, which was called Blenheim, to commemorate the greatest of his victories. But the taxes pressed very much heavier upon the people, and the national debt, William of Orange's legacy, was increased. And certainly, if the people were not benefited by these, which are called "splendid victories," the poor queen was still less so. She remained always in leading-strings, and harassed to death by the perpetual home-battles of her rival ministers Harley and Godolphin, and the still more petty and miserable squabbles of her fierce tyrant, Sarah Duchess of Marlborough.

At last Harley told her that the Duchess was queen instead of herself, which made Anne angry, and she sent away the Duchess, and would not allow her to have a place at court, or to see her again. Then the Duke of Marlborough and Godolphin were no longer ministers; but Harley and Bolingbroke, the Tory ministers, took their places. This was what, for so many years, these ambitious and dishonest men had been plotting for; but just as every one thought that now the young Stuart prince would be named Anne's successor, the queen fell very ill, and died before the ministers could get her to say that she would perform this act of justice; and as she had already said that her cousin George of Hanover should be king after her, Harley and Bolingbroke were obliged to give way, and to leave the power which they had been coveting all their lives, and for which they had committed so many bad actions, after they had enjoyed it only three days.

One very useful thing was done in Anne's reign; and as it put an end to many quarrels and jealousies, it was a lasting benefit to our country. This was the union of Scotland with England by Act of Parliament. When James the First came to the throne, Scotland ceased to be a separate country from England. It had the same king and government as England; but still it had not the same laws; and the Scots complained very much when they were obliged to obey the English laws instead of their own.

With Anne's consent her ministers and Parliament ordered that the Scots should now obey the same laws as the English people, or wherever this was not possible or advisable, from the different habits and circumstances of the two countries, that the Scots should be excused from obeying some particular laws. The Scottish members of parliament looked after their countrymen, and took care to mention in Parliament whenever they found that any new law was bad for their country; so that the Scots found themselves really much better off after the Union than they were before it. Some of the Scottish gentlemen, however, were very unhappy, because they loved to keep up the particular customs and national habits of Scotland; and among these, Andrew Fletcher of

Saltoun was the foremost. When the Union Act was signed, he exclaimed with bitter tears, that "Scotland was sold by traitors, and that now it was not fit for honest men to live in!" and then he got on his horse, and left his home at Saltoun, and went to die as an exile in France. He never came back to Scotland again. In the end, however, every one was glad that the Legislative Act of Union had passed.

Anne was a very kind and charitable queen to the poor. She had less money than any queen of England ever had before; but she spent so little of it upon herself, that she was able to pay her sister's debts, and to give away a great deal every year to distressed tradesmen, and old servants and soldiers. All the poor loved her very much indeed, and they always called her "Good Queen Anne." And if, as is certain, there is no better queen than one who loves and cherishes her *poor* subjects, and wins the blessings of those who have no court to pay her, and no rich presents to offer her, we must declare that the ignorant and homely Queen Anne's reign was of great benefit, and that all the misery she suffered from her insolent women and her miserable ministers, which must have made her shed many bitter tears in private, did not sour or narrow her kind and charitable heart.

There is a droll story told of her, which perhaps you will like to hear, as it shows also her kindness in entering into the ways and feelings of her subjects. This will be a very fit place for it.

Prince George of Denmark, the queen's husband, went once to pay a visit to Bristol; and when he had looked at the chief buildings of the city, he went on the Exchange, where the Bristol merchants transact their business. All the rich merchants looked at the prince, who had only one officer with him; and either because they did not feel sure of his being Prince George, or because they were too shy to speak to so great a personage, they all finished their business and went away, without asking him to dine with any of them.

There was only one inferior merchant left, named John Duddlestone; and when the honest man saw that all his grand companions were gone, and the prince was left alone, he felt that it was very inhospitable. So he went up to the prince, and said that he heard he was the queen's husband, and that he was sure it was only because they were too bashful that his brother-merchants had not asked him to dinner. He added, that he was only a poor plain man, but that if Prince George would go home with him and dine upon roast beef and plum-porridge, he was heartily welcome. The prince was pleased with this frank invitation, and he went home with John Duddlestone. When they got to the house, John cried out, "Dame, dame! come down I say and put on a clean apron, for the queen's husband is come to dine with us!" So down accordingly came Dame Duddlestone in a clean blue apron, and the prince feasted with this honest pair. When he went away, Prince George invited John and his dame to come and dine with him at Windsor Castle, and bade them goodbye, with many thanks. Some time after, John actually went to London on horse-back and took his wife behind him. They dined with the queen and prince, and after dinner the queen bade John Duddlestone kneel down, when she struck him with the *accolade*, or stroke of knighthood, and imitating his wife's manner of speaking, said to him, "*Ston up, Sir Jan!*"

Besides the ambitious Duke of Marlborough, with his soft and treacherous voice, and his fierce revengeful duchess (who was an open infidel), and the profligate group of ministers, there were several other remarkable persons in this reign, who were writers as well as courtiers. Swift was among the boldest, cleverest, and worst of these. Addison wrote very beautiful prose, and his papers in the Spectator will always be among the English classics. Pope was the best poet of the time, and among the best of his poems which you may read, is his version of Homer's Iliad. Dr. Johnson also wrote many works, which, though ponderous and artificial, are beautiful examples of latinised English.

Among the admirals was Admiral Rooke, who took Gibraltar; and it has always belonged to the English since Queen Anne's time. Although it is so far off, it is very useful for us to have Gibraltar, because, as it is on a very high rock and strongly fortified, and as the strait is narrow, the soldiers in the fort can prevent ships from passing in or out of the Mediterranean Sea.

You know that numbers of ships are passing all day through the straits of Gibraltar, bringing currants, and oranges, and almonds, and silk, and many other goods from Greece and Italy, so that it is very useful for us to have this *key*, as it is called, to hinder them in case of war.

This was the only useful conquest in Queen Anne's reign.

Good Queen Anne by Charles Jervas

Chapter LI.

The Hanoverian Kings
From 1714 to 1727

THE newly restored Whig ministers sent a message to the Elector of Hanover, as soon as Anne was dead, begging of him to come to England as quickly as he could. It was not in the Elector's nature, however, to do any thing quickly, and it was seven weeks before he got to his new kingdom, where he was proclaimed king, as George the First. The first thing he did was to choose a new set of ministers; and to every body's surprise, the ambitious soft-voiced Duke of Marlborough was not one of them. One of the chief new ministers was Sir Robert Walpole, who was witty and accomplished. He was, however, a bad man, and a very dishonest statesman.

On the Tory side, the leaders were Lord Bolingbroke, and a great friend of his, whom he made as bad as himself. His name was Sir William Wyndham, who was a most celebrated orator, and his speeches in the English Parliament will always be remembered for their wit and beauty. It mattered very little what ministers governed the country then; for ever since the time of Charles the Second, there had been scarcely one honest minister, or scarcely even one honest member of parliament. They were not ashamed to take money openly from any one who would pay them; and unless they had pensions and presents given them, they would not vote, or do their duty as members. Some of them even were base enough to take money from the king and from the Jacobites too; so that they betrayed each party by turns. Certainly you will feel ashamed to hear such things of the noblemen and gentlemen

George I by Godfrey Kneller, 1714

of our country, and will look back to the happy time of Catholic England, when the just and noble Eoldermen used to meet in King Alfred's Witan, or when the brave barons used to sit round the Plantagenet kings, all together trying, "with pure hands and a clean heart," to cause justice to be done throughout the land.

The profligate ministers of George the First thought very little about these things. Their chief ambition was to become rich; and to do this, they helped a number of dishonest merchants, and of very foolish people, to set on foot a speculation called "the South-Sea Scheme," by which they proposed to get a great treasure of wealth in the South-Sea Islands and South America. Every one ran to join in this foolish project, which soon became a kind of madness. Whole families sold their property, and lent the money to the South-Sea Company, expecting to gain enormous fortunes. But very soon the company became bankrupt; and thus not only the greater part of the people were ruined, but the nation became bankrupt. The public debts could not be paid, and the distress was very shocking. Lord Sunderland, the minister who was the most to blame, was not punished, though he was proved guilty.

To add to the distress, there was a civil war for a little while. Prince James, who was generally called the Chevalier St. George, landed in Scotland, and soon collected an army round him to try to get back his crown. Lord Mar was his chief friend in Scotland, and Lord Derwentwater and Lord Nithisdale helped him in England. The prince was proclaimed king as James the Third, at Scone, and for a little while every one thought he really would be king. But Lord Mar managed so badly, that his troops were every where beaten, though he might easily have won several battles; and the prince sailed back again to France. Before he went, he wrote a letter to the Duke of Argyle, who had been his chief opposer, with all the money he had left, and asked him to divide it among some poor people, whose cottages he had burned. You will think that it was like the son of the good King James and Mary Beatrice, to behave in so noble and charitable a manner.

"The Chevalier St. George, commonly called The Pretender" in *Cassell's Illustrated History of England, Volume 4,* John Cassell

George the First behaved neither nobly nor charitably, but with great cruelty. He condemned all the noblemen who had fought for the Prince to be put to death, and all the common people to be put in prison. All the prisons in the north of England were filled with these unfortunate people, who suffered the most cruel and inhuman hardships. The prisons were filthy and unwholesome dens, where even an animal could scarcely live, and they were often left to die of hunger in the greatest misery. Very many of these poor wretches were taken out of prison to be hanged and quartered; and perhaps this was the greatest act of George's mercy. Lady Derwentwater and several other ladies went and threw themselves at his feet to beg the pardon of the condemned lords, but George would not hear them. When the brave and good Lord Derwentwater was led to execution, he prayed for the restoration of the ancient Stuart line; and when they offered him his life, if he would leave his faith, he answered that he would rather die a thousand deaths than forsake the true religion. Kneeling down, he repeated three times, "Dear Jesus, be merciful to me!" and his head was cut off at one blow. The people gave a loud groan when they saw he was dead, for he was Charles the Second's grandson, and very much beloved.

Lord Nithisdale escaped through the courage and ingenuity of his brave wife, who took another lady, whom she called her maid, in two suits of clothes with her to the prison. When the gaoler was gone, Lord Nithisdale put on the suit of clothes which the lady wore over his own, and his wife went away with the sham lady, who pretended to cry

The escape of Lord Nithisdale, disguised as a woman, from the Tower of London, 1716. Hilary Morgan / Alamy Stock Photo

very much, that she might hide her face in her handkerchief. By this means he escaped to France.

By his cruel and cowardly want of mercy George the First made himself more disliked by every one. As it was, he had very few friends. His coarse, brutal manners, his ignorance of English, which he never took any pains to learn, and contempt of the laws and constitution of his own kingdom, offended the noblemen and gentlemen. His profligate life and habits of drunkenness made every one sorry and ashamed for him. He had a good and kind wife, named Sophia of Zell, whom he shut up in a castle in Germany for seventeen years, because some wicked people had accused her of crimes which she had never committed; and he was always quarrelling with his son, the Prince of Wales.

Nothing succeeded well in this reign. A great league was made between some of the chief kings of Europe, in which Spain, Austria, Russia, and Prussia united against England. The English sent Sir Charles Wager to blockade the Russian fleet at Revel, but they did not succeed. Another fleet was sent against Spain, but the ships all decayed at anchor, for the sailors died of fever. The admiral of this unfortunate fleet was Admiral Hosier, who died with his men; and many beautiful sea-songs are still sung about him and Portobello, where he and his poor sailors died.

At last George the First died a miserable death. His poor wife wrote him a letter just before she died, in which she called upon him to meet her before the Judgment-seat of God; and this letter was given to him when he was in Germany, just as he was setting out in his coach to go to Osnaburg. It struck him so much with horror and remorse, that it threw him into a fit, and when the coach stopped at Osnaburg he was dead.

CHAPTER LII.

Prince Charlie

From 1727 to 1760

THE Prince of Wales succeeded his father as George the Second. He had more talents and industry than his father, and a better disposition, but he lived quite as profligate a life. Walpole was made prime minister, and continued all his dishonest practices, in which he was joined by his brother-ministers.

Sir William Wyndham and Mr. Pulteney were the opposition ministers; that is, the ministers who chiefly were at the head of the other party. Some Acts of Parliament which were passed in this reign tell us a sad tale of the vice and misery which deluged once-merry England. Ever since William of Orange had encouraged the people to drink gin, and to make it cheap, the drunkenness from ardent spirits had become the common amusement of our poor countrymen. This led to every other vice, and to most dreadful misery and disease. When the Houses of Parliament were consulting about making some laws to try and stop this miserable frenzy for gin, a great many things were told which make one shudder to read, and which show us what a populous and civilized nation must become without the guiding and purifying influence of the Church and the sacraments.

Besides gin-drinking, the love of smoking had become also a kind of madness, and many thousands of brave and active young men were engaged in smuggling tobacco instead of following an honest trade. Two Scotchmen, named Robertson and Wilson, were seized in Edinburgh for this offence, and one of them was hanged. As this made the people very angry, they raised a riot, and the captain of the troops fired at them and killed some of them. For this he was sentenced to be shot, because he had not warned the people beforehand of what he was going to do, but he was reprieved. This so enraged the people, who wished him to be shot, that they broke into the prison and hanged him. This is always called the Porteus riot, from the name of the captain.

There was war abroad as well as at home. The Spaniards had a good many colonies in South America, and they brought from there a great deal of logwood and redwood, which were used in dyeing cloth of a fine black, and purple, and red color. The English thought they should like to go and fetch some of this logwood from the American woods in their own ships, instead of buying it from the Spaniards, and they sent some men to cut logwood trees in Campeachy Bay. The Spaniards did not wish to lose their trade, and they began to fight with the English soldiers, and the English went to war with Spain. Commodore Anson was sent out with a good many ships, and he sailed quite round the world, as Sir Francis Drake had done. Another admiral, named Vernon, was very unfortunate, and was shamefully beaten by the Spaniards at Carthagena. There was a third, named Admiral Byng, who was more unfortunate still. He went to fight the

Spaniards in the Mediterranean, and because he did not do all that the Parliament ordered him to do, he was shot when he came home to England.

At last, both Spain and England were tired of war, and peace was made between them. There was no peace, however, for England, but the next war was a just and generous one. The Emperor of Austria, Charles the Sixth, died, and left only a daughter, named Maria Theresa. He asked the kings of Europe to promise and acknowledge her as his successor, and they agreed to it by a treaty which is called by the hard name of the Pragmatic Sanction. But when Charles was dead, the kings were base enough to break the treaty, and to take slices of Maria Theresa's dominions for themselves. She was obliged to fly to Hungary, where she went into the Hungarian Parliament as the nobles were all assembled, with her little boy in her arms, and said to them: "Hungarians, I have nothing to trust to but your faithfulness, and I am come with my son, to place myself in your keeping." When they saw their beautiful and good empress, without a friend to fly to, or a place to put her child in safety, and knew that she had base enemies on every side of her, the brave and chivalrous Hungarian nobles drew their swords, and as they clashed them together, they shouted out, "We will die for our *king* Maria Theresa!"

England was the only country generous enough to help Maria Theresa and her brave Hungarians. An army was sent, and beat the French at the battle of Dettingen; and soon afterwards in some other places, so that she was firmly seated on her father's throne.

There was war in England itself too. Prince James was dead; but he had married a Polish lady, and they had two sons, one was named Charles Edward, and the other Henry.

Henry became a priest and went to Rome, where he was made a Cardinal, and is always called Cardinal York. He lived to be very old, and died at Rome. Charles Edward came to Scotland, to try to get back the English crown. He was a very handsome and pleasing young man, very gentle and kind and good; but it was a pity that he came, for now the house of Hanover was so firmly seated on the throne, that every one wished for peace and quiet, that they might plow their land, and reap their corn, and give their children bread, for the long and continual wars and disturbances had caused great distress.

The Battle of Culloden by David Morier, 1746.

Charles Edward went and lived in the palace at Holyrood in Scotland for some time just like a king, when the nobles gathered round him, and he got together a considerable army. He then came to Preston Pans, where he gained a complete victory over the Duke of Cumberland, who was sent against him. He even came as far as Derby; but he found that no one cared much about him, and he went back again to Culloden, where his army was quite cut to pieces by the

Duke of Cumberland. He escaped with great difficulty, and was hidden for a long time in the hills and caves of Scotland. At last he escaped through the courage of Flora Macdonald, a very brave and beautiful young lady, who called him her servant, and rode with him a long way in disguise, till he could get to the sea-shore, and go back to France, where he died. A great many beautiful Scotch songs were written about "Prince Charlie;" and for a long time the Scotch drank his health as "Charlie over the water." Nothing could quench their faithful untiring love for the old line of the Stuart kings.

The Duke of Cumberland, who was George's second son, behaved with the most disgusting cruelty after the battle of Culloden. He set up whole lines of gibbets along the roads, and left the poor people hanging on them. A large district, for fifty miles, was burnt entirely barren; so that neither men, nor women, nor children, nor cattle, nor corn, were left upon it. The prisons were crammed with the miserable inhabitants, who were condemned to be hanged, torn asunder, and their hearts thrown into the fire. All who escaped this cruel death were shipped on board transport vessels, and sold as slaves in the West Indies. It is scarcely to be believed that such atrocious outrages were committed in England such a short time ago; but it is still more difficult to believe that Englishmen could sit in Parliament and see such things done, without daring to lift a voice to protest against them. One Scotchman only was found, named Duncan Forbes, to speak in honest indignation, and he was so ill treated in consequence, that he died of a broken heart.

But happily a better minister now appeared, who, however his motives might be mixed with ambition, still really loved his country, and employed all his great energies and talents for what he honestly thought its good. This was William Pitt,

Lord Chatham, who joined the opposition against Walpole; and having taken office with the Duke of Newcastle, became in the end prime minister himself. Lord Chatham was one of the most powerful and brilliant orators that have been known in this country; and in his bursts of indignant eloquence, and his strong and vivid apostrophes[27] to those he opposed, he has often been compared to Demosthenes. It is strange that although scarcely a fragment of any of his speeches remain, for they were not allowed to be written down then as they are now. Yet still, the remembrance of his majestic attributes, his beautiful voice, his eagle eye, and his overpowering torrent of indignant scorn with which he overwhelmed every dishonest or petty opponent, will never be forgotten in the English Parliament.

Under Lord Chatham the foreign bands of German and Hessian troops which the Hanoverian kings brought in really to enslave England, were for ever disbanded, and instead of these, militia were raised all through the country. These were farmers, shopkeepers, and peasants, who were commanded by the noblemen and gentlemen of their own counties, whom they knew and loved; and they were obliged to serve for ten years. The people were very glad to do this for their dear country, and to get rid of the hated foreigners, and they loved Lord Chatham for trusting the defence of their country to themselves.

He managed the foreign wars so much better than the former minister, whose dishonesty it really was that had caused our armies and navies to be beaten. They had given the command of the ships and regiments of soldiers to young men who knew nothing about fighting or managing a vessel,

[27] The nature of an apostrophe should here be explained to children.

William Pitt, 1st Earl of Chatham after Richard Brompton

because they were their own cousins, or uncles, or brothers, or of noble family. It was quite enough then for a young officer to be related to some great man in office, to become a commanding officer, however badly he behaved. The brave old officers who were not nobly born were never rewarded; and they were not employed when they ought to have been, and often died in great poverty and neglect. Lord Chatham said that this should be no longer the case; and he took great pains to find out the really good and brave officers in the army and navy, and when he had had them tried, he gave them the command of ships and regiments, whether they were well-born or not. This act of justice not only made the people love him still more, and benefited numbers of brave and honest men, but it also made our armies and navies much better than they were before; for bad generals and admirals always make bad soldiers and sailors.

This led to new conquests. You perhaps recollect, that in Elizabeth's reign a number of merchants got leave to conquer part of India, and to govern it under the queen; and that they were afterwards called the East India Company. I dare say, too, that you have often heard of East India Directors, and have perhaps seen the India House in London, where they transact their business. You know that they must have a great deal of business to do, because the trade with the East Indies is very great. Sugar, and rice, and ivory, and many costly woods for dyeing, muslins and shawls, and silk and cotton, besides diamonds and rubies, and many kinds of fruits, are brought from India. The East India Company has a great number of ships, which are always going backwards and forwards to fetch these things, and to carry back other goods to India.

In George the Second's reign, some other merchants thought they should like to have a share in the trade with that rich country; and they went and traded in India without asking leave of the East India Company, who went to war with them, and many Englishmen were killed by their own countrymen, for the sake of a little money. After a while, however, they agreed to join their money together, and to call themselves the United East India Company, which it has ever since continued to be. This new company began to conquer a good many of the native chiefs, who were called nabobs and rajahs; and Lord Chatham sent a number of soldiers to help them to fight, and some brave generals, the chief of whom was Lord Clive.

The name of the Indian viceroy was Surajah Dowlah, a cruel and bad man, who marched suddenly upon the English at Calcutta in time of peace, and cutting a good many of them to pieces, and shut one hundred and forty-six men up in a room 20 feet square, called the Black Hole. The wretched men were soon raving mad, and began to fight with one another to get room to stand by two little slits in the wall, which were the only air-holes. In the morning only twenty-three ghastly men staggered out of this dreadful prison. One hundred and twenty-three dead bodies lay upon the floor.

Lord Clive fought a good many battles with Surajah, and performed wonderful deeds of courage and ingenuity. He beat the Indians so completely, and frightened them so much, that they always called him "the Daring in War." He had the French to fight with as well as the Indians; for they had several important settlements in India, especially at Pondicherry and Trichinopoli. Lord Clive beat them and their brave general Lally so entirely, that the French had not a single settlement left in India. At last Surajah was assassinated by some of his own countrymen; and the English gained a great deal of his territory, and made peace with the natives. It is sad to think that the enormous riches gained in this war, and the treasures of gold and precious stones, and rich stuffs and furniture, which were brought to England, were not all fairly and honestly gained. It is very sad to think what treachery and cruelty our countrymen were guilty of there. Lord Clive brought an immense fortune home with him; but he was never happy, and soon put an end to his life.

The conquests he had made were very important for our country. If you look in the map, you will see what a vast country India is. It is 1900 miles long, and 1500 miles broad; and contains 140,000,000 of inhabitants; that is to say, there are as many people as there are in Russia, Prussia, Austria, and France put together. Part of it, as on the Indus, is like an enormous park full of valuable trees. Rohilcund is full of corn and mango-groves. Bengal is covered with rice-plains, which stretch for hundreds of miles; and in the Deccan the rich maize, and many other kinds of grain, reach far above a man's head. In the mountains grow the banyan-tree, which can shelter 7000 men; forests of the stately teak-tree, with its white blossoms; the cotton-tree, the faupalin, which gives cocoa-nuts, oil, vinegar, matting, and cordage; besides innumerable varieties of gigantic shrubs, many of which are useful, as well as full of beauty. Every year there are two harvests on the same soil; and the earth and mountains are rich in coal and iron mines, zinc, saltpetre for making gunpowder, gold, diamonds, rubies, and emeralds.

In this vast and rich country, fifty-eight different kinds of nations, with different languages, live, the greater part of them now subject or tributary to our country. And if our dear country had been Catholic, and had carried the blessings of the true Faith to all those Pagan millions, what a glorious conquest would then have been the conquest of India, and what an unperishing treasure, far above Golconda diamonds and virgin gold, might England have laid up for herself!

Just as England was victorious over all her enemies, George the Second died suddenly at Kensington.

Chapter LIII.

Better Times–The American War

From 1760 to 1789

THE king who succeeded George the Second was his grandson. Frederic, the Prince Wales, died; and the cruel Duke of Cumberland, who fought with "Prince Charlie," died too; so the son of Prince Frederic of Wales succeeded, and was called George the Third. He was very unlike his grandfather and great-grandfather. He was a good man, who lived quietly and happily with his queen, and was very kind and charitable to every one who was in distress, or whoever applied to him for help. He was, too, born in England, and brought up like an English gentleman, which was a very good thing for the country. His reign was a very long one, sixty years long; and so many important things happened in it, that we must divide it into several chapters. The first will be about the American War.

You recollect that while Elizabeth reigned, Sir Walter Raleigh took some towns in America; and during Charles the

First's reign, a great many of the Puritan party left England, and went with their families to settle in America. Sir Walter Raleigh called that part of America which he found, Virginia; and the Puritans called what they peopled, New England. In Charles and James the Second's reign, a very good Quaker, named William Penn, went and settled in another part of America, which was called after him Pennsylvania. All these colonies had grown prosperous and rich and powerful, and had their own habits and customs, and grew a great deal of corn, and had several useful manufactures.

The wars which England was engaged in cost a great deal of money; and the ministers thought it would be a good plan to tax the American colonies to pay for these wars. The colonists thought it was not fair to tax them for wars which did them no good; and they refused to pay the money. There were great disturbances for a long time in America about these taxes; and for some time George the Third and his ministers were so busy making peace with the rest of Europe, that they did not see what was going on, and what mischief they were doing. At last peace was really made, and was called the Peace of Paris. It was settled at this peace, that England was to keep the Canadas, all the islands in the St. Lawrence, many others in the West Indies, and Minorca. The French were to take back some of their towns in India, but they were to build no forts; and they were to catch as many codfish as they pleased at Newfoundland, while the English were to cut logwood whenever they wanted it.

This was a very fair arrangement; and when it was made, the English ministers began to think of putting down the disturbances in America. But this was not so easily done. Lord North, who was then one of the ministers, was so foolish as to send a shipload of tea to Boston in America, and

Better Times—The American War

soldiers to force the people to buy the tea, and pay the tax upon it. The Boston people were so angry at this, that they threw all the tea into the sea; and while it was swimming in the bay, they covered the officers with tar and feathers; which is a cruel and brutal punishment.

As soon as the ministers and people in England heard of this behaviour, they got a large army together, and said that war should be declared instantly with the rebellious colonies. But the best and most just of the ministers said that it was a bad and unjust war, and that it would disgrace our country for ever. Lord Chatham was the foremost to condemn it. He was very old and very ill; but he came into the House of Lords, and spoke with his usual indignant and startling energy. "I rejoice," he said, "I rejoice that the Americans have resisted injustice and oppression! Three millions of men so slavish and degraded as they must have been *not* to have resisted, would have been enough to make slaves of us all!" Afterwards, in a voice of thunder, and an eye which made every one shrink, he spoke the memorable words, which will always be quoted for their eloquent power: "If I were an American, as I am an Englishman, I would never cease from my efforts, nor rest for one moment from my toil, till the last British soldier had left the American shore: no, never!" Another great statesman, Mr. Burke, took the same side as Lord Chatham, and spoke strongly against this unjust and foolish war; but the rest of the ministers and members of Parliament seemed to be too much degraded by long profligacy and dishonesty to be able to understand them, or scarcely to listen to them.

The Americans sent Benjamin Franklin to England to talk with the ministers, and to try to get the unjust taxes repealed. Franklin was a plain honest printer, very simple and straightforwar, but an acute and learned man. He was shocked and disgusted by the cold flippant manner in which the interests of his country were treated. He went back to America, and said that their only hope now was in war. The colonists had been, on the whole, very patient. They had done all they could to get a full hearing, and to represent their case respectfully to their king and the parliament of their mother country. But when they found that no attention was paid them, and that they were looked upon as a handful of ungrateful men, whose case was too contemptible to be attended to, they prepared for war with the greatest courage and energy. The men who led them were chiefly Jefferson, Henry, and two Adams; but the greatest and the best was George Washington.

There were two great battles fought at Lexington and Bunker's Hill, in which the English lost a great many soldiers. Lord Clinton and Lord Howe were the English generals. There was another, named General Burgoyne, who was obliged to surrender to the Americans at Saratoga.

This was sad news for England. The ministers had affected to despise the colonists; but I think they were so ignorant of the matter, that they could not have known General Washington, who was one of the wisest and best generals who have ever lived.

When the surrender of Saratoga was known, the French remembered Pondicherry, and the Spaniards thought of Gibraltar, and they both rejoiced, and made a treaty to help the Americans. When this was known, some of the base men who had been so eager for war with the colonies began to be frightened, and to talk of making peace. This was too much for Lord Chatham. He was on a sick-bed, on his death-bed; but he got up, and was carried into the House of Lords, when his still piercing eye made all the cowards tremble; and again he said, "I rejoice, I rejoice that the grave has not yet closed over me, and that I can stand forth again in my country's cause, and lift my voice against the dismemberment of this ancient and most noble monarchy. If we cannot keep peace with honor, why do we hesitate to declare war? If we must fall, let us fall like men." The Duke of Richmond attempted to answer him, and Lord Chatham rose once more. His eye kindled, he trembled with emotion, but his strength failed, and he sank back fainting. He had spoken his last words.

Never was this great statesman so needed as when his remains were laid in Westminster Abbey. Russia, Prussia, Denmark, and Sweden, joined in an armed neutrality, which meant really an enmity. Holland soon joined the neutrality; and they all combined in carrying war-stores to America to fight against England. A great many brave admirals and generals were sent from England; among whom were Admirals Rodney, Hood, and Drake, and Lord Cornwallis, who commanded part of the army. But brave as they were, and with plenty of good soldiers, they could do nothing. Lord Chatham's words had come true. It was an unjust war, and it brought disgrace upon England. Disgrace at the beginning and disgrace at the ending; for Lord Cornwallis was obliged to surrender, as General Burgoyne had done; and the brave and good General Washington put an end to the war.

The Americans, who loved him very much, wished him to be their king, but he said he did not think a monarchy would be a good kind of government for them. Together, the colonists devised a new government, a republic, in which Washington would live like any other citizen. This was noble and generous of Washington; but it is a great pity that he agreed to such a mistake, and with his countrymen raised up the most dangerous and least lasting kind of government .

As soon as the English troops came home, they found fresh work ready for them. The Spaniards were trying to get back Gibraltar. They took Minorca, and went on with a large army and stores to Gibraltar, where there was a desperate battle. The English, under Rodney, won. Lord Howe went to them too with provisions, and powder, and shot, and the French and Spanish were obliged to give up trying to get back Gibraltar.

While all these wars were going on, our countrymen disgraced themselves most sadly at home. Some of the ministers wished to do away with one or two of the cruel laws against Catholics; and because they did so, the brutal and ignorant populace raised a frightful clamour. They were led on and encouraged by a mad nobleman named Lord George Gordon; and the mob collected in London, and burnt Newgate prison, which had cost 100,000 pounds, and was just finished. They burnt many noblemen's houses, and stole their furniture, and drank their wine; and having set some spirit-distilleries on fire, the people knelt down to drink the burning spirits that were running in streams down the streets. Many of these poor deluded and ignorant creatures were killed in the act of doing this. Lord George Gordon, the Protestant champion, afterwards became a Jew. These riots are always known as the Gordon riots, and are a lasting disgrace to our countrymen.

It is difficult to believe the excess of degradation into which England had fallen. Every night bands of robbers and murderers stopped the carriages in London, and openly took the money and watches and jewels from ladies who were in them. Although the watch knew some of these very men quite well, when they saw them riding about, they dared not take them up. Every night there were innumerable robberies and murders; for there were no policemen to watch and guard the streets, which were not lighted at all with lamps; and which were so badly paved, that they were full of large holes, and pools of mud and rubbish.

The next time you walk in Regent Street and Oxford Street, in the evening, and find the smooth wide pavement lit up with the brightest gas, you will wonder to think how different London was in George the Third's time. The statesman who tried to make this wretched state of our towns better was named Sheridan. He was a dissipated, bad man, but kind and goodnatured, and very clever and witty. His speeches in parliament are celebrated for their wit and rich imagination.

Next there was another Indian war, in which the English behaved treacherously and dishonestly. The name of the governor of India was Warren Hastings, and he fought a great many battles with a brave and famous Indian chief named Hyder Ali. Hyder Ali was at last quite astonished and in despair at the courage and obstinate perseverance of his enemies. He had conquered a general named Baillie; but fresh armies constantly appeared; and he said in amazement, "The conquest of many Baillies will not finish these English. I can cut off their provisions, but I cannot dry up the sea."

Warren Hastings was tried when he came back to England for his injustice and cruelty to the Hindus. It was, however, a trick to get rid of him, rather than a real love of justice or humanity; for many of his accusers were much worse than himself, and he was acquitted.

There was now a new minister in England, who was in every way fit to take Lord Chatham's place. This was Lord Chatham's own son, William Pitt the younger, who, when he was only four-and-twenty years old, was made prime minister, and became one of the greatest orators that has ever been known. He had much older men to oppose him, with great talents, who had been trained statesmen for many years, and the foremost of them was named Charles Fox, who led the Whigs, or peace party. Mr. Pitt was almost alone. Every night there were long speeches made, and the Commons voted against what he wished; yet even when fifty or sixty votes were against him, he would not give up, because the king supported him, and the people loved him, and he thought he was right. He did not care for all the torrents of indignation and ridicule which were thrown upon him. He did not care when Fox called him "an ambitious young man," and the end, it was proved that he was right, and that he really was following the wisest course. Charles Fox's friends were turned out of parliament, and were laughed at, and called "Fox's Martyrs" and the "ambitious young man's" fame was firmly established. And now we must end this chapter.

Right Honourable William Pitt the Younger by Hoppner

CHAPTER LIV.

The French Revolution

FROM 1789 TO 1820.

THIS second chapter of George the Third's reign will be about the French Revolution; and you will find it a very interesting one. At all events, as it is important for you to know, you must pay great attention to it.

For a long time France had been governed very badly. The King of France who succeeded Louis the Fourteenth was a weak, bad man, and he allowed a number of wicked men and women to do just as they pleased. They governed the country, gave away all the offices, and treated the poor in a most shameful manner. The peasants were treated like slaves by the nobles, and the farmers and shopkeepers were not much better off. They were even obliged to pay taxes for many things which the nobles were not. They had no one to speak for them in the French Parliament, as our poor and middle classes have; and the king never knew how they went on, or what kind of life they led. As long as the nobles were good religious men, and the kings not extravagant, the peasants were well treated and happy; but at last the nobles became so dreadfully impious and wicked, that very many of them became infidels, and talked, and wrote, and lived in a manner which was directly contrary to religion. A number of bad men who called themselves "philosophers," because they pretended to love wisdom, helped to make every one more wicked, by laughing at the priests and at all good and pious men; so that it was thought a very fine thing by the young nobles not to practice their religion, and that going to Mass and to confession was only fit for women and children. For a long time these "philosophers" did all they could to persuade the king to send away the Jesuits, because they knew that they were the best soldiers and guards the Church had; but as long as Louis the Fourteenth lived, he would never listen to the "philosophers," or have any thing to do with them. When Louis the Fifteenth became king, however, he was so weak as to let them do what they pleased, so long as they did not disturb his life of disgraceful pleasure. The Jesuits were banished out of France: and very soon after, by the constant and bitter efforts of these same infidels, their order was suppressed altogether for a short time. When these body-guards were got rid of, the "philosophers" found every thing else very easy. They wrote a great many little books, called pamphlets, in which they pretended to be the friends and advocates of the people, and told them they were treated like slaves, and ought to rise up against their cruel masters. By their masters they meant the clergy and the nobles.

The poor, ignorant, and almost savage people read these poisonous books greedily, and soon began to like them very much. They read some things in them that were true; and those few things that were true made them believe all the others that were untrue. Their evil passions were roused up not only against the bad and cruel nobles, but against the good king; and not only against those clergy who were too rich, and not fit to be priests at all, but against the whole Church, and against religion itself.

Louis the Fifteenth died, and a young king succeeded him who was very good, and pious, and full of kindness and charity to all his poor unhappy subjects. His name was Louis the Sixteenth; and he had a queen named Marie Antoinette, who was one of the most beautiful and the best women in the world, but who had proud and haughty manners, and who did not at all understand in what state the country was. Poor Marie Antoinette! she had been brought up to think that kings and queens ought to be allowed to do just as they pleased, and that every body and every thing must give way to them. She had never seen any thing round her but grand nobles, and rich polite clergymen, and fine palaces, and silk dresses embroidered with gold and precious stones. She knew nothing of the savage passions that were burning like a volcano under a flowery soil, or of the terrible want and misery which had fed them, and driven her people to madness. The king, too, had been brought up in great ignorance of the state of France, though he knew more than the queen did; and he was very young, and had not much strength or energy of character. A great many Frenchmen had been in America during the American war, and amongst them one very brave officer named Lafayette; and they had heard and seen so much about the *rights of citizens* and liberty, that when they came back to France, they were more disgusted than ever with their own bad nobles, and their wicked way of life, and tyranny to the poor.

After a while, the merchants and townspeople began to

gather together, and to speak in large meetings about being *represented*, that is, having some one to speak for them in Parliament. More and more people joined them, and they called themselves the States-General, and asked the king to change the constitution, and to allow the States-General to remain as the French House of Commons. It was to be called the *Tiers Etat*, or Third Estate, that is, the gentry and shopkeepers, who had never had any one to represent them in Parliament, because in France the constitution was formed only of the king and the nobles. The king promised to make some changes in the constitution. But the people were not satisfied with that, and when the king said that they must not meet any longer in the hall where they were, they went away to the *Jeu de Paume,* or tennis-court, and there they sat and spoke in spite of the king. This National Assembly was now become very dangerous, for most of the cleverest and most famous men in Paris of that time belonged to it. Amongst these, one of the foremost was a profligate infidel named Mirabeau, whose talents and energy had tremendous power against the Court. They ended by seizing the king, and shutting him up in his own palace, and then put every one of his friends whom they met in the streets to death. Very often, when the poor queen looked out of the window, she saw some faithful soldier or friend hanging dead upon the nearest lamp-post. The Church-property was seized too; and all through the provinces the clergy were all driven away, and the nobles were besieged in their castles, cut to pieces, burned alive, and eaten by the savage mob, who were now become like raging fiends instead of men. At last they cut off the gentle, good king's head, and afterwards took out the beautiful Marie Antoinette, and cut off her head too, though she had done nothing but pray for them. They cut off the head of the king's sister, Madame Elizabeth, as well, who was so good and kind that no one could ever find a single fault with her. They put a great many noblemen, and their wives, and sisters, and children to death. The cruellest thing of all was, that they took the Dauphin, the king's eldest son, and shut him up, and beat him, and at last starved him to death. All Paris was streaming with blood, and was full of savage men and frantic women, called *Poissardes,* who were drinking and dancing like fiends, with their hands covered with blood. They grew tired of the constitution they had made, and broke it up. The first party who had made the constitution were called the Girondists. The next party were called the Jacobins, and they put all the Girondist leaders to death, and settled a Convention, which was governed by the wickedest of all the Revolution leaders. His name was Robespierre, and he began what is justly called the Reign of Terror. All the provinces and towns which disapproved of the king's death were now punished in the most shocking way. Lyons was burnt to ashes, and the poor people were tied together in long rows, and shot. Toulon was besieged, and the inhabitants were saved from being shot only by getting into the English ships which came to help them, and being carried away to England. This was very cruel; but what happened next was much more cruel. In the west of France, at the mouth of the Loire, and in Poitou, there is a large tract of woody land called La Vendee, and sometimes *Le Bocage,* or the Grove, because it is full of high hedgerows and narrow winding lanes, with tall trees on each side. It was behind these high hedges of La Vendee that in the past, the Black Prince had drawn up his brave soldiers before the battle of Poitiers; but now there were much more bloody, and cruel, and disgraceful battles fought in La Vendee than the battle of Poitiers. For the French soldiers were sent there against their own countrymen, and were told to shoot every noble and every priest they met, and every noble's wife, or child, or servant; all, indeed, who loved the king and the king's friends. The brave peasants of La Vendee were ready to meet their cruel enemies. They had no arms except pikes and guns, and no horses. They did not know how to fight; and they had to fight against old and trained soldiers who had won many battles. But they loved God, and His Church, and the dear old faith, and their king; and they armed themselves every where to fight for them, and for their homes. They were led by a nobleman named Monsieur de Rochejaquelein, and his brave son Henri, another named Monsieur de Lescure, and by several peasants, the chief of whom was named Cathelineau, who was one of the best and noblest men ever heard of. They fought the troops, and beat them every where in the most extraordinary manner; and when they took any of them prisoners, they treated them very kindly. But after the most wonderful and noble deeds, which you will love to read about by and by, more and more troops were sent into La Vendee, and the brave peasants were cut to pieces, and hunted down like wild beasts. When the wicked mob in Paris heard that La Vendee was destroyed, they danced and sang with bloodthirsty joy.

The most awful scenes were then seen in Paris. The schools and colleges were shut up. The tombs at St. Denis were torn up, and the Altars were broken down and stripped. The Crucifixes and holy images were trampled upon. Sunday was blotted out of the calendar. Christianity was declared to be destroyed, and Reason was to be worshipped instead of Almighty God. A wicked woman was carried in triumph through the streets, and put upon the Altar in the church of Notre Dame, where the blaspheming crowds of madmen came to adore her as a goddess. They were given up by Almighty God to be possessed by Satan, who had begun and carried out these hideous schemes.

Every day the guillotine was set up, and never ceased its work, till in four months a million of human beings had been put to death. Robespierre was put to death himself at last, for his own companions could not endure his cruelty any longer. Then a new government was settled, called the Directory, and the army was given to a young Corsican soldier named Napoleon Bonaparte, who had beaten the English at the siege of Toulon. Napoleon won a great many battles in Austria, Spain, and Italy; and he chose the best generals, and made the best soldiers that had ever been seen. He gave away most of the kingdoms of Europe to his friends, and at last was determined to conquer England.

But England had brave soldiers and sailors, and plenty of good ships to fight with, and experienced admirals to command them. It was, however, a time of the greatest trial to our country, for there were disturbances at home as well as abroad. The Irish broke out into open rebellion, and a French army landed in Ireland to help the rioters, who were very badly and foolishly treated by the government. Lord Cornwallis defeated them, and he was the first who behaved kindly to them, so that they gave up fighting against England. The Irishman who persuaded the French to land in that country was named Wolf Tone. Next, there were great troubles among the merchants and bankers; and so many banks broke, that the Bank of England itself was in danger of being bankrupt, which would have hindered the king from paying the soldiers and sailors, besides doing a great deal more mischief, which you cannot understand yet. Mr. Pitt ordered that the Bank should pay no more money, and that saved our country from ruin; and by care and good management the merchants and bankers settled their affairs, and every thing was right again. After that danger was over, the people began to grow discontented, and the worst of them wished to have a revolution in England, like the one in France, that all the wicked men might rob, and murder, and live just as they pleased. Mr. Pitt's courage and firmness again saved the country. He persuaded the Parliament to pass a law saying that every rioter and disturber of the peace should be taken up and put in prison without a warrant, which usually can never be done. This is called "the Suspending of the Habeas Corpus Act," which you will understand when you are older, as well as why it was thought so necessary, and why it was so difficult and dangerous a thing to do.

Nearly as soon as peace was secured, there was a mutiny in the fleet at Portsmouth. The admiral ordered the sailors to weigh anchor against the French, but no one would move. It was found that they had been very cruelly treated by the officers; and when this was proved, the officers were punished, and sent away from the fleet. As soon as full justice was done, the sailors all returned to their duty, and asked to be led against the French. Afterwards, there was a worse mutiny at the Nore; and as it was found that the sailors there had no reason for their bad conduct, as those at Portsmouth had, they were punished. In all these circumstances, which at such a time of danger were very trying, and which might in one week have caused the ruin of the country, Mr. Pitt showed that he had the courage, and energy, and firmness, and love of justice, which proved him to be a great statesman. He was never afraid either to pardon or to punish; and as soon as it became necessary to do either, he did it fully and at once.

Chapter LV.

Nelson and his Battles Peninsular War and Waterloo.

EVERY one felt confidence in Mr. Pitt; and whenever he sent out admirals and captains for the ships, the sailors felt sure that they were brave, and that they knew how to command, and they obeyed them promptly and cheerfully. The name of one of the new commodores was Horatio Nelson, and one of the captains who generally fought with him was Captain Collingwood. Nelson became afterwards one of the greatest and bravest admirals that have ever been known in any country. The first sea-battle was fought at Cape St. Vincent, which the English won. The next was at Camperdown, which they won too. There was great joy in England about these battles, for the people began to hope more than ever that the cruel monster Napoleon would be beaten at last. He was now in Egypt, which he was trying to conquer for his own, and to take India from the English. Nelson went after him with a large fleet, and sailed into the Nile, where he found the French fleet hiding in the Bay of Aboukir. The English had fewer ships and fewer men than the French; but Nelson set this right by getting round nine of the largest French ships, and beating them completely, until they sailed away from the rest of the fleet. By the time this was done, the sun went down, and it was dark. But it was not dark upon the Nile, for all night the flash of the cannon threw a broad glare upon the water, and the people gathered on the shore could see the grand and terrible scene quite distinctly. About the middle of the night the French admiral's ship, named L'Orient, blew up, and took fire. The flames shot up like a huge pillar of fire into the sky, and every one stopped fighting, and held his breath at the awful sight. It was then that Casa Bianca was killed, about whom and his son a beautiful poem has been written, which is set down for you here. It is the pleasantest thing to think of in that terrible battle of the Nile.[28]

---

[28] *The boy stood on the burning deck,*
  Whence all but he had fled;
The flame that lit the battle's wreck
  Shone round him o'er the dead.

Yet beautiful and bright he stood,
  As born to rule the storm;
A creature of heroic blood
  A proud through childlike form.

The flames rolled on; he would not go
  Without his father's word;
That father, faint in death below,
  His voice no longer heard.

He called aloud, "Say, father, say,
  If yet my task is done!"
He knew not that the cheiftain lay
  Unconscious of his son.

"Speak Father!" once again he cried,
  "If I may yet be gone;

The next battle Nelson fought was in the Baltic Sea, at Copenhagen. The Danes had made an alliance with France against England, and Nelson was sent to punish them. Sir Hyde Parker was the first admiral. His ship struck upon some shoals, and he was obliged to stay idle while Nelson was fighting. Since he was afraid Nelson was being beaten, he put up the signal-flag to leave off fighting. Nelson had only one eye; and when they told him that the flag was up, he put his telescope to his blind eye, and said, "I don't see the signal; keep mine flying for close battle; nail it to the mast. That is

And" — but the booming shots replied,
 And fast the flames rolled on.

Upon is brow he felt their breath,
 And in his waving hair,
And looked from that lone post of death,
 In still but brave despair.

And shouted but once more aloud,
 "My Father! must I stay?"
While o'er him fast, through sail and shroud,
 The wreathing fires made way.

They wrapt the ship in splendour wild,
 They caught the flag on high,
And streamed above the gallant child,
 Like banners in the sky.

There came a burst of thunder-sound;
 The boy! oh, where was he?
Ask of the winds, that far around
 With framents strewed the sea;

With mast and help and pennon fair,
 That well had borne their part:
But the noblest thing that perished there
 Was that young and noble heart!

Mrs. Hemans.

the way to answer such signals!" He beat all the Danish ships in such a way, that they could not fire a single gun: and this one battle put an end to the war with Denmark.

Very soon Napoleon began to prepare in earnest for invading England. More than 450,000 soldiers were gathered together to pour down upon our coasts, while gun-boats, arms, and cannon were gathered together in great numbers, ready to cross the channel at a moment's notice. The English were not idle. Riots, discontents, murmurs, mutinies, and political quarrels, were all forgotten. All hands were at work together, and all hearts united, in earnest and diligent preparation for the enemy. 300,000 volunteers eagerly came forward, from the highest nobles to the poorest peasants, all entreating to be allowed to defend their country; and every one agreed that the word *peace* should never be mentioned as long as one French soldier should remain on English ground.

It was a time of the greatest peril and excitement. Napoleon's scheme was to send a fleet towards the West Indies; and when Nelson should be tricked into pursuit of him, he should come back again, and land the whole French army in England. It was a bold and desperate scheme, and it very nearly succeeded. Nelson had actually pursued the French Admiral Villeneuve some way across the Atlantic; but finding he had escaped him, he turned back towards Spain, where, at Cape Trafalgar, he found Villeneuve drawn up in line of battle. The English, as usual, had much fewer ships than the French; but Nelson was there, and his glorious old flag-ship the *Victory* was there too, and upon its mast was nailed Nelson's flag, "England expects every man to do his duty." After a fiercer and hotter battle than had yet been fought, the French began to give way. Just as the victory was nearly certain, a French rifleman saw an officer walking up and down the *poop*, or raised hind-part of the *Victory*, and as he wore so many stars and ribbons, he thought it must be Lord Nelson. He fired at him, and Nelson fell. "They have done for me at last, Hardy," he said to his favorite captain. They took him down on the lower-deck, and raised him up; but nothing would stop the blood from flowing. Suddenly the sailors overhead gave a loud *huzza!* and Nelson heard that the French were lowering all their flags, and surrendering themselves prisoners. Full of joy to think that England was saved, he said, "Thank God, I have done my duty!" and immediately after expired. This great victory, in which twenty thousand prisoners were taken, put an end to Napoleon's projects against England. He went on making war against Austria, Prussia, and Russia. Among other atrocious cruelties, he took the venerable Pope prisoner, and shut him up in a castle in the Maritime Alps, near Savona. But from the moment that he laid his sacrilegious hands on the Vicar of Christ, he met with nothing but disasters. Nelson was dead, it is true, and there were no more sea-fights like the battles of the Nile and Trafalgar. But there was an English general who fought as well on land as Lord Nelson fought by sea. This was Sir Arthur Wellesley, who had fought a great deal in India, and who had distinguished himself by his sound judgment, and clear, calm understanding, as much as by his singular courage. He was sent to fight the French generals in Spain, and he beat the very best of them, who were named Ney, Soult, Mortier, and Massena. He took the castles of Ciudad Rodrigo and Badajos, in the midst of a storm of bursting powder-barrels, subterraneous fires, pitfalls, and all kinds of terrible destructives, which the French had prepared for their arrival. Nothing could stop the English soldiers; and the bravest of Napoleon's armies were swept before them.

Three other great battles were fought, at Salamanca, Vittoria, and the Pyrenees. The storming of St. Sebastian will always be a foul stain upon our country. The soldiers were enraged at the desperate resistance they met with; and when they took the town, they killed nearly every one they met, without mercy. There was another battle at Corunna, in which the brave and good Sir John Moore was killed.

These victories roused all Europe against Napoleon, whose atrocities and waste of human life had wearied out every one. Russia, Prussia, and Austria united with England against him, and took at last Paris. So Napoleon was obliged to fly to Elba, and Louis the Eighteenth was restored to his throne; and there was great rpjoicing all over the Continent, and most of all in England. The Emperor of Russia and the King of Prussia came to England, and, with Sir Arthur Wellesley, who was now made Duke of Wellington, they went in state with George the Third to the House of Lords and to St. Paul's. This war is always called the Peninsular War, because it was fought in the peninsula of Spain and Portugal.

But almost before the rejoicings were over, Napoleon astonished every one by appearing again in the south of France, and calling his old troops round him. Poor Louis the Eighteenth was obliged to fly as fast as he could to England. The Duke of Wellington was sent out again with an army to Belgium, to meet the proud and restless monster, who never seemed happy but when he was in the midst of bloodshed. The armies met at a place called Quatre Bras, and the French were driven back. The next day Wellington moved on to a safer ground, having on one side the old castle of Hougoumont, on the other a farm called La Haye Sainte, and behind it the village of Waterloo. The French first tried to take La Haye

Sainte, but were hindered by Ponsonby, who dashed upon them with his brave cavalry, and scattered them. He was killed, and most of his gallant soldiers were left dead on the field. Napoleon then sent his famous cavalry, or cuirassiers, to break the English center; and as often as they came on, with loud cries and flashing swords, the English gunners left their guns, and went in among the squares of foot-soldiers, whom the cuirassiers could not break. As soon as the French turned, the gunners ran out, and poured a storm of grape-shot upon them. This went on for a long time, and it was very hard work. Every time the French galloped upon them, whole ranks of soldiers were left dead on the field. The Duke stayed by them all the time; and each time he cried out in his clear, steady voice, "Stand fast, 95th; what would they say of us in England?"

"Never fear, sir," the brave soldiers answered; "we know our duty." At last Napoleon was enraged to find that nothing could move these iron squares of foot-soldiers, and he ordered his own guard, always called the "old guard," to move forward against them. The old guard had never yet been conquered; and now every one thought the English troops were going to be crushed. All day long they had done the hardest work, standing still to be shot at, and filling up the ranks of their dead companions, till they were weary of what seemed a waste of their lives for no useful end. If they had not had such confidence in their general, they never could have endured it. But now Wellington saw that the time was come to move. He took off his cap, and said, "Forward, guards, and at them!" He was answered by a *huzza*, which sounded like thunder to the French; and they poured steadily forward with such irresistible fury, that the invincible old guard were soon seen flying down the slope in all directions.

The Prussians, under Blucher, coming at that moment, the whole force joined in pursuit; and Napoleon turned his horse's head and fled in despair. Nine times that night the French prepared their tents, and lay down to rest; and nine times the shouts and glittering swords of the Prussians forced them to fly again. Forty thousand Frenchmen were either wounded or lay dead on the field of Waterloo.

This great battle ended the war in which Europe had been plunged for thirty years. Napoleon surrendered to the English, and they sent him to the island of St. Helena, where he died. His second reign in France is always called the Hundred Days, because it lasted just that time.

The Duke of Wellington had a good deal of money given to him, and a house called Apsley House, in London, where he generally lives. It is close to Hyde Park; and when you go to London you can look at it, and remember how bravely he fought to save Europe from a cruel tyrant, and especially at the battle of Waterloo.

All the officers and soldiers who fought in the battle had a silver medal given to them. They were all exactly alike; and although the Duke has many fine stars and orders, most likely he values his little Waterloo medal, with its blue ribbon, more than them all.

Just as peace was made all over Europe, George the Third died at Windsor Castle, after reigning sixty years. It is the longest and one of the most important reigns in our history. For many years before he died, the kind good old king had been insane, and he suffered very much. But at all times, and all his life, he was the same simple, straightforward, kind man. Although in many things he was not a good king, yet he loved his people sincerely, and always tried to do what he thought most for their real good.

Chapter LVI.

The Breaking of our Chains

From 1820 to 1830

There is very little to be said about the next king. He was George the Third's son, and was crowned George the Fourth. He was very handsome and graceful, and was generally called "the finest gentleman in Europe," because his manners were so polite and dignified. But you know that a true gentleman must be a good Christian; and as George the Fourth led a very bad life, we cannot call him a real gentleman. When he was Prince of Wales, he married a Catholic lady, named Mrs. Fitzherbert, but he behaved very badly to her; and afterwards he behaved very badly to his queen, Caroline of Brunswick. She was very pretty and goodnatured and agreeable, but was too fond of dancing and laughing. George soon grew tired of her; and he pretended that she was a wicked woman, and tried to send her away. She was tried in the House of Lords, and two very clever and learned lawyers defended her, named Lord Brougham and

Lord Denman. Lord Brougham was afterwards made Lord Chancellor, and Lord Denman became the chief judge in the Court of Queen's Bench. The Queen was found not guilty; and the people, who loved her very much, made bonfires, and illuminated the whole of London.

Soon after, George the Fourth went to Westminster Abbey to be crowned, and the Queen went to be crowned with him. But he had ordered the horse-guards to send her away, and not to let her come in; and this insult grieved poor Queen Caroline so much, that she fell sick and died a few days after.

The most important event in the reign of George the Fourth was the passing of the Catholic Relief Bill. You remember that James the Second had done all he could to persuade the Parliament to repeal the Test Act, which hindered Catholics from taking any office in this country; and that he offended a great many of his subjects by this just wish. In the time of George the Third, Mr. Pitt had tried several times to persuade the king to allow a law to be made by which Catholics could become members of parliament; but the king would never consent. He was too old and too prejudiced to allow what seemed to him a very dangerous change in the laws. But in George the Fourth's reign, the Catholics began to speak for themselves, especially in Ireland, where, as there are 7,000,000 Catholics, and only some hundred thousands of Protestants, the injustice was much heavier and more evident.

The persons who were most zealous and active in obtaining the act of justice that Catholics should be allowed to have Catholic members to speak for them in Parliament, were two gentlemen named Daniel O'Connell and Richard Lalor Sheil. Mr. O'Connell was brought up at the Jesuits' College at St. Omers in France, and Mr. Sheil was educated by the Jesuits at Stonyhurst in England. Both of them had

THE BREAKING OF OUR CHAINS

Daniel O'Connell: The Champion of Liberty; a poster in Philadelphia 1847

great talents and wonderful powers of oratory, which, you now know very well, means speaking well and eloquently in public. But Mr. O'Connell had very much greater energy and activity of character than his countryman; and this gave him besides a singular power over the minds and hearts of others. He could, in fact, by a single speech, excite 300,000 people to open rebellion, or persuade them to the most complete submission. It is this wonderful art of governing and controlling the passions and emotions of others which

Sir Robert Peel, by Henry William Pickersgill, detail

will cause the name of Daniel O'Connell to be always remembered in Ireland.

Certainly you have not forgotten the brave Duke of Wellington. He was a statesman as well as a soldier; and he and another statesman, named Sir Robert Peel, at last passed the Catholic Relief Bill; and Catholic noblemen and gentlemen began to sit in Parliament again. At the same time the famous Test Act was repealed. These laws showed that our countrymen were grown a great deal wiser than they were in George the Third's time, and when they committed the disgraceful outrages of the Gordon riots.

George the Fourth died at Windsor. He had shut himself up for a long time before his death; and as he had never shown any love for his people, or for any one but himself, no one was sorry when he died.

Chapter LVII.

The Constitution Changed, But Yet the Same.

From 1830 to 1837.

THE next king was George the Fourth's brother, the Duke of Clarence; and he was called William the Fourth. He was an old man when he became king, and was very like his father, George the Third. He was so kind and goodnatured and straightforward, that every one loved him. He had, too, the honest, frank manners of a sailor; for William the Fourth, like James the Second, had been a sailor for many years.

Nearly as soon as he became king, a fresh change was made in our constitution. As he lived only a few years ago, it is impossible to tell yet awhile what will be the effects of this change; for it will most likely lead to several, which we cannot foresee now. It requires time, and sometimes even nearly a century's time, to show what effects a change in the constitution of a country will have upon it; and this is why it is so difficult to make really wise laws, and why it is seldom that really great statesmen can be found to govern a country. This is why, too, Minos and Solon and Lycurgus, whom you read about in ancient history, were so famous. They were great *legislators,* or law-makers.

The change in our constitution was made in this manner. England, you know, but as we shall repeat again, is divided into a number of counties or shires, with one or more large towns in each, which are called *boroughs.* These divisions and their names are as old as the time of our wise Anglo-Saxon forefathers who made them; and they divided them into hundreds besides, which are smaller divisions: so that every part of the country might be governed by its own governors, and justice be done to all. Each shire was governed by a magistrate called a *Reeve,* or a *Shire-reeve,* which is now become shortened into *Sheriff.* Each borough was governed by another magistrate, whom we now call the Mayor. Every shire chose a member to speak in Parliament, called the Knight of the Shire; and every borough chose a citizen called a Burgess or Commoner, who was to speak for his fellow-townsmen. Every knight was obliged to have 600 pounds a-year of his own, and every burgess 300 pounds a-year.

Now, of course, as the land in the shires became better cultivated, and as more villages and hamlets sprang up among the woods and cornfields, there were many more people in them. As more manufactures were found out, and new countries discovered, large towns sprang up to weave silk and cotton and woollen enough, and to make knives and swords, and needles and machinery, and tools of all kinds, for the ships to carry to sell in all parts of the globe.

But these large towns, where the busy hum of incessant toil

went on from daybreak till dark night, were not boroughs, so they had no burgesses to speak for them in Parliament, and they thought this very unjust. The people of Birmingham and Manchester especially thought so, and they met together in great crowds of hundreds of thousands, asking to be heard. William the Fourth was quite ready to hear them. He sent away the Duke of Wellington and Sir Robert Peel, who did not wish any change to be made in the boroughs, and he made Lord Grey his minister. Lord Grey chose for his Chancellor Lord Brougham, who defended poor Queen Caroline so well when she was tried, and when she had scarcely any friends. Lord Althorp[29] and Lord John Russell were the chief leading ministers in the House of Commons.

They made a law called the Reform Bill, which settled that a great many new boroughs should be made, and more members for the shires or counties; and they asked the Lords to pass the bill. But they *threw it out,* that is, they said it should not be a law; and there was an end of the Reform Bill for the present.

This made the people very angry indeed. They besieged the House of Lords, and threw stones at a great many of the Peers as they went along the streets. They burnt the Duke of Newcastle's castle at Nottingham, took possession of Derby, and set fire to Bristol. It is difficult to say what would have happened, if the king had not been firm and brave. He went himself to the House of Lords and dissolved the Parliament; that is, he sent them all away, and new members were to be chosen. Lord Grey asked him to make a great many new lords, that the Reform Bill might be sure to become a law. The king would not do this, but he asked some of the lords himself not

---

[29] Afterwards Lord Spencer, elder brother of the Honourable and Reverand George Spencer, Father Provincial of the Passionists.

to vote against it, and persuaded some others; and as they all saw that he was steady to his resolution of changing the law, they gave way, and the Reform Bill was passed.

And now you must understand why this made a change in the constitution, for at first sight it seems to be no change at all. It increased the democratic part of the constitution, and gave it more power than it had ever had before. In the time of Cromwell, the Parliament usurped a power which did not belong to it, and which in reality belonged to the king. But every one knew that this was a power usurped, and that it was an injustice. By this injustice, the democratic power was increased only for a little while, and by violence. But when the Reform Bill had passed, a great deal more power was given to the House of Commons, by increasing its members, and by choosing many more of them from the middle classes of the country. This power being given by the law, is therefore made theirs by right; which is a much greater power in reality than one which may seem greater, but which is usurped, or taken by violence. It caused too a change in people's minds. Many of them began to think that as so great a change had been made, a greater one might come by and by; and that as there were now more men who could choose members to speak for them in Parliament, perhaps in a little while every man, even the very lowest, might do the same, or perhaps be in Parliament himself. This excited men's pride and ambition to speak of many matters, and to give opinions about them, which they were quite unable to understand. The votes and opinions of the House of Commons began to draw the House of Lords with a greater and stronger power, and, as it were, to *force* it to agree to what it proposed. This may lead to many other consequences which we cannot yet foresee; but some of them you will be able to understand by yourself when you are a few years older.

Several other new laws were made in William the Fourth's reign, but they are not written down here, because, though they made great changes, they had very little effect on the constitution.

There were several revolutions in different parts of Europe. The Netherlands revolted from Holland, and became an independent kingdom, called Belgium. They chose for their king Leopold of Saxe Cobourg, who had married the Princess Charlotte, the daughter of George the Fourth and poor Queen Caroline.

Greece had been for a long time fighting with the Turks, who had taken possession of it. The English had helped them to be independent; and amongst others who fought for the Greeks was a famous poet named Lord Byron, who was one of the cleverest and most unhappy men of the time. By and by you must ask your parents to choose for you some parts of Childe Harold, and a few of his other poems, which give the most beautiful descriptions of Italy and its celebrated cities. Greece became quite independent in William the Fourth's reign, and Otho of Bavaria was made its king.

One of the last and best things that was done in this reign was, that all the negro slaves in our West Indian Islands were made free. The English nation agreed to pay a very large sum of money, twenty millions of pounds, to buy these poor slaves of the planters, that they might be set free. A great many celebrated men had been trying to obtain this for a long time, and among the chief was Lord Brougham. And at last it was done; and in one day in August, 1836, there was not a single slave in all our plantations. They all became free blacks, who worked for wages, as laborers do in England.

There were also many useful and valuable discoveries

made in George the Fourth's and William's reign. Sir John Ross sailed to the North Pole, which no one had ever done before; and you will like to read the account of his travels and sufferings, which he has written himself.

A great deal of new country has been explored in New Holland and in New Zealand; and fresh colonies have been founded in both those large countries.

Two brothers, named Lander, went into the middle of Africa, and discovered the source or rising of the river Niger, which had never been known before.

And since then a great deal of new country has been conquered in India and China by the English; so that now we have lands and towns and colonies all round the globe.

Besides this, large steam-boats have been built, so as to go across the Atlantic Ocean to America in fourteen days, instead of three months, which is the time a ship takes to make the voyage. A quicker way has been found, too, of going to India, through the Mediterranean, across the Isthmus of Suez, and down the Red Sea, which shortens that long voyage very much. Formerly it took our countrymen a whole year to go to India, because they had to go all round Africa.

Railways have been made, too, all over England, and in many parts of Europe, so that every one can come and go more quickly, and send letters and goods, corn and provisions, and coal, more cheaply and faster. This is a great benefit in very many ways; and the chief of them is, that it is of great service to the Church, by helping the Bishops and other superiors to go quickly all through their own dioceses, and to travel to other places when they are wanted.

A beautiful new light, called gas, was invented for lighting streets and houses. The streets of our towns were all well paved and cleaned, and guarded from thieves by policemen;

The Constitution Changed, But Yet the Same.

so that even ladies can now walk about London as safely as if they were shut up in their own parks or gardens. In short, it would be impossible to write down all the improvements that were made.

But the very best thing is kept till the last, and this is the one we can never be thankful enough for. Instead of being imprisoned and fined, and put to death, or hunted down like wild beasts, our Bishops and clergy are now to be found in every town, openly professing and glorying in their sacred office, and performing all their duties fully and without hindrance. Instead of hiding our Altars and Tabernacles in caves or garrets, we now see our churches springing up again in every corner of our country, and sending forth the sound of their sweet bells upon the wind to cheer and console those faithful souls, who have been scattered here and there in England, like grains of salt in a mass of corruption and decay; or like a few seeds of corn long hidden in the dark earth, which are now yielding rich fields of ripening grain.

The names of many celebrated men ought to be mentioned during these two reigns, and the succeeding one of her present majesty Queen Victoria, the niece of William the Fourth. Among them, the chief are the poets Lord Byron, Sir Walter Scott (whose historical novels are the best that have ever been written), Campbell, Rogers, Shelley, Coleridge, Southey, and Wordsworth. Of these, Byron had the finest genius and sense of what is beautiful in every way; and Wordsworth's poetry is the most instructive, and has the best influence. He founded a completely new school of poetry, and has a great many disciples, the very best of whom is Keble, who wrote the *Christian Year*. Coleridge and Southey wrote even more beautiful prose than poetry.

The chief natural philosophers and men of science were Sir

Humphry Davy, Watt, Brewster, Airy, Faraday, Brindley, and Rennie. Sir Humphry Davy made a great many discoveries in electricity and galvanism, and in chemistry. He was celebrated for the clear and exact manner in which he reasoned upon what he observed in his experiments, and this led him to make several discoveries which saved the lives of thousands of our countrymen. The most beautiful instance of this was the perseverance with which he followed up by reasoning, step by step, some experiments which he made upon the bad air in mines, and which led finally to the invention of the safety-lamp, which put an end to the terrible explosions of what is called fire-damp in mines.

In painting, and sculpture, and architecture, England made some progress; but it is impossible for any country, cut off from the Church, to possess that genius in art which only the Church can inspire. English painting has for a long time dwindled down to mere mechanical efforts to imitate natural objects; and until the love of our blessed Lady and the glorious chorus of the Saints and Soldiers of the Church inspires our dear country with love, art must continue in this degraded state.

Among English Catholics, who are only now again struggling into life, there cannot be many names that are celebrated. There are several whom you must not forget, and who have had to contend not only with poverty, but with every other difficulty, which must be an obstacle to a minority in a rich and highly populous country. Pugin has made the greatest efforts for the revival of the study of architecture in this country, and has labored with unwearied industry to promote a taste and knowledge of purely Christian art.

Among writers, Digby has the most successfully toiled for the same end; and when you read his *Ages of Faith* or *Mores*

Catholici, his *Broad Stone of Honor,* and *Compitum,* you will see how much he has studied and labored for this generous purpose, trying to make men love only what is holy and pure and noble.

The best modern historian is the Catholic historian of England, Lingard; and two of the best of the modern poets were Catholics, Moore and Griffin. One of the most eloquent of the eloquent contemporaries of Pitt was the Catholic statesman, Grattan; and one of the most celebrated pleaders and wits of the Irish bar, Curran, was also a Catholic. Burke was brought up in a Catholic college.

Many other names might be mentioned; but there is space only for one, which you all know, and venerate and love. Among the celebrated theological writers of the present time, Bishop Wiseman stands in the foremost rank; and his works have obtained, not only an eminent and enduring celebrity for himself, but the most solid and lasting benefit to religion.

He was born at Seville, in Spain, and spent the chief part of his life in Rome;[30] which gave him the great advantage of a thorough training in the practices and temper of countries which, from their first conversion, have never lost the Catholic Faith, nor ever doubted its glorious truths.

At an age when the generality of men are still pursuing their studies, he published his Lectures on the Connexion between Science and Revealed Religion, a work which immediately achieved for him an European reputation; and the *Horae Syriacae,* written when he held the Professorship of Oriental Languages in the University of Rome— a chair which requires no ordinary learning and gifts to fill. The celebrity thus gained was afterwards sustained and increased by his controversial writings, the eloquence of his preaching,

---

[30] Bishop Wiseman went to Rome at the age of sixteen.

and his vast and untiring efforts for the general good of the Church.

Bishop Wiseman came to England in 1840, renouncing a life of learned and elegant and keenly enjoyable literary occupations, surrounded by men of like sympathies and pursuits—by whom he was warmly admired and appreciated—to give up the rest of his life to the toilsome object of restoring our dear country to the Faith, amongst and against a thousand obstacles and perplexities. Ever since, he has earnestly and unceasingly devoted his splendid acquirements and the inexhaustible resources of his genius to this great end.

For this end, whether publicly, by preaching and exhorting in crowded churches, weaving, as it were, a tissue of grand and noble and gorgeously-colored design—slowly building up and bringing out to view those magnificent types of truth and beauty which enchant thousands; or whether, in more private and hidden ways, by awakening souls to a higher spiritual life, or leading them into the Fold of the Church, or loosing them from the bonds of sin—making himself at once the tenderest father to sinners, and with children the gladdest child; the conversion of England has been the constant theme of his thoughts, his prayers, his life.

And for this end, much as he has done, he is still doing more; for although he has, in the very prime of life, fulfillled the work of a ripe old age, he continues to labor as if he were now only beginning his first course.

Chapter LVIII.

The End, and our Present Condition

YOU know, dear children, some of the colleges in our country; but perhaps you do not know the names of them all. There are now no less than ten Catholic colleges where boys are educated, and where young men are trained for the priesthood. Their names are, St. Edmund's in Hertfordshire, Stonyhurst in Lancashire, St. Mary's in Staffordshire, St. Peter and Paul and St. Gregory's in Somersetshire, St.Cuthbert's in Durham, St. Lawrence's in Yorkshire, Mount St. Mary's in Derbyshire, St. Edward's in Lancashire, and the Immaculate Conception in Leicestershire. The chief of these colleges are St. Edmund's, Stonyhurst, and St. Mary's. Stonyhurst is under the direction of Fathers of the Society of Jesus, to whom also Mount St. Mary's belongs. There are besides a great many lesser schools for boys.

It could scarcely be expected that the English Catholics, who are few and poor, should be able to compete with the rich and powerful dignitaries and professors of a wealthy protestant country in the matter of education; and yet, in spite of all the robberies and persecutions which seemed to have stripped them of every means of exertion, such is the undying energy of our holy religion, that in the late Government-examination for schoolmasters, nearly the only successful candidates for the first class were two Catholics. The knowledge required for this class was really considerable. This fact shows that if the condition of our schools is necessarily low, their case is very hopeful, and their means such as to give cheering prospects of improvement.

There are now above forty convents of different orders of religious women in this country, and thirteen convents for religious men, besides three houses of Fathers of the Oratory, the children of the great and sweet and loving Roman Saint, St. Philip Neri, who are secular priests living in community with one aim and spirit, but with only one vow.

Besides religious, there are upwards of six hundred and seventy priests in Great Britain,[31] where not a century ago a price would have been set upon the head of every one who should be found.

But these are not all the blessings which Almighty God is showering upon England, who so little deserves that the true Faith should again revisit her ungrateful shores. Within the last twelve years the prejudices of many good and learned Anglican clergymen and laymen have given way to their honest researches after the truth, both in history and religion; and their hearts, in consequence, have been turned with great earnestness towards the Church.

They began to doubt whether much that they had heard from their childhood was not a completely false view both of the Church and their own state of faith. Their eyes became

---

[31] Not, of coure, reckoning Ireland.

opened to the fact, that the Reformation, of which the English had been in the habit of boasting as the spread of light and purity of doctrine, was only a new form of ancient heresies which had been long since condemned and cast out by the Church. Following out this fact, they found that that Church, one, unchanging, infallible, indivisible, spoken of by the Apostles, and described by the Prophets with the same characteristics, if it existed at all in this world, was no other than the Church of Rome. Either our Lord's words concerning His Church were not true, or the Roman Church is she; for she alone (as they reasoned out step by step) has the four marks of truth,—she alone is One, Holy, Catholic, Apostolic.

When this truth became a conviction in the minds of these excellent men, who, following the clear guidance of God in their conscience, were led, in the most wonderful manner, to the just conclusions at which they arrived, they acted upon His teaching; and renouncing the shadow-Church in which they had been educated, they returned in flocks to the Church who had baptized them, and who joyfully claimed and welcomed her long-lost children.

You will learn to love and value the names of these devoted converts a great deal more when you cease to be children; and to give you now the long list of nearly two hundred persons who, during the last five years only, have returned to the Church, would only tire you. The best known among them are, Mr. Newman, Mr. Oakeley, and Mr. Faber. Mr. Newman and Mr. Faber are now Fathers of the Oratory, and Mr. Oakeley is a Missionary priest. Father Newman is one of the greatest scholars and most learned writers in Europe; but he is beloved by those who know him for other qualities than learning or scholarship. For, as we can only justly and reasonably conclude, it is no light or common grace to be, chosen out and led on in the extraordinary way in which he, who was the chief guide and teacher of the rest, was led. When we follow and dwell upon the calm, hidden, and silent manner in which such a mind as his was gradually grounded and built up in the true Faith, without a human teacher, we can only lift up our hearts in thankful joy to God, for the wonderful ways in which He leads His own, and take fresh courage to renew our prayers and labors for our country. For, if He has raised up such as these for Himself, without the help or knowledge of man, will He not lead many more by the same paths; or can we, with any faith, doubt that He is preparing greater blessings for England?

John Henry Newman, by Sir John Everett Millais

Appendix

[It will be evident that the Genealogy and the short statistical account accompanying it are to be made use of by the instructor, rather than by the child alone.]

NORMANS AND PLANTAGENETS.

THREE NORMANS—ONE BLOIS—FOURTEEN PLANTAGENETS.

William the Conqueror = Matilda, daughter of Baldwin V. Earl of Flanders.

- Robert, Duke of Normandy, 1134. = Sibilla of Conversana.
- Richard, killed in hunting.
- *William Rufus*, 1100.
- Matilda = of Scotland, 1118. ⟂ *Henry Beauclerc* 1135. = Adelais of Brabant.
- Adela = Stephen, Earl of Blois.
- Other daughters.

From Matilda = Henry Beauclerc:
- William. = Matilda of Normandy.
- Henry IV. = Matilda Emperor of 1167. Germany, 1126.
- William.
- Baldwin.
- Eustace, Earl of Boulogne, 1152.
- Constantia of France. = William, Earl of Boulogne.
- Two daughters.

From Adela = Stephen:
- Theobald, Earl of Blois.
- Henry, Bishop of Winchester.
- *Stephen*, 1154. = Maud of Boulogne.
  - Matilda. Eleanor. Joan.

William, = Joan Earl of Flanders. Savoy.

Henry II. 1189. = Eleanor of Aquitaine.
- Geoffrey, Earl of Nantes.
- William.
- Henry = Margaret, daughter of Louis VII.
- *Richard* 1199. = Berengaria of Navarre.
- Geoffrey, Earl of Bretagne. = Constance of Bretagne.
- *John* 1216. = Isabella of Angouleme.

Arthur, murdered by John.

Henry III. = Eleanor of Provence.

Edmund the Humpbacked, Duke of Lancaster. Margaret. *Edward I.* 1307 = Eleanora of Castile.

Elizabeth. John, Earl of Gloucester. *Edward II.* = Isabella of France, the **She-wolf**.

APPENDIX

Genealogical table: Descendants of Edward III and Philippa of Hainault.

- **Edward III.** = **Philippa of Hainault.**
  - **Edward, Prince of Wales (Black Prince), 1376.** = **Joan of Kent.**
    - **Richard II.** = (1) **Anne of Bohemia**; (2) **Isabella, la Petite Reine.**
  - **Lionel, Duke of Clarence.** = **Elizabeth de Burgh.**
    - **Philippa** = **Edmund Mortimer, Earl of March.**
      - Roger. = Eleanor Holland. — Edmund. — Elizabeth. — Philippa.
        - Edmund. — Roger. — Anne. — Eleanor.
  - **John, Duke of Lancaster.** = **Blanche, daughter of great grandson of Henry III.**
    - **Philippa, Queen of Portugal.**
    - **Henry IV. 1413.** = **Mary Bohun.**
      - **Henry V. 1422.** = **Katherine of France.**
        - **Henry VI.** = **Margaret of Anjou. 1472.**
          - Edward, murdered after the battle of Tewkesbury. = Anne Nevil, daughter of the King-maker.
      - Thomas, Duke of Clarence.
      - John, Duke of Bedford.
      - Humphrey, Duke of Gloucester.
  - **Edmund, Duke of York, 1402.** = **Isabella of Castile.**
    - **Edward, Duke of York.**
    - **Richard, Earl of Cambridge.** = **Anne Constance of March.**
      - **Richard, Duke of York, 1460.** = **Cicely Nevil.**
        - *Edward IV.* 1461. = **Elizabeth Wydeville, 1492.**
          - *Edward V.* 1483, murdered by Richard III.
          - Richard, Duke of York.
          - Elizabeth.
        - George, Duke of Clarence, 1477.
          - Earl of Warwick, executed by Henry IV.
          - George.
        - *Richard III.* 1485. = **Anne Nevil.**
          - Edward, Prince of Wales (died young).
  - **Thomas, Duke of Gloucester.**

457

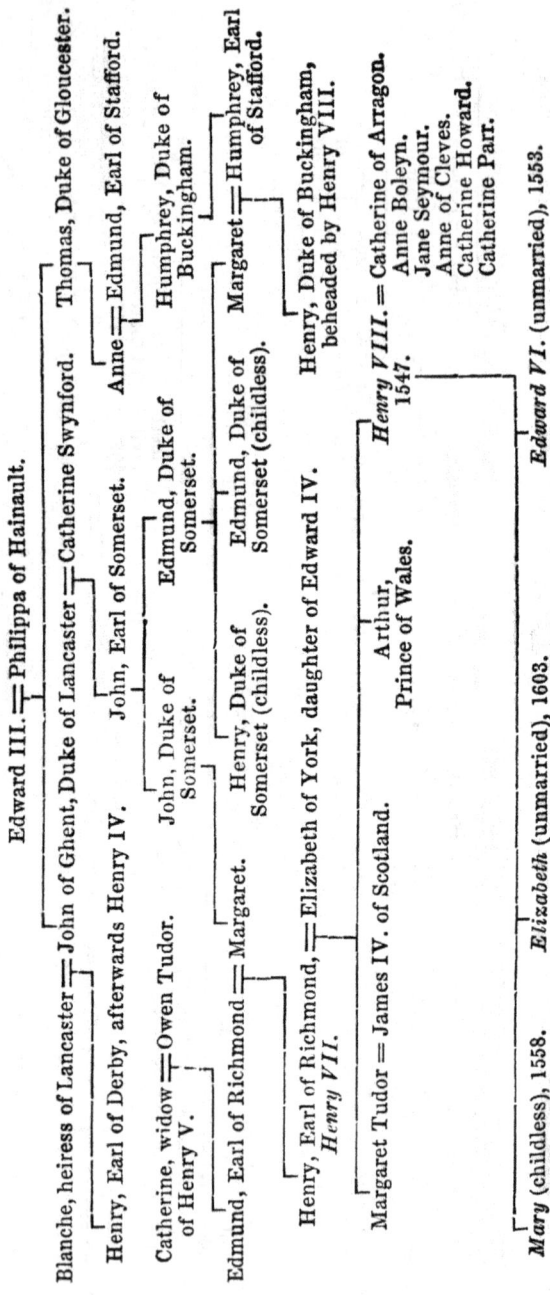

APPENDIX

HOUSE OF STUART.
SIX SOVEREIGNS.

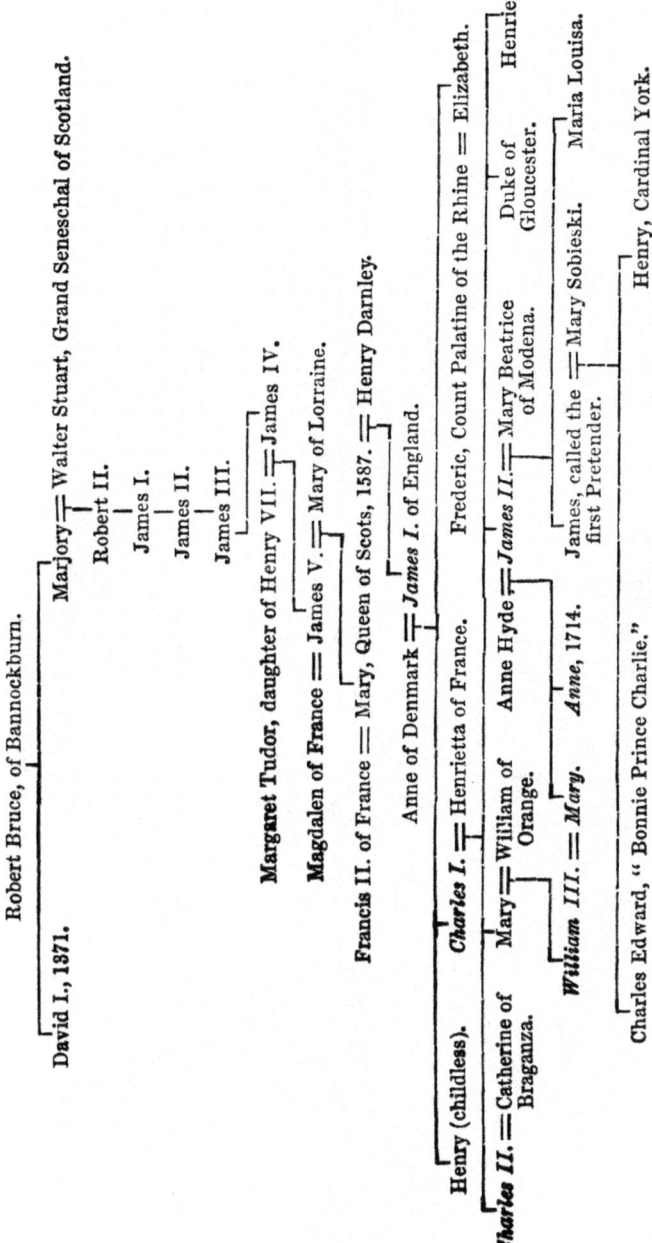

459

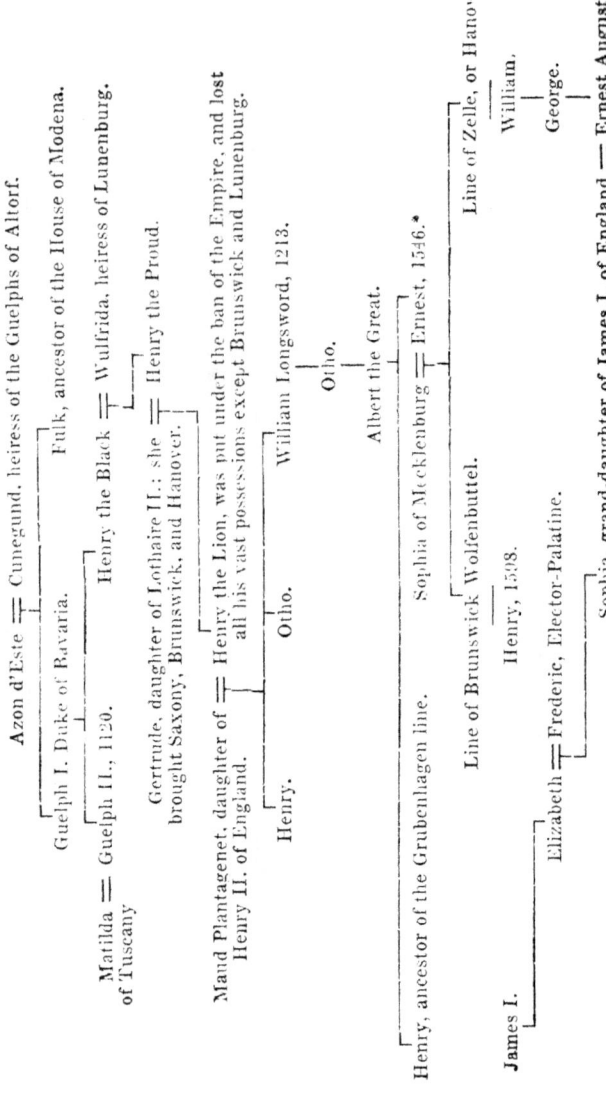

APPENDIX

Sophia of Zelle, or Brunswick = George I. of England.

- Sophia, 1757.
- Wilhelmina of Anspach = George II.
  - Augusta of Saxe Gotha = Frederic, Prince of Wales.
    - George III. = Charlotte of Mecklenburg.
      - George IV. = Caroline of Wolfenbuttel.
        - Princess Charlotte = Prince Leopold.
      - Frederic, Duke of York.
      - William IV. = Adelaide.
      - Edward, Duke of Kent. = Victoria.
        - Albert, Saxe Cobourg and Gotha = Victoria.
          - Victoria Adelaide, Princess Royal.
          - Albert Edward, Prince of Wales.
          - Alice Maude.
          - Albert Ernest.
          - Helena Augusta.
      - Ernest, Duke of Cumberland, King of Hanover.
      - Duke of Sussex.
        - George.
        - Two daughters.
      - Duke of Cambridge.
        - George.
        1. Charlotte A.
        2. Aug. Sophia.
        3. Elizabeth.
        4. Mary.
        5. Sophia.
        6. Amelia.
      - Duke of Gloucester.
    - Augusta.
    - Edward, Duke of York.
    - William, Duke of Gloucester. — Three daughters.
    - Henry, Duke of Cumberland.
  - William, Duke of Cumberland.
  - George, died young.
  - Five daughters.

www.ingramcontent.com/pod-product-compliance
Lightning Source LLC
Chambersburg PA
CBHW060447170426
43199CB00011B/1126